GREEK TRAGEDY AND POLITICAL PHILOSOPHY

Rationalism and Religion in Sophocles' Theban Plays

In *Greek Tragedy and Political Philosophy*, Peter J. Ahrensdorf examines Sophocles' powerful analysis of a central question of political philosophy and a perennial question of political life: Should citizens and leaders govern political society by the light of unaided human reason or religious faith?

Through a fresh examination of Sophocles' timeless masterpieces – *Oedipus the Tyrant*, *Oedipus at Colonus*, and *Antigone* – Ahrensdorf offers a sustained challenge to the prevailing view, championed by Nietzsche in his attack on Socratic rationalism, that Sophocles is an opponent of rationalism. Ahrensdorf argues that Sophocles is a genuinely philosophical thinker and a rationalist, albeit one who advocates a cautious political rationalism. Such rationalism constitutes a middle way between an immoderate political rationalism that dismisses religion – exemplified by Oedipus the Tyrant – and a piety that rejects reason – exemplified by Oedipus at Colonus.

Ahrensdorf concludes with an incisive analysis of Nietzsche, Socrates, and Aristotle on tragedy and philosophy. He argues, against Nietzsche, that the rationalism of Socrates and Aristotle incorporates a profound awareness of the tragic dimension of human existence and therefore resembles in fundamental ways the somber and humane rationalism of Sophocles.

Peter J. Ahrensdorf is professor of political science and adjunct professor of classics at Davidson College. He is the author of *The Death of Socrates and The Life of Philosophy: An Interpretation of "Phaedo"* and the co-author of *Justice Among Nations: On the Moral Basis of Power and Peace.*

GREEK TRAGEDY AND POLITICAL PHILOSOPHY

Rationalism and Religion in Sophocles' Theban Plays

Peter J. Ahrensdorf

Davidson College

CAMBRIDGE
UNIVERSITY PRESS

CAMBRIDGE UNIVERSITY PRESS
Cambridge, New York, Melbourne, Madrid, Cape Town,
Singapore, São Paulo, Delhi, Tokyo, Mexico City

Cambridge University Press
32 Avenue of the Americas, New York, NY 10013-2473, USA

www.cambridge.org
Information on this title: www.cambridge.org/9781107699120

First published 2009
Reprinted 2009, 2010
First paperback edition 2011

A catalog record for this publication is available from the British Library.

Library of Congress Cataloging in Publication Data

Ahrensdorf, Peter J., 1958–
    Greek tragedy and political philosophy : rationalism and religion in Sophocles'
    Theban plays / Peter J. Ahrensdorf.
       p.   cm.
    Includes bibliographical references and index.
    ISBN 978-0-521-51586-3 (hardback)
       1. Political science – Greece – Philosophy. 2. Rationalism – Political aspects.
    3. Religion and politics. 4. Sophocles – Criticism and interpretation.
    5. Sophocles – Political and social views. 6. Political plays, Greek – History
    and criticism. 7. Politics and literature – Greece. 8. Greek drama (Tragedy) –
    History and criticism. I. Title.
    JC73.A37   2009
    320.01–dc22   2008037006

ISBN 978-0-521-51586-3 Hardback
ISBN 978-1-107-69912-0 Paperback

To Alejandra

Contents

Acknowledgments

Many have contributed to the genesis of this book, and it is a pleasure to express my thanks to them. Chapters 1 and 2, which were published previously in somewhat different versions, have been revised and expanded for this book. Chapter 1 originally appeared as "The Limits of Political Rationalism: Enlightenment and Religion in *Oedipus the Tyrant*," *Journal of Politics*, 66:3 (August 2004), pp. 773–99, copyright © 2004 Southern Political Science Association, and is used here with the permission of Cambridge University Press. Chapter 2 originally appeared as "Blind Faith and Political Rationalism in Sophocles' *Oedipus at Colonus*," *Review of Politics*, 70:2 (Spring 2008), pp. 165–89, copyright © 2008 *Review of Politics*, and is used here with the permission of the editors of *Review of Politics* and University of Notre Dame. I thank *Journal of Politics* and *Review of Politics* for kindly granting me permission to use this material.

I thank Davidson College, the Earhart Foundation, and the National Endowment for the Humanities for their generous financial support. My thanks also go to Beatrice Rehl, my editor at Cambridge University Press, who provided me with most valuable and timely advice, encouragement, and assistance. I also wish to express my gratitude to the anonymous reviewers at the Press, who offered me extraordinarily judicious and beneficial suggestions and criticisms, and helped me improve the manuscript in crucial ways.

I thank Kristen Schrauder of Davidson College and Shari Chappell of Cambridge University Press for their assistance, and Ronald Cohen, whose conscientious and meticulous editing helped polish the manuscript and prepare it for publication.

It was my tremendous good fortune to study Sophocles at the University of Chicago with Allan Bloom. Through his classes, his writings, and his example, he taught me the importance of seeking wisdom from the great poets, as well as the great philosophers, of the past. It was also my privilege and pleasure to study Sophocles at Chicago with David Grene.

I thank the lively, engaging, and energetic students of Kenyon College and Davidson College who took my classes on Sophocles and taught me much about his plays. I also learned a great deal from my fellow teachers of Sophocles at both institutions, especially Stephen Wirls. I am grateful as well to Fred Baumann, David Bolotin, Werner J. Dannhauser, Steven J. Kautz, Rafe Major, Judd Owen, Richard S. Ruderman, Brian J. Shaw, and Devin Stauffer, who graciously read portions of my manuscript and offered me exceptionally incisive comments, salutary advice, and friendly encouragement.

Finally, I wish to express my gratitude to my family for all the help they have given me. My wonderful children, Lucia and Matias, have helped me more than they can know, especially by supporting me with such love, patience, and good humor. My wife, Alejandra Arce Ahrensdorf, has offered me the most constant, generous, and indispensable support of all. Throughout the many years of this project, she has always given me the benefit of her wise counsel, her courageous spirit, and her loving heart. She is always an inspiration to me, and I owe her more than I can possibly say. I dedicate this book to her.

GREEK TRAGEDY AND POLITICAL PHILOSOPHY

Rationalism and Religion in Sophocles' Theban Plays

Introduction

Since the end of the secular, Cold War struggle between liberalism and communism, conflicts around the world have increasingly reflected a religious challenge to liberalism and its rationalist thesis that reason is our "only Star and compass" (Locke 1988, 182). The abiding political importance of religion is a central fact of our time, and yet that fact is surprising, not only given the hypothesis that the end of the Cold War would usher in an "end of history" – "the end point of mankind's ideological evolution and the universalization of Western liberal democracy as the final form of human government" (Fukuyama 1989, 4) – but also, and more importantly, given the confidence of the Enlightenment founders of liberalism that, in Tocqueville's words, "Religious zeal ... will be extinguished as freedom and enlightenment increase" (2000, 282).[1] In the light of the apparent tendency of modern political theory to underestimate the power of religion, it seems reasonable to consider the pre-modern, classical analysis of religion and political enlightenment. As this book will show, that analysis is set forth with singular clarity and power in Sophocles' Theban plays.

The importance of the issue of religious anti-rationalism and political rationalism in Sophocles has been recognized most emphatically in modern times by Nietzsche, the deepest philosophic source of post-modernism. Indeed, when Nietzsche launched his attack on the Western tradition of liberal, democratic rationalism – an attack so momentous for the post-modern world (see Rorty 1989, 27–30, 39–43, 61–6, 96–121; 1991, 32–3) – he did so in the name of the

---

[1] Tocqueville himself did not share that confidence. See 2000, 283–4, 510–11.

tragic grandeur of Sophocles' and Aeschylus's heroes. Nietzsche argued that, in contrast to the cowardly, dogmatic rationalism and shallow optimism of the scientific world view, founded and embodied by Socrates, the tragic world view, set forth by Aeschylus and Sophocles, courageously and honestly faced the world as it truly is: chaotic, cruel, and ultimately impenetrable to human reason.[2] Yet the tragic human being was not broken by this vision of cosmic indifference and conflict, but rather lovingly affirmed "the infinite primordial joy of existence," as well as "the eternal suffering" at the heart of Being, and celebrated "the playful construction and destruction of the individual world as the overflow of a primordial delight" (1967, 105, 112, 142). The "pessimism of *strength*" of the tragic poets and their heroes enabled them to found and perfect a tragic culture, open to the sorrow of existence and the mystery of being and yet life-affirming, "saying Yes to life even in its strangest and hardest problems."[3] This tragic age of the Greeks constituted the most profound and noble culture human beings have ever created, one "sure of our astonished veneration" (1967, 88; see also 87; 93–4).

But that culture was destroyed by Socrates, who replaced it with a rationalistic culture, one based on the optimistic, anti-tragic, "faith" or "illusion" that reason "can penetrate the deepest abysses of being"; that happiness is the proper goal of life and that reason can lead human beings to happiness; and hence that the life based on reason is the best way of life for a human being (1967, 95–7; see also 86–8, 91). Socrates is consequently "the one turning point and vortex of so-called world history" (96). The culture he founded remains our culture, characterized by "the triumph of *optimism*, the gradual prevalence of *rationality*, practical and theoretical *utilitarianism*, no less than de-mocracy itself" (21, emphases in text; see also 109–14, 91). The triumph of Socratic political rationalism, however, foreshadows "*the over-all degeneration of man*," for Socratic culture is not only deluded in its rationalistic understanding of the world and in its self-contradictory "faith" in reason but, more importantly, is degraded by its incapacity to

---

[2] 1967, 17–8, 89–90, 94–7, 106; see also 1954a, 473–4, 478; 1969, 272–3.

[3] 1967, 17–18, emphasis in text; 1954a, 562–3; see also 1968, 434–5, 448–53.

face and experience the ennobling tragedy of human existence (1989, 118, emphasis in text; see also 54, 103–4, 112–4, 158–9).

To avoid the final victory of the democratic, peaceful, subtragic, subhumanly happy "last man," Nietzsche, who dubs himself "the first *tragic philosopher*," calls for a rebirth of tragedy, the re-establishment of a tragic, warlike culture that is based on a rejection of political rationalism, an "affirmation of passing away *and destroying*. . . . [and a] saying Yes to opposition and war" (1954b, 128–30; 1969, 273, emphases in text; see also 274). "Yes, my friends, believe with me in . . . the rebirth of tragedy . . . The age of Socratic man is over . . . Only dare to be tragic men; for you are to be redeemed" (1967, 124; see also 99, 106, 121–3). If the rationalist Socrates prefigures the subspiritual, subhuman last man, the anti-rationalist, "suffering hero of Greek tragedy, Oedipus or Prometheus, is the original model for Nietzsche's *Übermensch*, the superman."[4]

The principal example Nietzsche gives of a human being who exemplifies the tragic world view is Sophocles' Oedipus.[5] In the first place, Oedipus has the courage to confront the world honestly, "with intrepid Oedipus eyes" (1989, 161). Furthermore, "Sophocles understood the most sorrowful figure of the Greek stage, the unfortunate Oedipus, as the noble human being who, in spite of his wisdom, is destined to error and misery but who eventually, through his tremendous suffering, spreads a magical blessing that remains effective even beyond his decease" (1967, 67). "The wise Oedipus" achieves the greatest wisdom and nobility because, through his suffering – an unjust suffering, unprovoked by "sin" – he comes to understand, to accept, and ultimately to affirm the utter cruelty and mystery of the world and the inability of reason to comprehend the world or to guide our lives (42, 68–9; see also 46, 73). Most importantly, "the most sorrowful figure of the Greek stage, the unfortunate Oedipus," also finds comfort, a metaphysical and pious comfort, in the mystery of being (1967, 67).

---

[4] Silk and Stern 1981, 296. See also Dannhauser 1974, 114–15. On the importance of Sophocles, and especially his Oedipus, for Nietzsche's thought, see Silk and Stern 1981, 162, 255–7, 272.

[5] The other visionary tragic hero Nietzsche praises, Prometheus, is a god (1967, 69–72).

For he "is confronted by the supraterrestrial cheerfulness that descends from the divine sphere" (68). "In the Old Tragedy, one could sense at the end that metaphysical comfort without which the delight in tragedy cannot be explained at all. The reconciling tones sound purest, perhaps, in the *Oedipus at Colonus*" (108). Accordingly, "Sophocles in his *Oedipus* sounds as a prelude the *holy man's* song of triumph" (70, emphasis in text). Nietzsche argues on the basis of his account of Oedipus in particular, as the tragic hero who rejects reason and ultimately finds hope and salvation through suffering (1974, 219), that Sophocles was an anti-rationalist. In this way, Nietzsche invokes the purported anti-rationalism of Sophocles, the poet traditionally regarded as the greatest of the tragic poets,[6] to support his overall thesis that a spiritual renaissance of humanity can be founded on the rejection of Socratic rationalism.

But was Sophocles truly an opponent of rationalism? Did Sophocles present his Oedipus as a model human being who wisely and nobly rejects reason? Did Sophocles anticipate Nietzsche in teaching that human life is fundamentally tragic and that the universe is fundamentally mysterious and hence impenetrable to the human mind? Or was Sophocles, like his younger contemporaries Socrates and Thucydides, a believer in the private, rational life of the mind but skeptical concerning the practical possibilities of a popular, *political* rationalism or enlightenment?

The brilliant, richly provocative, and deeply influential interpretation of Sophocles by Nietzsche is not as clearly grounded in convincing, detailed, textual analysis as one might expect. For example, in *The Birth of Tragedy*, Nietzsche bases his entire interpretation of Sophocles' *Oedipus the Tyrant* and *Oedipus at Colonus* on the claim that Oedipus's solving of the riddle of the Sphinx proves that he is unequivocally wise and that his wisdom was the wisdom of a "holy man" (1967, 42, 46, 67–70). But, in the text of *Oedipus the Tyrant*, Oedipus claims that he solved the riddle of the Sphinx through unassisted human reason alone and consequently denies the claims to wisdom made by religious

---

[6] See, for example, Xenophon *Memorabilia* 1.4.3, as well as Segal's helpful historical account of the reputation of Sophocles' *Oedipus the Tyrant* in particular (2001, 144–57).

prophets and oracles (390–8).[7] In this book, I assess the interpretation of Sophocles by Nietzsche on the basis of a detailed textual analysis of the Theban plays – *Oedipus the Tyrant*, *Oedipus at Colonus*, and *Antigone* – the very plays on which Nietzsche bases his interpretation of Sophocles as a critic of rationalism. My approach to the plays does not assume that individual characters, such as Oedipus or Teiresias, are the spokesmen for Sophocles but rather that the poet's thought can only be uncovered by examining each character's speeches within the context of the overall drama of each play.

Since Nietzsche especially – whom Harold Bloom, for example, calls "the truest guide to *Oedipus the King*" (1988, 4) – the view of Sophocles as a proto-Nietzschean or religious enemy of rationalism has tended to prevail among a wide variety of thinkers and scholars.[8] Heidegger, for example, affirms that it is Oedipus's "passion for disclosure of being," the "fundamental passion" of "the science of the Greeks," that leads to his "downfall" (1980, 107). Bernard Knox claims that *Oedipus the Tyrant* "is a reassertion of the religious view of a divinely ordered universe" against the "rationalism" of "the

[7] Many scholars have offered fascinating and thought-provoking interpretations of the Theban plays, which are based in large part on the supposed content of the riddle of the Sphinx and Oedipus's answer (for example, Vernant and Vidal-Naquet 1988, 113–40, 207–36; Benardete 2000, 71–82, 126–35; Schwartz 1986, 198–9; Wilson 1997, 14–18; Rocco 1997, 46–51). Benardete goes so far as to claim that "Any interpretation of Oedipus has to face this riddle: What is the necessary connection between Oedipus's solution to the riddle of the Sphinx and Oedipus's two crimes?" (2000, 126). However, since neither the content of the riddle nor Oedipus's solution appears in any of Sophocles' extant plays but only, as far as we know, in much later sources, I think it safer to interpret the Theban plays without reference to the riddle's supposed meaning. Regarding the classical sources for the content of the riddle, see Vernant and Vidal-Naquet 1988, 468. In Vernant's account, Diodorus Siculus, who lived in the first century B.C., seems to be our oldest known source for the content of the riddle: "What is that thing which, while still being the same, is two-legged, three-legged, and four-legged?" (4.64.3–4).

[8] As Segal observes more broadly, "From Nietzsche on, Greek tragedy has been felt to hold the key to that darker vision of existence, the irrational and the violent in man and the world" (1986, 45). According to Silk, Nietzsche represents "the very apex of modern theorizing about 'the tragic'" (1996, 10).

fifth-century philosophers and sophists" (1998, 47–8). Charles Segal
is less sure of Sophocles' piety but nonetheless emphatic regarding
his rejection of rationalism: "The verbal ironies of *Oedipus Tyrannus*
reflect both the ultimate failure of Oedipus to solve the true 'riddle' of
the play – the riddle of the meaning of life in a universe governed by
chance or by distant and mysterious gods – and the very incoherence
of a universe that *logos*, reason-as-language, cannot make intelligible"
(1986, 73).[9]

Over the past two decades, trailblazing studies of Sophocles' political
thought by J. Peter Euben (1986, 1990, 1997) and Arlene Saxonhouse,
(1986, 1988, 1992) have challenged this scholarly consensus by
stressing that there are important similarities and continuities between
Sophocles and Socratic thought.[10] However, while I am indebted to their
work in important ways, I go further than they do in arguing that,
although Sophocles is cautiously critical of *political* rationalism – namely,
the attempt to base political society on reason alone – he clearly points to
the need for a *theoretical* rationalism – namely, the attempt to steer one's
own life by the compass of unaided reason.[11] For example, Euben does
suggest that there may be "an affinity between especially this tragedy
[*Oedipus the Tyrant*] and Socratic political theory" (1990, 127n 72;
consider also 30–1, 108, 202–3). But Euben tends to emphasize, more

---

[9] Consider also Reinhardt (1979, 130–4); Dodds (1968, 25–8); Gould (1988);
  Ehrenberg (1954, especially 66–9, 136–66); Lattimore (1958, 94–5);
  Waldcock (1966, 168); Vernant and Vidal-Naquet (1988, 104–7); Wilson
  (1997, 171–2); and even Whitman (1971, for example, 146, 251 [but see
  also 123, 134]) and Rocco (1997, 34, 38–9, 43, 55–6, 64). For an older
  view, which stresses the affinity between the classical tragic poets and the
  classical philosophers, consider Racine's remark in his preface to *Phèdre*: "Their
  theater was a school where virtue was no less well taught than in the schools of
  the philosophers" (1965, 32).

[10] Consider as well Bolotin (1980) and Tessitore (2003).

[11] It is striking that Nietzsche himself on occasion seems to wonder whether
  Sophocles is not closer to Socratic rationalism than he is to Aeschylus's (purported) anti-rationalism: "in tragedy from Sophocles onward . . . we are already
  in the atmosphere of a theoretical world, where scientific knowledge is valued
  more highly than the artistic reflection of a universal law" (1967, 108; consider as well 85, 87, 92).

than Sophocles' theoretical rationalism, the extent to which his play presents Oedipus as "living proof of the limits of rationality and the presence of the divine" (115; see also 26–7, 101, 105, 122–3; 1986, 28, 35; 1997, 194–6, 199–201). Moreover, although I completely agree with Saxonhouse's argument that the play is a warning against *political* rationalism – that is, "attempting the transformation of the world on the basis of abstract, calculating reason alone" – I am inclined to disagree with her suggestion that the play is also, at least partially, a critique of the theoretical, Socratic pursuit of wisdom through reason alone (1988, 1272; see especially 1263, 1265, 1270–3).

My own study of Sophocles leads me to conclude that Sophocles is not a critic of rationalism, that he does not endorse the denunciations of reason made by such characters as Teiresias and the blind Oedipus, even though he also does not simply endorse the secular, anti-conventional, political rationalism represented by Oedipus's "tyrannical" rule. I argue, for example, that Sophocles believes that the downfall of Oedipus in *Oedipus the Tyrant* is ultimately caused, not by his dedication to reason, but by his abandonment of reason and his turn to piety. But Sophocles also believes that political rulers will inevitably abandon reason in favor of pious hopes when confronted with such mortal political crises as Oedipus faces at the beginning of that play. Similarly, I show that it is not the religious, anti-rationalist Oedipus who is the hero of *Oedipus at Colonus*, but rather the humane and enlightened Theseus, whose states-manship constitutes a middle way between an immoderate political rationalism that dismisses the power of religion – exemplified by Oedipus the Tyrant – and a piety that rejects reason – exemplified by Oedipus at Colonus. Finally, I argue that Antigone ultimately demonstrates her superiority to Creon, not only through her heroic piety but also through her heroic willingness to question her most cherished convictions about justice and about the possibility of an immortal happiness. The *Antigone*, I suggest, invites one to ascend from the pious heroism of Antigone to the humane wisdom of Sophocles. The true model of rationalism to be found in the Theban plays, I conclude, is Sophocles himself, who presents the problem of politics, reason, and piety with a genuinely philosophic clarity, calm, and depth, but whose rationalism differs from Socrates and even from Thucydides, most notably, in its somber reserve. I close my study with an examination of the teachings of

Nietzsche, Socrates, and Aristotle concerning the relation between tragedy and philosophy. I argue that, notwithstanding the claims of Nietzsche to the contrary, the rationalism of Socrates and Aristotle is not simply optimistic, that it is indeed sensitive to the tragic dimension of human existence, and that it therefore resembles in fundamental ways the somber rationalism of Sophocles.

I *Oedipus the Tyrant* and the Limits of Political Rationalism

CRIME AND PUNISHMENT?

On the very surface, *Oedipus the Tyrant* appears to be a story of the triumph of justice over injustice. As the title of the play emphasizes, most unmistakably to its democratic Athenian audience, Oedipus is a tyrant – a man who ascends to power and rules outside the limits imposed by human and divine law.[1] He violates the most sacred of laws – the laws that protect the family – and commits the most atrocious and monstrous of crimes by killing his father and sleeping with his

---

[1] See, for example, Thucydides 6.15, 53, 59–61; Xenophon *Hiero* 4.5, 7.10; *Hellenica* 5.4.9, 13, 6.4.32, 7.3.4–12, especially 7; Isocrates *Nicocles* 24. These passages call into question Knox's suggestion that Oedipus's "title, *tyrannos* . . . must have won him the sympathy of the Athenian audience" because Athens aimed to become the tyrant of Greece (1998, 99; see 58–77). Oedipus is consistently referred to as a tyrant throughout the play (380, 408, 514, 535, 541, 588, 592, 873, 925, 1096). The only time that he is referred to as a king is immediately after it is discovered that he is the son of King Laius (1202). The Corinthian messenger does say that Oedipus will also be named the tyrant of Corinth, even though he is ostensibly the son of the former ruler Polybus (939–40). But perhaps it is already known there that he is not the true son of Polybus. Oedipus does call Laius a tyrant (128, 799, 1043), but he also calls him king and clearly indicates that Laius was a member of the royal family and the heir to the throne of Thebes (257, 264–8). The fact that Oedipus refers to Laius as tyrant as well as king may indicate that the word "tyranny" has a somewhat broad meaning in the play. But it also would seem to be in Oedipus's interest to blur the distinction between a ruler who is heir to the throne by birth, as Laius is, and one who is not, as he is not.

mother.[2] Through such crimes, Oedipus seems most clearly to violate those divine laws, which, the chorus declares, are "lofty ones, through heavenly aether born, whose only father is Olympus; nor did any mortal nature of men give birth to them, nor will forgetfulness ever put them to sleep; great is the god in them, and he grows not old."[3] Through such crimes, Oedipus seems most clearly to exhibit the *hubris* that, the chorus explains, begets a tyrant (873).[4] The downfall of Oedipus the tyrant, therefore, seems, at first glance, eminently just and specifically a triumph of law over tyranny.

Yet a more careful reading of *Oedipus the Tyrant* calls into question this initial impression of the play as a simple condemnation of Oedipus. For Oedipus seems to be a truly great ruler, one who combines what no other Sophoclean hero combines: genuine wisdom with a genuinely noble devotion to others.[5] When a cruel monster, the Sphinx, threatened Thebes with destruction unless someone could solve her riddle, it was Oedipus alone who had the wisdom to solve a riddle that even the soothsayers could not solve (390–400). But by saving Thebes, Oedipus displayed not only his wisdom but also his nobility. For Oedipus saved Thebes from destruction even though he was a foreigner and a wayfarer who had no evident interest in or obligation to Thebes. Later in the play, Oedipus appeals to Teiresias's self-interest and sense of civic duty by urging him to help the city to which he belongs and "which reared you" (310–3, 322–3). But Oedipus's original intervention to save Thebes cannot have been motivated by any such self-interest or sense of duty. It seems rather to have been an act of sheer generosity, free of any self-interest or obligation, a vivid expression of Oedipus's conviction

---

[2] Consider Plato *Republic* 568d4–569c9, 571a1–575a7, especially 571c3-d4; *Laws* 838a4-e1. See Wohl 2002, 250.

[3] 863–71; see also 899–910.

[4] See also Benardete 2000, 72–3. As Wohl puts it, "Oedipus's tyranny . . . represents a metaphysical position, an illegal relation to being and power . . ." (2002, 259).

[5] Oedipus seems to combine the intelligence or wisdom characteristic of Sophocles' Odysseus, Ismene, and Chrysothemis with the nobility characteristic of his Neoptolemus, Ajax, Antigone, and Electra.

that "to benefit a man from what one has and can do is the noblest of toils" (314–15).[6]

To be sure, Oedipus does become the tyrant of Thebes as a direct consequence of saving the city from the Sphinx. But, as Oedipus emphasizes, he never asked the Thebans to make him their tyrant. The Thebans freely chose him to be their ruler, even though he was a young foreigner unknown to them, because he had saved their city from destruction (380–9; consider also *Oedipus at Colonus* 539–41). Oedipus did not acquire his tyrannical power in the usual manner, by force or wealth or guile (see *Oedipus the Tyrant* 540–1), but seems rather to have graciously accepted it as a recognition of his wisdom and nobility and to have generously and even selflessly agreed to devote himself to the good of his newly adopted city.

Oedipus's tyrannical rule over Thebes is, moreover, evidently superior to that of his predecessor, the hereditary king, Laius – whose murder the Thebans never even investigate during the many years after the intervening crisis of the Sphinx has passed[7] – as well as to that of King Creon, who becomes ruler solely by reason of his family ties with Jocasta and Oedipus, who appears to be wholly indifferent to the public good in *Oedipus the Tyrant,* and whose rule quickly collapses into chaos as a consequence of his disastrous conflict with Antigone (see 124–36, 255–8, 264–8, 729–37, 754–64; and also 577–600; *Antigone* 155–61). Since Oedipus became tyrant of Thebes, the city has evidently prospered under his rule for some fifteen years. He evidently enjoys broad support from the people, for he is praised throughout the play as a ruler who is both wise and devoted to the city (*Oedipus the Tyrant* 31–57, 103–4, 497–511, 689–96, 1196–1203, 1282–3, 1524–7). Once the city is threatened for a second time with destruction – from a plague – the Thebans look to Oedipus again to save them. When he is

[6] Euripides' Jocasta (*The Phoenecian Women* 45–54) says that Creon declared that the man who solved the riddle of the Sphinx should marry the queen, but there is no such suggestion in Sophocles' account.

[7] It is understandable that the Thebans neglected to investigate the killing of their king while the Sphinx threatened to destroy their city. But the fact that they neglected to investigate the regicide after the threat had passed suggests a certain indifference to his reign, as Oedipus himself may suggest at 133–6 and 255–8.

told by the oracle at Delphi that he must find and punish the killer of
Laius to save the city, he devotes himself zealously to this task,
pledging, for example, that he will punish the killer even if he should
turn out to be a member of his own family (249–51). He publicly
abases himself before Teiresias in order to persuade him to help solve
the murder (300–15, 326–7). When the soothsayer refuses to help,
Oedipus is indignant, not on his own behalf but on behalf of the city
(339–40; see also 322–3, 330–1). When Teiresias enigmatically tells
Oedipus that he destroyed himself when he defeated the Sphinx and
subsequently became tyrant of Thebes, Oedipus responds, "But if I
saved this city, it [my destruction] is of no concern to me" (442–3; see
also 669–72). Finally, when Oedipus concludes that he is the murderer
of Laius, and hence the cause of the plague, he abdicates his power
without hesitation and punishes himself. Oedipus appears to be a wise
and noble ruler who is willing to sacrifice everything – his family, his
pride, his rule, even his very happiness – for the sake of his city.[8]

---

[8] Oedipus's charge that Creon had Laius killed and is conspiring with Teiresias
to overthrow him may seem foolish and unjust (see, for example, Lattimore
1958, 92; Vellacott 1971, 161; Vernant and Vidal-Naquet 1988, 106; but
for defenses of Oedipus, see Whitman 1971, 130–1; Benardete 2000, 129–
31). Indeed, at the end of the play, Oedipus himself decries his own treatment
of Creon as "evil" (1419–21). Yet, given that Oedipus has no reason at the
beginning of the play even to suspect that he has killed Laius or committed
patricide and incest, his suspicion of Creon at the time is not unreasonable. As
the brother of the young queen, Creon was the presumptive heir to Laius's
throne and therefore presumably had the motive, as well as the means, to have
Laius killed (124–5). Creon never investigated the killing of Laius, even
though it was suspected that a Theban hired the killers (126–40). Furthermore, Creon urges Oedipus to summon Teiresias, who proceeds effectively to
call for Oedipus's overthrow by accusing him publicly of being the killer of
Laius – and hence the cause of the plague ravaging Thebes – as well as of
patricide and incest to boot. Now, as the man who would have succeeded Laius,
as a native Theban, and as an older man, Creon has good reason to resent the
foreign and young Oedipus for having become ruler of Thebes (consider
639–41, 674–5). As the brother of Oedipus's wife, Creon is also, presumably,
the natural successor to Oedipus. It is true that Creon denies to Oedipus that
he has any ambition whatsoever to replace him (577–602). But it is also true
that he has every reason to deny to the sitting tyrant of Thebes that he has any
ambition whatsoever to replace him (consider also Creon's spirited remarks at

Furthermore, Oedipus appears to be greatly devoted to his family as well. Even though he was the heir to the throne of Corinth and, by his own account, the "greatest" man in the city, he left Corinth and thereby apparently sacrificed all of his hopes of ever becoming a ruler, in order to avoid fulfilling the Delphic Oracle's prediction that he would kill his father and sleep with his mother (774–97, 822–33, 991–1013). He evidently loves his wife, "dearest" Jocasta, and reveres her, he says, even more than he does the Theban elders (950, 772–3; see also 700, 800). And although Oedipus may seem somewhat indifferent toward his sons, he expresses what seems to be a profound fatherly love for, in his words, "what is dearest" to him, his daughters Antigone and Ismene, a love to which even Creon bears witness (1458–1514). Indeed, Oedipus's last words in the play are his plea to Creon: "Never take these girls from me" (1522).

Finally, even though Oedipus did commit patricide and incest, he did so unknowingly, since he had no idea that Laius was his father and Jocasta his mother.[9] Once he learned from the Delphic Oracle that he would kill

---

626–30, 673–5). And Creon does in fact replace Oedipus and become ruler of Thebes without expressing any hesitation or reluctance about ruling whatsoever, either in this play or in *Oedipus at Colonus* and *Antigone*. Finally, as Oedipus points out to the chorus, even if he is not absolutely certain that Creon is conspiring against him, he cannot afford to investigate Creon at his leisure but must act swiftly to defend himself and his rule (618–21).

[9] Oedipus repeatedly argues in *Oedipus at Colonus* that, since he committed patricide and incest unwittingly, he cannot be justly blamed for these crimes (see, for example, 270–4, 521–3, 546–8, and 962–99 as a whole). The Second Messenger in *Oedipus the Tyrant* also stresses the importance of the distinction between willing and unwilling acts (1227–31). On the case for Oedipus's "essential moral innocence," see, for example, Dodds 1968, 18–22. Dodds, however, goes on to argue that, even though Oedipus knows he is morally innocent, he rightly punishes himself out of "a sense of guilt" (23–4; see Wilson 1997, 145–9). Consider as well Kitto 1958, and compare 47, 49–50, and 57–8 with 62–3. For an ingenious argument that Oedipus knowingly killed his father and slept with his mother and hence that "every disaster here sprang from human choice," see Vellacott 1971, 238, and as a whole. In order to square this thesis with the overwhelming impression of the text that Oedipus is ignorant of these crimes, however, Vellacott asserts, without sufficient evidence and in somewhat contradictory fashion, both that Oedipus represses, in his own mind and heart, the knowledge of his guilt and

his father and sleep with his mother, he made every effort, at considerable sacrifice, to avoid those whom he had every reason to believe were his parents. Moreover, given his ignorance of his parents, his actions are altogether defensible. While Oedipus is certainly a spirited man, he kills Laius only in response to his unprovoked, violent attack, as he emphasizes both in this play (804–13) and *Oedipus at Colonus* (270–4, 521–3, 546–8, 962–99). His marriage to Jocasta, the widow of the dead king, was proposed by the Thebans themselves and was presumably motivated by their understandable desire to add legitimacy and hence stability to this young foreigner's rule (consider *Oedipus at Colonus* 525–6, 539–41; see also *Oedipus the Tyrant* 255–68). One must add as well that, however political that marriage may have been in its origins, it is evidently marked by genuine affection between Oedipus and Jocasta (consider 577–80, 700, 772–3, 800, 861–2, 911–23, 950).

How, then, can such a wise and noble ruler and human being deserve to suffer the terrible fate of discovering that he has committed patricide and incest; of losing his power, his city, and his beloved wife; and of living the rest of his life as a blind wanderer? How can Oedipus be justly held responsible for crimes he committed against his will? It would seem that, insofar as Oedipus is wise, noble, and wholly undeserving of his downfall, Sophocles' play does indeed, as Nietzsche suggests, teach us that the world is cruelly indifferent to human beings and fundamentally incomprehensible to human reason.[10] But is it true that Oedipus is wise, noble, and in no way responsible for his downfall?

FROM ENLIGHTENMENT TO THEOCRACY

The immediate causes within the play of the chain of events that leads to Oedipus's downfall are, first, his sending of Creon to the Delphic

---

that he consciously and deliberately orchestrates the gradual revelation of his guilt to the Thebans by, for example, merely pretending to be angry with Teiresias and Creon (see 119–22, as well as 137, 167–9, 198–9, 225, 233).

[10] Consider as well Arthur Waldock's conclusion: "There is no meaning in the *Oedipus Tyrannus*. There is merely the terror of coincidence, and then, at the end of it all, our impression of man's power to suffer, and of his greatness because of this power" (1966, 168). See also Nussbaum 1992, 262–3, 285–7.

Oracle to learn how Thebes might be saved from the plague – an action that immediately precedes the opening of the play – and then his summoning of Teiresias, early in the play. If Oedipus had not sought assistance from the oracle and soothsayer of Apollo, he would not have been led to investigate the killing of Laius, to decree that the killer be exiled or killed, to conclude that he was the killer, and to punish himself. To be sure, the revelation by the Corinthian messenger that Polybus and Merope are not his true parents does lead Oedipus to conclude that he has committed incest and patricide. But even by the time of that revelation, his decision to turn to the oracle and the soothsayer for help has committed him to trying to save Thebes by punishing the killer of Laius, has exposed him to the public accusations of Teiresias that he is guilty of regicide, patricide, and incest, and has placed him on the verge of discovering that he is the killer of Laius (see 216–75, 305–9, 350–3, 362, 449–60, 644–73, 697–706, 744–5, 747, 836–63, 1041–52). What then is the significance of Oedipus's turn to the gods for assistance?

To address this question, let us return to that fact about Oedipus the title of the play emphasizes – that he is a tyrant – and consider more carefully the distinctive character of Oedipus's rule. The defining act of Oedipus's political career is his victory over the Sphinx and his subsequent accession to power in Thebes, not by birth or through force, but by reason of that victory (see, for example, 31–57, 505–11, 1196–1203). Oedipus's victory over that monster puts him in the company of such heroes as Heracles and Theseus, who also won fame by vanquishing monsters.[11] What is distinctive about Oedipus's victory over the Sphinx, however, is that it is a purely intellectual victory, one of brains and not at all of brawn. He solves the riddle and thereby defeats the monster and saves Thebes. Although Oedipus is sufficiently strong to kill five men single-handedly, what makes him great is not his strength but his mind.[12]

---

[11] See *Trachinian Women* 1–41, 555–77, 680–722, 831–40, 1010–4, 1058–61, 1089–1111, 1162–3; *Philoctetes* 1418–20; *Oedipus at Colonus* 562–9; Plutarch *Theseus* 6–20.

[12] 798–813, 438–41; see also 390–8, 1524–7. As Saxonhouse remarks, "His strength lies in his mind and his own authority rests on that intellect" (1988,

But Oedipus's triumph over the Sphinx is not only a victory of brains over brawn, but also one of human reason over divine revelation. As Oedipus declares to the soothsayer Teiresias: "Since, come, tell me, where were you a clear soothsayer? How, when the chanting dog was here, did you not utter something for these townsmen here, to release them? Indeed, the riddle was not for the first man who came along, that he should solve it, but a divination was needed, which you were not able to bring to light, either from birds or from something known from the gods. But I came, the one who knows nothing, Oedipus, and put a stop to her, hitting the mark with my judgment, without having learned from birds" (390–8). Oedipus affirms here not only that Teiresias, the soothsayer of Apollo and the representative of divine wisdom, failed to solve the riddle of the Sphinx but that he, Oedipus, solved it through human reason alone.[13] In this way, he seems to deny not only the veracity of soothsayers and oracles but also the need for divine assistance, since unassisted reason is sufficient to save such political communities as Thebes from such deadly monsters as the Sphinx. Oedipus's unconventional rule, or tyranny, seems to herald, then, the liberation of human wisdom and prudence from the benighted rule of soothsayers and oracles.

The chorus of Theban elders sets forth the conventional view that it is the gods – led by Zeus, the "lord of all things," whose rule is "deathless, eternal" – who are the true rulers of human beings, who protect the city from harm, punish the wicked, provide humans with eternal, divine laws, and reveal their will to human beings through their oracles and soothsayers (904–5, 497–9, 158–67, 188–215, 863–72, 879–903). Teiresias, for example, is said by the chorus to know all that Apollo knows and is described as "the divine seer . . . in whom alone of human beings the truth has taken root" (284–6, 297–9). Indeed, the elders place such importance on the oracles and soothsayers that they declare that, if the oracles and soothsayers prove to be false, they will lose all faith in the gods' care for humans (897–910).

1264). Lattimore suggests that "his tragedy is the intellectual's tragedy" (1958, 95). See also Wilson 1997, 178; Rocco 1997, 34–41; Van Nortwick 1998, 25.

[13] See, in contrast, the priest's more pious account of Oedipus's defeat of the Sphinx at 31–9, 46–53.

Under the reign of Laius, the soothsayers and oracles held such sway
that they convinced the king and the queen to kill their only son and to
remain childless (711–22, 1173–6; see also 114–5, 558–63). Later,
Creon, who originally persuaded Oedipus to seek Teiresias's assistance,
stresses that, in contrast to Oedipus, he will seek divine guidance for all
of his decisions as ruler.[14] Oedipus's rule is preceded and followed by
pious kings under the more or less continuous sway of oracles and
soothsayers. In contrast, under Oedipus's rule, his wife Jocasta does not
hesitate to deny publicly the veracity of all soothsayers and oracles:
"Now you release yourself of the things you speak of and listen to me
and learn why you can find no mortal being who possesses a soothsayer's
art."[15] She suggests as well that there is no afterlife for human beings
(955–6; cf. 971–2). Later, she goes so far as to express, again publicly,
the atheistic view that the true rulers of humankind are not gods
but chance: "Why should a human being be afraid, for whom chance
rules and there is no sure foreknowledge of anything?" (977–9). And
although Oedipus never goes quite this far, on one occasion he does
publicly deny the veracity of the Delphic Oracle in particular, as well as
of soothsayers as a whole (964–7). More importantly, the play suggests
that, during the fifteen years or so between his accession to power and
the coming of the plague, Oedipus never consulted oracles or soothsayers but ruled by his own wits alone. Oedipus's decision to send
Creon to consult the oracle of Apollo at Delphi is taken only as a last
resort, when he is at his wit's end because he can think of no other
possible way of saving Thebes from the plague (58–72). Even though
Teiresias has been honored by the Thebans as a wise soothsayer since
before his accession to power, Oedipus has evidently regarded him as a
charlatan, has consequently never asked him for advice, and does so now
only at the behest of Creon.[16] Oedipus's rule, then, during the fifteen

---

[14] 555–7, 1422–31, 1438–45, 1515–20; see also *Antigone* 163–4, 278–89,
304–14, and especially 991–5. Accordingly I cannot agree with Reinhardt's
suggestion that Creon "represents the rational, enlightened *bios* of the age"
(1979, 121; see also 132).

[15] See 707–9; see also 723–5, 857–8, 973, 975. Under Oedipus's rule, even the
chorus expresses a momentary doubt concerning the truthfulness of soothsayers
(497–501).

[16] 558–63, 284–6, 297–9, 390–8, 555–7; compare 300ff. with *Antigone* 991–5.

years or so from his defeat of the Sphinx until the coming of the plague, marks an experiment in political enlightenment or rationalism, during which religion is separated from politics, and reason rather than revelation is the ruler's sole star and compass.

Oedipus's rule also seems to represent the elevation of reason over blood. Oedipus is the ruler of Thebes, even though he is not – apparently – a member of the royal house or a native Cadmeian (see 14, 255–68; see also Knox 1998, 54). His rule is based, then, on a rejection of the conventional view that only native members of a community can be counted on to care for it. His title to rule is objective merit – his superior intelligence and character – rather than birth, and his devotion to Thebes – which seems to surpass by far the devotion felt by any one else in the play – springs entirely from his soul, and not from his body.[17]

Finally, Oedipus's rule represents an elevation of reason over age. For he is young when he becomes ruler, in his early twenties at most, with a mother still young enough to bear four children. Convention would ordinarily prevent such a gifted young man from ruling over the inferior but older Creon, for example, on the grounds that the old are wiser than the young. In the *Antigone*, Creon speaks for the conventional view when he asks indignantly, after being challenged by his son Haemon: "Should we at our age be taught to think by a man of such an age in his nature?" (726; see also 639–40, 742; *Oedipus at Colonus* 1291–8). Indeed, the announcement of the death of Polybus during

---

[17] See 63–4, 93–4. Whereas Oedipus refers to the city (πολις) seven times in his scene with Teiresias (302, 312, 322, 331, 340, 383, 442), Teiresias never refers either to the city or to its suffering as a result of the plague, and refuses to help Oedipus solve the murder of Laius and end that suffering (see Benardete 2000, 73, 128). Creon claims to be indifferent to political life and hence, it would seem, to the good of his city (see 582–602), though his later political career suggests that he may be hiding his public spiritedness and ambition from the tyrant Oedipus. Even Jocasta, who is the last character in the play to refer to the plague (634–6; but see 660–8), later urges Oedipus to desist from questioning the herdsman who was Laius's servant, even though that would mean closing the investigation of Laius's murder and hence abandoning all efforts to save the city from the plague (1054–72). Finally, everyone in the play, except for Oedipus, seems to be remarkably indifferent to the unsolved murder of Laius, even though that crime would seem to be against the whole community.

the play reminds us that, in the ordinary course of things, if Oedipus had remained in Corinth, he would not have become ruler until now, when he is in his mid- to late-thirties (*Oedipus the Tyrant* 939–42). Yet he is chosen to rule by the Thebans simply by the sheer force of his virtue and wisdom.

Oedipus's tyrannical rule thus marks a great rebellion against the kingdom of darkness – the traditional rule of soothsayers, oracles, gods, kings, and elders – and the victory of enlightenment over superstition, reason over blood, wisdom over age. It constitutes an experiment in political rationalism, the attempt to free politics from the unreasonable constraints imposed by convention and law, human and divine. The true meaning of Oedipus's tyranny, then, is not that it is a rule of force – it is not – nor even that it is the rule of one, but rather that it is that form of rule that is freest from convention, law, and tradition and that is guided most of all by unaided human reason. In this light, the tyrannical character of Oedipus's rule is essential to its greatness, for its tyrannical character makes possible its enlightened character. Oedipus is the tyrant insofar, but only insofar, as he is the purely rational ruler.

But insofar as Oedipus's tyranny constitutes an experiment in political rationalism, the opening of the play marks the end of that experiment. For the actions with which the play virtually opens and that ultimately lead to his downfall – sending Creon to the Delphic Oracle and summoning the soothsayer Teiresias – mark Oedipus's break from the unassisted human reason he has relied on up till now and his turn for guidance to the oracles, the soothsayers, and ultimately the gods. It is not, then, Oedipus's rational, tyrannical rule but rather his abandonment thereof that leads to his downfall.

Yet, given Oedipus's own experiences with the Delphic Oracle and Teiresias, his turn to them for help is surprising and even bewildering. For when he turned to the oracle of Apollo for assistance as a young man and asked it who his parents were, the oracle refused to answer, even though it went on to underscore the vital importance of knowing an answer to this question by stating that Oedipus would kill his father and sleep with his mother (779–97). The oracle was therefore exceedingly cruel to Oedipus, for it told him that he would commit the crimes of patricide and incest but it refused to give him the information that would enable him to avoid doing so. Moreover, Oedipus knows that, when Thebes faced destruction before at the hands of the Sphinx, Teiresias, the soothsayer of Apollo, was unable to save the city (390–8). Oedipus's only experiences with oracles and soothsayers up until now would seem to point to the conclusion that it is unreasonable for human beings to look to the gods for assistance either because the gods are whimsical and cruel beings or because, as Jocasta declares, it is not the gods but chance that rules over human affairs, that the gods do not exist, and those, like the oracle and Teiresias, who claim to be their spokesmen, are charlatans (977–9).

The play as a whole seems also to point to the conclusion either that the gods are whimsical and cruel or that they do not exist and the oracles and soothsayers are fraudulent. If the oracle at Delphi truly speaks for Apollo, then Apollo is guilty of extreme cruelty toward Oedipus. By telling Oedipus that he will kill his father and sleep with his mother, Apollo virtually commands him to flee his parents (786–97, 994–8, 1001, 1011, 1013). But by refusing to reveal to him who his parents are, Apollo makes it impossible for Oedipus to obey this command. In the end, Apollo leads the unwitting Oedipus to kill his father and sleep with his mother when he seeks to avoid doing so, just as, in the *Ajax*, Athena leads the unwitting Ajax to slaughter the Greek army's livestock when he seeks rather to kill his enemies.[18] Indeed, Apollo's treatment of Oedipus seems more clearly unjust than Athena's treatment of Ajax, since it is not prompted by any even alleged misdeed on Oedipus's part.[19] Furthermore, one wonders, why would Apollo send a plague to Thebes only now, some fifteen years after the crimes which he ostensibly wishes to punish have been committed? What possible purpose is served by waiting, while Oedipus and Jocasta have four children, before revealing and punishing Oedipus's incest and patricide (see 558–69 and also 1207–12)? Here, too, Apollo seems wantonly cruel toward Oedipus and his family. Finally, if Teiresias truly speaks for Apollo, then Apollo is cruel here as well. For Teiresias does not clearly and compassionately explain to Oedipus that, although he has committed patricide and incest, since he has done so unwittingly

---

[18] See 774–833, 992–1013, 1329–30; *Ajax* 1–126.
[19] Consider *Ajax* 127–33, 749–80. But see also 455–6, 121–6.

and involuntarily, he is not truly responsible for those crimes. Instead, Teiresias speaks coyly, in riddles, and with evident malice about his crimes, and thereby ensures that Oedipus will go through the excruciating, drawn-out agony of angrily denying, then fearfully suspecting, and finally painfully concluding that he is guilty of incest and patricide.[20] Moreover, Teiresias harshly blames him for those crimes and taunts him for his ignorance, rather than pointing out that precisely his ignorance would seem to absolve him of responsibility for his crimes (364–7, 372–3, 412–28), as Oedipus himself will go on to argue in *Oedipus at Colonus* (270–4, 521–3, 546–8, 962–99). Finally, it is Teiresias alone who suggests to Oedipus that he should punish himself for these involuntary crimes by blinding himself (*Oedipus the Tyrant* 415–9, 454–6). The play thus suggests that if the gods exist, they are cruel beings indeed.

But the play also suggests that the gods may not exist at all and rather that, as Jocasta contends, the soothsayers and oracles are fraudulent and that blind chance governs the universe. First, it is important to note that, in contrast to the *Ajax* (1–133) and the *Philoctetes* (1409–71), gods or divine beings never appear on stage in *Oedipus the Tyrant*. We never see the gods but only hear of them from the oracles and the soothsayers. Yet these are, at the very least, fallible. Not only does Teiresias undeniably fail to solve the riddle of Sphinx – he himself never denies this failure – but the oracle that Oedipus will kill both his father *and his mother* proves to be false, at least literally (see 390–8, 438–42, 1171–6; but consider 1252–64). Moreover, the oracles contradict one another. The oracle of Apollo at Delphi states to Creon that many killed Laius, while Teiresias, the soothsayer of Apollo, claims that only Oedipus killed him (106–7, 305–9, 350–3, 362).[21] Indeed, we never even learn with certainty that Oedipus killed Laius,

---

[20] See, for example, 350–5, 362–4, 435–40, 449–62, 551–68, 703–6, 726–48, 836–47, 1182–5; compare also 316–44 with 447–8.

[21] Vellacott nonetheless asserts that the authority of the Delphic Oracle is "infallible" and that "everyone" believes Teiresias to be "infallible" and concludes from this assertion that Oedipus must have known all along that Laius and Jocasta were his true parents (1971, 118, 161: see also 148, 152, 158–9, 163, 165, 171).

since the key witness is never asked about the killing (compare 834–62 with 1039–53, 1119–85).[22] But even if Oedipus is guilty of patricide as well as incest, Teiresias, who has had some fifteen years to investigate, could have learned of this on his own, from the herdsman, as Oedipus eventually does, rather than from Apollo.[23] Finally, we never learn with certainty whether the plague ended once Oedipus punished himself, and hence whether it truly was sent by the gods (see 305–9).[24] So many seemingly chance events are central to the story – the herdsman's pity, Polybus's childlessness, the Corinthian drunk (see 776), the meeting of Laius and Oedipus at the three roads, Oedipus's arrival in Thebes, the death of Polybus, the identity of the Corinthian messenger – that it is at least possible that the plague too is a chance event (as Jocasta seems to suggest at 977–8), a sign not of the gods' righteous anger at Thebes, or even of their simple cruelty, but rather of nature's harsh indifference to human beings.[25]

---

[22] See Benardete 2000, 101, 132–3; Ormand 1999, 127–8.

[23] I therefore disagree with Knox's claim that "The play takes a clear stand" in favor of "the truth . . . of prophecy" and hence constitutes a reassertion of piety against "the new concepts of the fifth-century philosophers and sophists" (1998, 43–4, 47; see also Gould 1988). Victor Ehrenberg argues that the play presents Sophocles' pious warning against Socratic and especially Periclean rationalism (1954, 66–9, 136–66). But Whitman challenges those who "treat the play as a vivid proof of Sophocles' simple faith and pure piety" and points out that "If Sophocles had wished to reawaken public religion, he could scarcely have chosen a worse way than by preaching the careless power of the gods and the nothingness of man – the very beliefs, in fact, which were themselves concomitants of the Athenians' lawlessness and moral decay" (1971, 123, 134; but see also, for example, 146, 251; consider as well Rocco 1997, 55–6, 63–4).

[24] In contrast, Homer indicates clearly in Book I of the *Iliad* that the plague sent by Apollo is withdrawn once Agamemnon has returned Chryseis to her father, the priest of Apollo, in obedience to the god's demands (9–100, 430–74).

[25] According to Segal, "The plague is not mentioned in the myth before Sophocles, and it may well be his invention . . . . Sophocles may have been influenced by the plague that broke out in Athens in 430" (2001, 27; see also 11–2; Whitman 1971, 49–50, 133–4; Lattimore 1958, 94–5; Rehm 1992, 111). For Thucydides' suggestion that the plague that befell Athens was a sign, not of the gods' anger, but of nature's indifference to human beings, see 2.54.

Since the play as a whole, as well as Oedipus's experiences in particular, suggest that the gods are either wantonly cruel or that they do not exist, and that their oracles and soothsayers are fraudulent, why does Oedipus abandon his rationalism and turn to the gods for help now? Why does Oedipus summon the very soothsayer Teiresias who, by Oedipus's own account, has always been a charlatan (compare 390–7 with 300–15; see also 432)? Why does Oedipus turn for help to the very oracle that refused before even to tell him who his parents were?

The immediate cause of Oedipus's turn to the gods for assistance is the plague. The plague constitutes the greatest crisis of Oedipus's rule, for it threatens Thebes with complete destruction. As the priest puts it, "The house of Cadmus is emptied and black Hades grows rich in groans and wails" (29–30; see 14–57, 151–215). Oedipus responds by explaining that he has thought long and hard about the crisis, has considered every possible remedy for the plague, and has discovered only one – namely, to send Creon to Apollo to learn how he may save the city (58–72). Oedipus speaks here as though he has arrived at the conclusion through reason – after "considering well" (εὐ σκοπων–68) – that the only way that Thebes can be saved from destruction is by turning to the oracle of Apollo for help. But as we have seen, Oedipus's own experience with both the oracle and the soothsayer of Apollo would seem to suggest that it is unreasonable to turn to the gods for help. As he knows, Apollo either declined or was unable either to tell him who his parents were or to save Thebes from the Sphinx. Oedipus's reason, then, would seem to lead to the conclusion that there simply is no remedy for the plague and that the plague may destroy Thebes or may peter out, but that Oedipus is helpless before its deadly power.

Oedipus, however, evidently cannot accept that conclusion. He rejects what would seem to be the rational conclusion that, just as individual human beings are mortal, so are political communities. Oedipus cannot face the death of the city to which he is so devoted. He cannot face the possibility that the world or the gods are indifferent to its fate. Therefore, when reason points to that possibility, he rejects reason and fervently embraces instead the pious hope and belief of the chorus that it is beneficent and moral gods, rather than indifferent gods or blind chance, who rule over human beings. Not only does Oedipus send Creon to the oracle of Apollo to learn how to save the city from destruction; he also declares that he himself would be evil if he did not obey Apollo in all things, he prays to Apollo to save Thebes, he prays that the gods punish those who do evil, and he affirms that he will be a just ally to Apollo, that the Thebans can only succeed with the god's help, and that Teiresias, the soothsayer of Apollo, is the only possible savior of the city (76–7, 80–1, 246–54, 269–72, 135–6, 244–5, 145–6, 303–4). When Oedipus learns from the Delphic Oracle that Apollo requires that he solve the murder of Laius in order to save Thebes from the plague, Oedipus does not attempt to question on his own either the sole witness to that murder or even his wife Jocasta, but rather follows Creon's advice that he summon Teiresias, the soothsayer of Apollo.[26] Most importantly, Oedipus prays that, for those Thebans who are just, "May Justice, your ally, and all the gods benefit you forever" (273–5). In all these ways, Oedipus affirms that the gods rule over humans, that they are just, that they punish the wicked and reward the good, and that they bestow on the latter the reward of everlasting happiness (consider also 816, 830–3). Oedipus responds to the seemingly unavoidable death of all that he cares about by abandoning his political rationalism and by affirming that human beings can escape death and dwell with the gods "forever" if only they will act justly and piously.

Through the example of Oedipus, Sophocles suggests that the problem of human mortality constitutes the fundamental obstacle to the attempt to rule either one's political society or one's own life by human reason alone. For reason requires us human beings to accept our mortal nature and the terrible fragility that that nature imposes on us. It requires us to accept that all that we care about – our country, our loved ones, ourselves – can be taken from us at any moment, and inevitably *will* be taken from us. Through the case of Oedipus, Sophocles suggests that such an austere resignation, which calls on us to deny our greatest hopes, is simply beyond the reach of virtually all humans. To be sure, through the case of Jocasta, Sophocles might seem to offer an example of one who accepts with equanimity the belief that blind chance governs our lives. Yet by claiming that life is easiest if one lives, not according to reason, but according to one's will or whim

---

[26] Compare 276–89 (and 555–7) with 116–23, 698–862, especially 754–68.

($ε\dot{i}κ\tilde{η}$–979), Jocasta herself suggests that she also finds the austerity required by reason too difficult to bear, and hence that she tries to avoid even thinking about the terrible power of chance (977–83). Furthermore, the fact that Jocasta prays to Apollo when she fears for Oedipus's well-being reveals that, like Oedipus, she embraces piety when what she loves most is threatened (911–23; see also 646–8). Through the examples of both Oedipus and Jocasta, then, Sophocles suggests that the human longing to protect what one loves from harm and from death, a longing that political rationalism cannot ultimately satisfy, will incline even seemingly rationalistic human beings to embrace the belief in just gods who rule over us and who reward the righteous with eternal well-being. For piety offers us humans the hope that the gods will protect those we love "forever" (273–5).

Yet, although Sophocles teaches that political rationalism tends to collapse in the face of death, and hence that reason is weak, he also suggests that we need reason in order to attain such happiness as is available to such mortal beings as ourselves. As the play shows, when Oedipus's rationalism would seem to dictate resignation in the face of the destructive power of nature, his desire to protect what he loves most – apparently Thebes – leads him to reject that rationalism and turn to the gods. But it is that very rejection of reason and turn to piety that ultimately lead to his downfall.[27]

NOBILITY AND SELF-INTEREST

The apparent reason that Oedipus cannot be resigned to the possible destruction of Thebes from the plague is his devotion to Thebes. As he says to the Theban priest, his soul groans for the suffering city (63–4). And to Creon he remarks, "For I bear the suffering more for these [that is, the chorus of Theban elders] than for my own soul" (93–4). Oedipus

---

[27] I therefore disagree with the thesis that it is Oedipus's passion for the truth that leads to his downfall. See, for example, Heidegger 1980, 106–7; Rocco 1997, 53. Consider as well Bloom's pithy formulation: "You shall know the truth, and the truth will make you mad" (1988, 4).

suggests that his soul's devotion to the city eclipses its concern for itself, and hence that his dedication to the city's good surpasses his concern for his own individual good. Accordingly, when Teiresias later says that, by solving the riddle of the Sphinx, Oedipus has destroyed himself, Oedipus responds: "But if I saved the city, it [my destruction] is of no concern to me" (442). This devotion to Thebes is especially remarkable since Thebes is Oedipus's adopted city. He does not owe Thebes the debt he would have if he had been raised there (see 322–3; but see also 1378–83). And Oedipus, of all men, knows well that it is possible for a man who loses one city to find his fortune in another. But it seems that his devotion is based, not on a felt duty to or dependence on Thebes in particular, but rather on his dedication to acting as befits a noble human being. As he says, "To benefit a man from what one has and can do is the noblest of toils" (314–15).

It seems to be Oedipus's dedication to nobility thus understood that leads him, when faced with the plague, to reject reason, to turn to the gods for help, and to believe that he deserves their help. By his account, a noble man not only strives to benefit others but does so successfully. But consequently the noble man requires power in order to benefit others and hence in order to be noble. Until now, Oedipus has possessed sufficient power to benefit the Thebans, first by saving them from the Sphinx, and then by ruling over them successfully. He has possessed sufficient power to be a noble human being. But now, by threatening to destroy the community that Oedipus has devoted his life to benefiting, the plague exposes the weakness of his powers and therefore the fragility of his nobility. As the Theban priest tells him: "Let us in no way remember your rule as one in which we stood upright and later fell, but in safety set this city upright once again . . . . Since if indeed you will rule this land, just as you hold power over it, it is *nobler* to hold power over a land with men than over one that is empty" (49–55; emphasis added). The priest here points out that if Thebes, the beneficiary of Oedipus's nobility, is destroyed, Oedipus will lose not only the honor due to him as the savior of the city but also in large measure his very nobility.

The plague thus poses a radical challenge to Oedipus's dedication to nobility. If, as reason suggests, there is no remedy for the plague, then it is not possible for him to rescue the city and hence to be noble. If Oedipus were to follow reason, he would have to accept the fact that it is not always possible to be noble, since being noble depends not only on himself but also on blind chance or whimsical gods. He would ultimately have to accept the fact that even his ability to avoid what he later calls the "basest" of deeds (1408) – patricide and incest – depends on powers beyond his control. It would seem, then, that the plague would lead Oedipus to question whether it makes sense for him to devote himself to nobility and to make all of the apparent sacrifices he makes for the sake of being noble. For if the city one toils nobly and selflessly to benefit is ultimately destroyed, are not one's toils futile and senseless? More broadly, if one's ability to be noble depends so decisively on capricious fortune or gods, is it reasonable to make nobility the goal of one's life and to sacrifice one's well-being for that goal?

Oedipus, however, does not respond to the plague by pursuing such questions. Instead he embraces the hope that there are gods who support nobility, who would make it possible for him to save the city from the deadly plague and to help it achieve an immortal well-being, and hence who would enable him to act nobly even under these most terrible circumstances (see especially 76–7, 80–1, 135–6, 145–6, 244–54, 269–75, 300–15). It seems that so great is Oedipus's dedication to nobility that he suppresses his all-too-reasonable doubts about the beneficence of the gods in order to remain true to that dedication. And it is that zealous dedication to nobility that leads him to decree that the killer of Laius must be punished, to discover that he is guilty of that regicide, as well as of patricide and incest, and to punish himself, and hence that leads to his downfall.

Yet, in the course of the play, Sophocles shows that Oedipus's concern for nobility is not in truth his deepest concern. For, after his confrontation with Teiresias, Oedipus abandons his noble devotion to the city. For example, while Oedipus refers to the city ($\pi o\lambda\iota\varsigma$) ten times up to and including that scene, he refers to it only once thereafter, and not at all during the last half of the play (4, 64, 72, 302, 312, 322, 331, 340, 383, 442, 629).[28] Similarly, while Oedipus refers

---

[28] At 1378, Oedipus does refer to the town ($a\sigma\tau\upsilon$) and tower of Thebes, and on 1450 he does refer to his paternal town ($a\sigma\tau\upsilon$), but in neither case does he refer to Thebes as a political community or *polis*.

repeatedly to the plague up through his quarrel with Teiresias, he refers
to it only once thereafter, and never during the last half of the play (58–
69, 93–4, 143–6, 216–8, 300–15, 330–1; 671–2). More importantly, while Oedipus focuses during the first two-thirds of the play
on solving the regicide of Laius, a crime against the city and, according
to the Delphic Oracle, the cause of the plague destroying the city,
Oedipus focuses during the last third of the play on discovering whether he is guilty of patricide and incest, crimes against the family and
crimes apparently unrelated to the plague destroying Thebes. Indeed,
so complete is Oedipus's forgetting of the city that, when he finally has
an opportunity to interrogate the only witness to the killing of Laius,
the event that has purportedly caused the plague, he forgets to ask the
witness about the regicide and asks only about his own parents' identity
(compare 836–62 with 1037–85, 1119–81). The two distinctive
characteristics of Oedipus as a ruler are his political rationalism and his
noble devotion to the city. But, in the course of the play, Oedipus
abandons both.

The moment Oedipus begins to abandon his noble devotion to the
city is shown in the scene with Teiresias. The key development here is
Teiresias's charge that Oedipus is the killer of Laius and hence the cause
of the plague. Now Oedipus responds to this charge with understandable outrage, given the malice with which it is clearly spoken, as
well as the contradiction between what Teiresias says and the accounts
reportedly given both by the Delphic oracle and the eye-witness (see,
for example, 350–3, 360–2, 435–42, 447–8, and also 100–7, 305–
9). And Oedipus responds with understandable chagrin and sorrow
when it becomes increasingly apparent that the charge is true (738,
744–5, 747, 754, 813–33). Yet one might expect that, given his
devotion to Thebes, Oedipus would at least feel relieved to learn who
the killer of Laius is, so that Thebes might be saved. But Oedipus never
expresses such relief.[29] Instead, he becomes concerned only with

[29] The closest Oedipus comes to expressing relief that, if he proves to be the killer
of Laius, at least the city will be saved from the plague, is at 669–72. There
Oedipus responds to the pleas of the plague-weary chorus of Theban elders that
he should believe Creon's protestations of innocence concerning the killing of
Laius by saying, "then let him go, even if I must die a perfect death, or be

establishing his innocence. When he first summons the sole eyewitness of Laius's death, he does not express any interest in asking the witness who killed Laius so that he might solve the murder and end the plague, but only seeks to know whether or not he, Oedipus, could be the murderer (836–47). When he speaks of his hope concerning the interrogation, it is his hope for his own innocence and not for the salvation of Thebes.

Oedipus's abandonment of his noble devotion to Thebes points to a fundamental ambiguity within his understanding of nobility. On the one hand, Oedipus emphasizes that the noble human being is one who is selflessly devoted to benefiting others. This is clearest when, in response to Teiresias's claim that Oedipus destroyed himself by solving the riddle of the Sphinx, Oedipus replies, "But if I saved the city, it [my destruction] is of no concern to me" (443). It seems clear as well when he says, "To benefit a man from what one has and can do is the noblest of toils" (314–15). Yet Oedipus also believes that being noble benefits the noble human being. A noble human being may receive recognition from future generations, as the Theban priest points out (49–55). Such a human being may enjoy an inner satisfaction from benefiting others. Perhaps most importantly, being noble may benefit one intrinsically, by simply making one a better person. Accordingly, at line 443, Oedipus suggests that, while his destruction does not concern him, he is concerned not only that Thebes be saved but that *he* be the one who saves Thebes and hence that *he* be noble. Similarly, when Oedipus originally sends Creon to the Delphic Oracle, he does so, he says, in order to learn, not merely how the city might be saved, but how *he* might save the city (69–72). Even at lines 314–5, while Oedipus certainly means to say there that benefiting *other* men is the noblest of toils, the literal meaning of his words is that "to benefit a man from what one has and can do is the noblest of toils." The sentence therefore may mean that benefiting a man, even and especially if that man is oneself, is the noblest of toils. The question arises, then, is Oedipus's

thrust out violently, dishonored, from this land. For I pity your piteous mouth, not his. This one, wherever he may be, will be hated." But even there his words are evidently bitter and grudging, as Creon points out (673–5), and no such words are repeated in the rest of the play.

concern for nobility motivated primarily by his desire to benefit others or himself? Now, Oedipus throughout the play emphasizes that to be noble is to be devoted primarily to others. He emphasizes – to others, but also to himself – that he is more concerned for others than for himself. But once it appears that *he* may be the cause of the city's suffering rather than being its savior, and hence that he may be ig-noble rather than noble, he seems to forget entirely about the suf-ferings of the city and to focus exclusively and, one must say, selfishly, on establishing his own innocence. This change suggests that, not-withstanding Oedipus's self-understanding, his concern for nobility has always been motivated primarily by a desire to benefit himself. It would seem, then, that Oedipus cannot resign himself to the de-struction of Thebes, not primarily because of his desire to save the Thebans from death and to help them achieve an immortal well-being, but rather, as the priest suggests, because of his concern lest *his* fame and *his* nobility perish along with the city, as well as because of his own desire for immortality (compare 58–67, 93–4, 442 with 49–57; see also 273–5).

The scene in which Oedipus learns of the death of Polybus, the man he believes to be his father, reveals especially starkly Oedipus's nar-rowly self-regarding nature, not only with respect to his city but also with respect to his family. When the messenger from Corinth arrives, he tells Jocasta that he brings good news to Oedipus, but also remarks that the news may cause distress as well (934–6). The messenger expects that Oedipus will be pleased to learn that he is ruler of Corinth but saddened by the death of his father. Here, however, is Oedipus's response to the news, after two questions about how his father died: "Ah! Ah! Why, then, lady, would someone look to the altar of the Pythian soothsayer, or the screaming birds above, according to whose guidance I was to kill my father? The dead man is hidden beneath the earth. And I am here and haven't touched a spear" (964–9). Now, it seems understandable that Oedipus is relieved that the oracle was apparently mistaken and that he (Oedipus) does not have the blood of his father on his hands. Oedipus, however, expresses no grief whatsoever over the death of his father, but only pleasure that he himself is not responsible for his death. Oedipus then goes on to consider momentarily the possibility that Polybus may have died because he pined for his son, because he loved his son and was heart-broken by his absence. "Unless through longing for me (τωμω ποθω) he wasted away. In this way he would be dead because of me" (969–70).

What is striking here is that Oedipus does not pause to express regret for having broken the heart of his father. He only considers here whether he might be deemed in any way responsible for his father's death. We see, then, that Oedipus's concern regarding the oracle that he would kill his father is not that his father would be harmed and killed but that *he* would be held responsible for his father's death. Later, when explaining to the Corinthian messenger why he fled Corinth after learning from the oracle that he would kill his father, Oedipus does not say that he wanted to prevent the death of his father but only that "I did not want to be the killer of my father, old man" (1001). Oedipus dreads not the death of his father, but rather being held guilty of causing that death.

Indeed, this scene makes it clear that, ever since Oedipus heard of the oracle, he has always longed for the deaths of his father and mother precisely so that he need no longer fear being considered guilty of patricide and incest. When Jocasta says that Oedipus should no longer worry about the oracle now that his father is dead, Oedipus says, "All these things would be nobly spoken by you if she who bore me were not alive. But now, since she lives, it is entirely necessary, even if you speak nobly, to shrink in hesitation" (984–6). And when Jocasta remarks, "But a great comfort is the grave of your father," Oedipus replies, "Great, I agree. But there is fear of she who lives" (987–8). Oedipus here indicates quite clearly that he wished for his father's death and now wishes for his mother's death. Yet, while he is terrified of being considered guilty of killing his father, he does not seem to feel at all guilty about having wished for the death of his father. Like Jocasta, he separates entirely the wish to commit a crime from the actual commission of the crime (see 976–83). Oedipus may link the wish for his father's death and the responsibility for that death at lines 969–70. For while I have translated those lines here as, "Unless *through longing for me* he wasted away. In this way he would be dead because of me," they may also be translated, more literally, as "Unless *through my longing* (τωμω ποθω) [for his death] he wasted away. In this way he would be dead because of me." Yet again, Oedipus does not seem to feel at all guilty about longing for his father's death but only about the possibility of being considered the cause of that death. This would seem to be so because Oedipus does not truly dread killing his father or even feeling guilty about killing his father. Oedipus's true fear is of being polluted by the crimes of patricide and incest, of being considered guilty by the gods of patricide and incest, and of being punished by them. Indeed, Oedipus goes so far as to suggest to the Corinthian messenger that he has "always" feared committing the crimes of patricide and incest lest he take upon himself the pollution of those crimes and lest Apollo punish him for them (1011–13). Earlier, he prays that the gods help him avoid committing those crimes and thereby save him from the "stain of misfortune" and, it seems, the divine punishment that would follow (823–33). And later, after he has discovered that he is guilty of those crimes, he expresses the fear of being punished in Hades for his crimes by being forced to confront his dead parents (1371–4; see also 971–2 and compare with 955–6). Indeed, within the play, Oedipus exhibits a singularly strong interest in the afterlife. He is the only character, apart from the priest, to speak of Hades (29–30). And each time he mentions Hades, he does so in order to reject the apparent suggestion first of Jocasta and then of the chorus that there is no afterlife (compare 971–2 with 955–6 and 1371–4 with 1367–8). Oedipus, then, does not dread committing patricide because he dreads harming his father but rather because he dreads harming himself, not intrinsically by, say, defiling or degrading his soul but rather by incurring the wrath of the gods, and not only in the here and now, but also in the hereafter. Consequently, Oedipus did not flee Corinth – and apparently sacrifice all of his apparent hopes and ambitions of becoming king – after he heard from the oracle that he would kill his father and sleep with his mother – out of love for his parents but rather out of love for himself.

Moreover, the scene in which Oedipus learns of the death of Polybus reminds us that he (Oedipus) did not sacrifice his ambition to rule when he left Corinth but actually advanced it. By bringing the "good" news that Polybus is dead and that Oedipus has been chosen as tyrant of Corinth, the Corinthian messenger reminds us that, if Oedipus had stayed in Corinth, he would not have become a ruler until now, some fifteen years since he became ruler of Thebes (934, 936–7, 939–40). During those years his position would have resembled that of Creon under Oedipus, able to pursue private pleasures but unable to fulfill his ambition to rule. But while Creon claims to eschew such ambition, Oedipus enjoys ruling (577–602). Furthermore, Oedipus says that, as a young man in his early twenties, he was already considered "the greatest man of the townsmen" in Corinth, and thereby suggests that he may have been considered greater than even his father Polybus, the ruler (774–6). Oedipus must have foreseen, as a young man, that in the ordinary course of things he would not be able to fulfill his greatness for many years, but would have to live in his father's shadow and wait until his death in order to become ruler. Perhaps he was especially sensitive to the oracle's claim that he would kill his father and sleep with his mother precisely because he already sensed uneasily a tension between his ambition and his position as a subject of his father the ruler.[30] At any rate, by leaving Corinth Oedipus made it possible for him to fulfill an ambition that would have been thwarted as long as he lived under his father's rule in Corinth. Moreover, when Oedipus left Corinth he did not leave his ambition aside. He clearly welcomed the opportunity to win glory by defeating the Sphinx and saving Thebes (390–8, 439–41). And although he did not ask to be made tyrant of Thebes, he also did not decline the Thebans' request. Accordingly, Oedipus's sacrifice of his position at Corinth was not the selfless act it seems at first. While Oedipus does express regret that he had to leave Corinth, he also acknowledges to the Corinthian messenger that it was "with good fortune," and hence fortunate for him that he left Corinth (822–33,

---

[30] Freud's richly thought-provoking thesis that Oedipus reflects "our first sexual impulses towards our mothers, and our first hatred and violent wishes towards our fathers" overlooks Sophocles' suggestion that it is not Oedipus's sexual desire but rather his political ambition that brings him into conflict with his father, as for example, Shakespeare's Prince Hal's political ambition brings him into conflict with his father (Freud 1927, 221–4; *Henry IV, Part One*, I.ii.199–221; II.iv.432–6; *Henry IV, Part Two*, IV.v.20–137; see also Saxonhouse 1988, 1262). Through the conflict between Laius and Oedipus, which takes place because each is so spirited that he is unwilling to give precedence to the other, Sophocles may mean to portray a potential conflict that always exists between at least spirited fathers and sons (800–13). For a critique of Freud's interpretation of *Oedipus the Tyrant*, consider Vernant and Vidal-Naquet 1988, 85–111.

994–9). Oedipus's departure from Corinth, then, was not noble but rather self-interested, inasmuch as he sought both to avoid being punished for killing his father and sleeping with his mother and to fulfill his ambition to rule.

THE INHUMANE PIETY OF OEDIPUS AND THE HUMANE RATIONALISM OF SOPHOCLES

But doesn't the end of the play vindicate Oedipus's claim to be a noble human being? Once he concludes that he has committed regicide, patricide, and incest, doesn't he punish himself and demand that Creon and the Thebans punish him, in compliance with the Delphic Oracle's commands concerning the salvation of Thebes from the plague, rather than defending himself on the grounds that he committed these crimes unwittingly and hence involuntarily?[31] Indeed, isn't Oedipus so horrified by the harm that he has done his loved ones that he punishes himself well beyond what was commanded by the Delphic Oracle by blinding himself (1327–31)? Doesn't Oedipus's punishment of himself show that he is noble, devoted above all, not to himself but to his family and city?

Oedipus himself suggests that his punishment of himself is a noble act. In response to the chorus's criticism of him for blinding himself, Oedipus first suggests that what he has done has been for the "best," and defends his action (1367–90). He then laments his birth, his patricide, and above all his incestuous marriage, which he calls the "basest" of deeds possible among human beings (1391–1408). At that point he breaks off by saying: "But indeed it is not noble to speak of what it is not noble to do, so, as quickly as possible, in the name of the gods, hide me somewhere outside [Thebes], or kill me, or cast me out into the sea, where you will never see me more" (1409–12). Oedipus evidently refers, not to his punishment of himself, but to his

---

[31] 1340–6, 1409–15, 1432–41, 1449–54, 1517–21. For this view, see, for example, Dodds's statement: "Oedipus is great because he accepts responsibility for *all* his acts, including those which are objectively most horrible, though subjectively innocent" (1968, 28; emphasis in text).

patricide and especially his incest, the "basest" of crimes, when he says that it is not noble to speak of what it is not noble to do. He suggests, then, that his punishment of himself is not only "best" but also noble. Indeed, it would seem that Oedipus emphasizes earlier that, while Apollo was responsible for his (Oedipus's) evils and his suffering, he, Oedipus, was solely responsible for blinding himself, because he wants to emphasize that he alone was responsible for this noble deed (1327–31).

If, however, one subscribes to Oedipus's earlier definition of nobility, if, that is, "To benefit a man from what one has and can do is the noblest of toils," then it seems that Oedipus's actions at the end of the play cannot be deemed noble (314–5). In the first place, we never learn whether the plague destroying Thebes ends after, and as a result of, Oedipus's punishment of himself. More importantly, Oedipus never even refers to the plague or expresses a wish or hope of ending it during the second half of the play. Accordingly, the end of the play does not show that Oedipus is nobly devoted to the city, for it does not show that he benefited, or even sought to benefit, the city by punishing himself.[32]

Nor does the end of the play prove Oedipus to be noble with respect to his family. Indeed, it shows that he positively harms his family. It is important to remember that Oedipus's first action, upon learning that he is guilty of incest and patricide, is to try to kill Jocasta, the woman he has loved as a wife and as the mother of his children for some fifteen years. He bursts into his home and shouts to his servants demanding to be given a sword and to know where Jocasta is. Then, crying terribly, with a sword in hand, he breaks into Jocasta's bedroom, evidently with the intention of killing her. And even though Jocasta hangs herself before he can kill her, it must be said that Oedipus does, in truth, seem at least indirectly responsible for her death. For even though Jocasta speaks as though she may intend to kill herself when she discovers that Oedipus is her son, and flees his presence, it is only when the distraught Jocasta hears Oedipus raging and threatening her with violence that she

---

[32] Oedipus does wish that he had never been born since then he would not have caused pain to himself or his loved ones, among whom he counts the Theban elders (1349–55; see 1321–6, 1337–9).

actually kills herself (see 1237–66, 1071–2). Yet Oedipus never blames himself at all for his mother's death. It is true that he blinds himself once he discovers that she is dead (1266–79). But he evidently planned to blind himself even before he entered the house (1183–5). One of the most striking paradoxes of the play is that, whereas Oedipus blames himself for committing patricide and incest, even though he did so unwittingly and hence involuntarily, he never blames himself for matricide, for causing his mother's death, even though he does so knowingly and hence, it would seem, voluntarily. Oedipus evidently blames Jocasta and seeks to punish her for having committed incest. The incest, and not Jocasta's attempted infanticide, is what Oedipus speaks of as he looks for her, according to the second messenger: "For he roams about demanding that we furnish him with a sword, and where he would find a wife no wife, a mother's double field for him and his children" (1257–9). Even after Jocasta dies, Oedipus refers to her as "evil" and "impious" (1397, 1360). But such blame of Jocasta is clearly unjust since she, like Oedipus, committed incest unwittingly and hence involuntarily. Indeed, her incest is even more excusable than his since, unlike Oedipus, she was never told by an oracle that she would commit the crime of incest and hence never had even a remote reason, as Oedipus did, to avoid marrying anyone who could even conceivably lead her to commit the crime of incest (compare 711–14, 720–2, 851–8, 1173–6 with 785–93).[33] Oedipus unjustly seeks to kill

[33] For the following reasons, it might seem that Jocasta learned that Oedipus is her son well before the arrival of the Corinthian messenger (but after her marriage to Oedipus), and kept his identity secret to protect her family and city: she notes that Laius's "form" or "shape" did not differ much from Oedipus's, she knew that her son's ankles had been pierced and must have known that Oedipus's ankles were pierced as well, and she claims quite emphatically and perhaps defensively that "many" mortals have slept with their mothers "in their dreams as well" as when awake (743, 717–19, 1030–38, 977–83). Yet the fact that she never heard the prophecy that she would sleep with her son; the fact that she reveals so casually, unnecessarily, and – it seems – innocently to Oedipus that he resembles Laius and that her son's ankles were pierced; and her apparent shock and violent grief at the messenger's revelation that he received the baby Oedipus from Laius's servant all suggest that she did not know Oedipus's true identity heretofore (705–19, 740–43, 1060–72, 1241–50).

Jocasta, apparently drives her to her death, and persists in blaming her unjustly even after her death, and therefore cannot be said to act nobly toward her.

Furthermore, Oedipus needlessly harms his daughters, not only by causing their mother's death, but also by blinding himself. Oedipus clearly cares for his daughters and, in a vivid and heart-rending speech, he expresses great sorrow and pity for the disgrace and desolation that will be their plight. Moreover, he beseeches Creon to care for them: "Son of Menoiceus, since you alone are left as father for these two – for both of us who bred them have perished – do not overlook them, beggars, without a man, your own kin, wandering, nor make these ones equal in my evils. But pity them, seeing them so young, destitute of all, except your part" (1503–9). Yet Oedipus needlessly worsens his daughters' plight by driving Jocasta to suicide and by blinding himself. Once Oedipus's crimes were revealed, he would, given the punishment he decreed for Laius's killer, have had to go into exile. But he either could have left his daughters under Jocasta's care in Thebes or he could have taken his family with him into exile, but with a man – a relatively young man in his late thirties – to protect them. Instead, by driving Jocasta to suicide and by blinding himself, Oedipus leaves his daughters with no choice but either to rely on their uncle for protection, perhaps for the rest of their lives, or to follow their disgraced and blind father into exile. By Oedipus's own account, it would be better for his daughters to stay in Thebes with Creon. But, to make matters worse, in his last words of the play, Oedipus selfishly begs Creon to let his daughters stay with him forever and hence to join him and take care of him in his long, hard exile (1522). The end of the play, then, does not vindicate Oedipus's claim to be noble either with respect to his family or his city.

Why does Oedipus respond to his discovery that he has committed incest and patricide by trying to kill Jocasta and then blinding himself? These actions do not appear to be a necessary part of his downfall.[34]

---

[34] In Homer's account, even after Oedipus is revealed to be guilty of patricide and incest, and after his mother's suicide, he remains as ruler of Thebes, albeit haunted by the Furies, and eventually dies in battle (*Odyssey* 11.271–89; *Iliad* 23.679–80).

Once Oedipus discovers and reveals his unwitting regicide, patricide, and incest, clearly he can no longer rule Thebes or even live there. He can, however, return to his earlier life as a wanderer, either alone while Jocasta and his children are with Creon in Thebes, or together with his family. As a still relatively young man Oedipus can presumably fend for himself and provide for his family and might even perhaps find his fortune, as he did once he left Corinth. The discovery and revelation of his unwitting crimes by themselves would thus seem to destroy Oedipus in his capacity as ruler of Thebes, but not in his capacity as the protector of his family or simply as a man who can fend for himself in the world. But then Oedipus tries to kill Jocasta – apparently thereby driving her to suicide – and blinds himself. By taking these actions, Oedipus makes it impossible for him to protect his family or take care of himself, and hence seems to ruin his family – at least his wife and daughters – and himself completely. Why, then, does he try to kill Jocasta and then blind himself?

Perhaps the most obvious explanation for Oedipus's impulse to punish Jocasta and himself is his sheer horror at their incest. After all, even though Jocasta argues that, if blind chance – rather than provident gods – governs human affairs, humans need not fear committing incest or other acts that violate purportedly divine law, she herself becomes horrified, deranged, and suicidal when she discovers her own incest (see 977–83, 1060–72, 1241–50). Oedipus goes so far as to call incest the "basest" of deeds that are possible among human beings, and hence worse even than patricide (1408). And, as we have seen, he also suggests that his punishment of himself for committing incest is a noble deed. Oedipus evidently believes that incest is so monstrous a crime that nobility and justice demand that it be punished to the greatest extent possible, under any circumstances, even if the crime has been committed involuntarily (see Dodds 1968, 23–5). Moreover, perhaps by punishing this atrocious violation of the most sacred laws so ferociously, Oedipus seeks to atone, not only for having committed such a crime, but also for having sought to rule tyrannically, on the basis of human reason alone rather than on the basis of convention and law. Once he sees with brutal clarity what it means to rule and to live free of laws – namely, that one must be willing, at least, to disobey even the most sacred law against incest – perhaps Oedipus recoils in horror and zealously punishes this horrible crime.

But why does incest inspire such horror? What makes incest so horrible, as Oedipus repeatedly stresses, is that it destroys relations within the family by confusing those relations: "Marriage, marriage, you begot us and, having begotten us, again raised up the same seed, and you displayed fathers, brothers, children, kindred blood, brides, wives, mothers, as many of the basest deeds as are possible among human beings" (1403–8); "For what of evils is missing? Your father has slain his father. She who bore him he sowed, there where he himself was begotten, and he acquired you from the same place he himself was born" (1496–9; see 1361–2, 1480–5). With these words, Oedipus echoes Teiresias's earlier, enigmatic characterization of the incest between Oedipus and Jocasta: "I say that unawares you are consorting most basely with your dearest ones, nor do you see where you are evil . . . . And unawares you are hateful to your own, beneath, upon, and above the earth, and the double-lashing, terrible-footed curse of your mother and your father will someday drive you out of this land, you who now see correctly, but then will see in darkness . . . You do not perceive a multitude of other evils which will make you equal to yourself and your children . . . . The man whom you have been seeking for a long time . . . will be shown to have been for his children at once brother and father, and to the woman who bore him son and husband, and of his father a fellow sower and killer" (364–5, 415–19, 424–5, 449–51, 457–60).

As a result of incest, the relations between husband and wife, parent and child, brother and sister, which should be clear, single, and above all pure, become confused, double, and impure.[35] Oedipus is both husband and son to Jocasta and father and brother to Antigone and Ismene. The incest renders him a hybrid or monstrous being – a kind of two-headed beast – with respect to his family: to Jocasta, half-husband, half-son; to Antigone and Ismene, half-father and half-brother. Following Teiresias, Oedipus suggests that this monstrous confusion of relations is not only physical but psychic.[36] Since Oedipus is

---

[35] For Oedipus's pious concern for purity, see 99, 256, 823, and 830.

[36] For this reason, I am inclined to disagree with Benardete's argument that "Teiresias, for all the effect he has, could just as well have remained silent about both Oedipus's patricide and incest" (2000, 133).

biologically both husband and son to Jocasta and father and brother to
Antigone and Ismene, he cannot love them, or be loved by them, as,
respectively, husband and father. The confusion of his physical relations
renders his love for them, and theirs for him, confused, monstrous, and
base. As Teiresias suggests, the discovery of the incest renders Oedipus
"hateful" to those who are "dearest" to him (366–7, 415–19). What
makes incest so uniquely horrible, then – even more so than patricide – is
that it seems to overturn and pervert the entire natural order of the
family, according to which relations within the family are pure, clear,
and single, in which one is, simply, son to one's parents, father to one's
children, brother to one's siblings. Perhaps Oedipus reacts to this crime
with such violence and horror because the crime itself is simply
monstrous and deserves to be punished as harshly as possible. Indeed, so
monstrously unnatural does incest appear that the chorus believes that
incest should be physically impossible, and wonders how such an act
could be permitted by nature: "Dear, glorious Oedipus, for whom the
same great haven sufficed for child and father to enter as bridegroom!
How in the world? How were the furrows ploughed by your father able
to bear you, wretch, in silence for so long?" (1207–12).[37]

Yet, as the play shows, such incest is indeed possible. Oedipus truly
is husband and son to Jocasta, father and brother to Antigone and
Ismene, and – inasmuch as he longed to be ruler first of Corinth and
then of Thebes – son and rival to his father. Furthermore, and more
importantly, Sophocles does not present Oedipus's relations with his
family as horrible or monstrous or base. Before he discovers that Jocasta
is his mother, Oedipus genuinely seems to love her and to be loved by
her in turn. Moreover, even after he discovers that Antigone and Ismene
are his sisters as well as his daughters, he still loves them, in his way, if
not simply as a father or brother, then at least as one who cares for them,
pities them, and begs others to help them. Sophocles' portrayal of
Oedipus's relations with his family invites one to ask: Are familial
relations pure, clear, and distinctive by nature or is their purity, clarity,
and distinctiveness primarily the product of law and convention? Does

---

[37] In Ormand's words, the horrified chorus here expresses "the realization that the
incest taboo is not a natural fact . . . [and] that this boundary is not a permanent, self-defined, natural fixture" (1999, 141).

love within the family necessarily require purity, clarity, and distinctiveness in order to be genuine? More simply, by portraying Oedipus's relations with Jocasta, Antigone, and Ismene as loving rather than as tawdry or monstrous, Sophocles undercuts the indignation and revulsion his readers would abstractly feel toward the crime of incest. In this way, Sophocles even encourages us to feel, if not horror, at least sadness and dismay, at Oedipus's zeal to punish the crime of incest. For by punishing Jocasta and himself, doesn't Oedipus needlessly harm those who are blameless and who, at any rate, have already been sufficiently harmed?

Sophocles' play also invites one to wonder whether, especially in the case of incest, there is not a crucial distinction between a conscious and an unwitting act. For if what makes incest so monstrous is that it confuses familial relations, it would seem that this would be so only of conscious incest. But Jocasta and Oedipus do not know that they are mother and son when they are wed. Indeed, in the strictest sense, they are mother and son only biologically and not at all psychologically or morally. There is no indication that their love for one another is anything other than the love between wife and husband. Their relations do not seem at all ambiguous or confused or impure.[38] In this way, too, it does not seem reasonable that Oedipus should feel such horror and revulsion and punish Jocasta and himself as he does for having committed incest unawares.

If Oedipus were to follow reason, it would seem that he would not punish or blame either Jocasta or himself for the crimes they committed unwittingly, as he himself argues in *Oedipus at Colonus* (270–4, 521–3, 546–8, 962–99). Oedipus's own response to the discovery that he has killed his father and slept with his mother points to such a rational conclusion. He declares: "Light, for the last time I look to you, I who have been shown to have been born from those from whom I ought not, to have mingled with those with whom I ought not, to have killed those whom I should not" (*Oedipus the Tyrant* 1183–5).

---

[38] Consider Vernant and Vidal-Naquet 1988, 108: ". . . the maternal figure in Oedipus' sentimental life can only be Merope . . . . [Jocasta] is in no way a mother to him."

Oedipus's words here indicate most clearly that, since he committed his crimes unwittingly and hence involuntarily, his resolution to punish himself for his crimes is, from the perspective of reason, unjust. For he blames himself here not only for incest and patricide but for having been born. Oedipus thereby tacitly acknowledges that he is as little responsible for his patricide and incest as for his having been born. Indeed, Oedipus has made every effort he could, not only to avoid committing those crimes, but also to lead a noble life. And yet he has been led, either by blind chance or cruel gods, to commit the basest of crimes (1403–7). All of this suggests, as the plague suggests, that human beings are playthings of chance or indifferent gods and hence that it is impossible for human beings to live nobly or to win the favor and protection of the gods. Reason would seem to dictate that Oedipus resign himself to the power of chance or of the gods, a power that is so great that it can lead human beings to commit the basest of crimes against their will. Reason would seem to dictate that he face and accept the weakness of nobility in the world and the indifference of the world to nobility. Yet, however sad and bleak such a conclusion might seem, the rational course in this case would also seem effectively to serve the interests of both Oedipus and his family. For it would enable him at least to provide for himself and for his family as well, albeit as an exile.

The Second Messenger makes this crucial point and thereby shows that he is the character who comes closest to speaking for the poet in the play. For he is the only character in the play who draws a clear distinction between the "involuntary" evils Oedipus suffers, such as having unwittingly committed incest and patricide, and the "self-inflicted" evils, such as blinding himself (see especially 1227–31 and 1280–5; see also Jebb 1966, 129). The messenger points out that Oedipus was "justly" prosperous when he ruled Thebes before, and acknowledges that the involuntary evils he committed brought an end to such prosperity (1280–5). But he also declares that "Of woes, those that give the most pain are the ones which are manifestly self-inflicted" (1230–1). The messenger stresses here that Oedipus's self-inflicted evils were wholly unnecessary, that they are much more harmful than the involuntary evils he has committed, and that it is these evils that seal his ruin. For if Oedipus had not blinded himself, he at least would have been able to care for himself and his family. Why then does

Oedipus reject the rational course and thereby ruin not only his family but also, it seems, himself?

It might seem that Oedipus rejects reason because of his dedication to nobility. For even if his punishment of himself is harmful to his loved ones, is it not at least a clear sign of his nobility insofar as, by blinding himself, he willingly punishes himself for his crimes, sacrifices his well-being, and thereby shows that he is superior to mere self-interest? But why, then, does he not simply kill himself once he discovers that he has committed incest and patricide? The chorus is surprised that he does not, "for you are better off no longer existing than living blind" (1368). But Oedipus emphatically rejects the chorus's suggestion that human beings cease to exist once they die, just as he had rejected Jocasta's suggestion that Polybus ceased to exist when he died. Instead, Oedipus affirms the existence of an afterlife and explains his decision to blind himself primarily on the grounds that there is an afterlife: "That these things are not thus worked out in the best way, do not instruct me, nor advise me any longer. For I do not know, seeing with what eyes, how I could look upon my father, once I was in Hades, nor upon my wretched mother, against both of whom the deeds wrought by me are too bad for hanging" (1369–74; compare 971–2 with 955–6). In this, his principal explanation for blinding himself rather than killing himself, Oedipus expresses the fear of seeing his parents in Hades, since his crimes against them deserve terrible punishments, punishments worse than death (see also 269–72). But Oedipus, then, presumably fears not only meeting his parents but also suffering terrible punishments in Hades. He refuses to commit suicide now lest he suffer not only the pain of facing his parents in Hades, but also the greater pain of suffering there terrible punishments inflicted by the gods for his crimes, crimes that are, in his view, the basest of deeds possible among humans and crimes that have rendered him most hateful to the gods.

Oedipus evidently believes that, by blinding himself rather than killing himself, he is not selflessly sacrificing his self-interest but rather acting in his self-interest by at least postponing the punishments awaiting him in Hades. Yet he will eventually die and go to Hades. Even at the end of this very speech to the chorus, he urges them to exile him or even to kill him, and thereby implies that he no longer fears so much the divine punishments awaiting him in Hades (1409–12). Oedipus must hope, then, that, by blinding himself, he has appeased the gods. He must hope that, by making the apparently noble sacrifice of his sight and hence his well-being, he has preempted the gods' punishment, won the gods' favor, and hence served his self-interest. Yet it is not clear that this hope is well-founded. For even if one were to assume, contrary to the evidence in the play, that the gods are benevolent beings, it is not clear that the sacrifice that Oedipus makes in the hope of being rewarded is a genuine sacrifice and hence deserving of divine rewards.

A key to understanding why Oedipus tries to kill Jocasta and then blinds himself is that both actions were prophesied by oracles and soothsayers. When Teiresias told Oedipus that he would discover that he had committed patricide and incest, he also told Oedipus that he would blind himself (415–19, 454–6). Furthermore, the herdsman reveals that Jocasta ordered him to kill the baby Oedipus because of an oracle that he would grow up to kill both of his parents (1171–6). Oedipus reacts to this news by immediately attempting to fulfill the oracle and kill his mother. Oedipus, then, responds to the discovery that he has committed incest and patricide, not by seeking to destroy himself but rather by seeking to avoid the gods' wrath and win their favor, above all in Hades. Whereas before he had prayed that, for those Thebans who are just, "May Justice, your ally, and all the gods benefit you forever," Oedipus now seeks to punish Jocasta and himself so as to secure for himself such eternal rewards (273–5). He seeks now to become the avenger of what the chorus suggests are the eternal, divine laws and thereby seeks to win the favor of Zeus, who is the "lord of all things" and whose rule is "deathless" and "eternal" (863–71, 903–5; cf. 738). Oedipus is led by his hope for avoiding everlasting punishments and securing everlasting rewards for himself to sacrifice the well-being of his family by attempting to kill his mother and to blind himself.

We see that Oedipus ultimately renounces his rationalism and turns to the gods, not because he cannot face the weakness of nobility in the world or the indifference of the world to nobility, but rather because he cannot face the indifference of the world to his deepest hope, his hope for personal immortality. It is his hope for immortality that leads him to react to the deadly plague by seeking to punish the killer of Laius so as to win the gods' favor. And it is his hope for immortality that leads him to react to the discovery of his incest and patricide by seeking to punish Jocasta and himself so as to win the gods' favor. So great is his hope for immortality that he would rather sacrifice his family and blind himself than relinquish that hope. What makes Oedipus truly blind, one might say, what makes him blind to his true self-interest and hence blindly selfish, is his hope for immortality and his unwillingness to examine that hope. Oedipus thoughtlessly holds the self-contradictory belief that he is selflessly noble and that he will be rewarded by the gods for his nobility. This belief leads him, in the end, to be cruel to his family and ultimately to himself.[39]

Oedipus's political and family life defies conventional categories and thereby reveals the limits, and even the falsehood, of convention. The young, unknown, Corinthian Oedipus was an excellent ruler of Thebes, evidently a better ruler than the Theban king Laius, even though he was not the conventionally legitimate ruler. Similarly, Oedipus was an excellent father and husband, evidently better than Laius, notwithstanding his violations of the divine laws that protect the family. But Oedipus cannot face the world without the clarity, and especially without the hope, given by convention. Oedipus can only live in a world governed not by blind chance but by purposeful, moral gods and in a family marked not by double and mixed but by single and pure relations. Convention makes what is by nature manifold seem simple and clear and what is by nature indifferent to human hopes seem supportive of them. Oedipus tries, in his way, to live according to nature and reason, but in the end he returns to traditional law and piety.

Through his account of Oedipus's life and fate, Sophocles indicates why a pure political rationalism – the attempt to govern political society in the harsh light of reason alone – must ultimately fail and why

---

[39] Consequently I must disagree with (1) O'Brien's claim that Oedipus "is willing to face the truth" (1968, 15); (2) Dodds's claims that Oedipus acts "from the highest motives" and that Oedipus exhibits "the strength to pursue the truth at whatever personal cost" (1968, 23, 28); and (3) Rocco's claim that Oedipus feels an "unquenchable desire for truth" (1997, 53).

tradition, convention, and piety are therefore necessary to political life
(see Saxonhouse 1988, 1272). While Oedipus goes very far in leading
his life according to reason alone, he cannot resign himself, as reason
dictates that he must, to the mortality of all that he cares about: his
city, his loved ones, himself. He simply cannot face the world without
the hope that there is some escape from the ills, and especially the
mortality, imposed on us by our human nature. Accordingly, in the face
of death, Oedipus's experiment in political rationalism collapses and he
returns to the pious belief – represented throughout the play by the
chorus – in the "deathless, eternal" rule of gods who reward the righteous and punish the wicked (904–5). Through the example of
Oedipus's tyranny, Sophocles suggests that politics must somehow
satisfy humans' longings for immortality and accommodate human
beings' hopes for immortality, and therefore that some element of piety
is necessary for a stable political society.

But the play does not simply celebrate piety, for it is Oedipus's
unreasonable, pious hopes and beliefs that lead him to harm those dearest
to him and himself, as the Second Messenger suggests, so needlessly.
Sophocles encourages us to sympathize with and even, in some measure,
to admire Oedipus's hope for immortality, for that hope reflects not only
a longing to escape death but also a longing to be worthy of escaping
death and hence a longing to be greater and nobler than a merely mortal
being. But however impressive that soaring hope might be, Sophocles
suggests that a genuine understanding and acceptance of our mortality,
such as the poet exhibits throughout the play, fosters the even more
impressive qualities of human wisdom and human compassion. However
mindful Sophocles may be of the limits of political rationalism, of the
prudence of accommodating pious longings within the political arena,
and of the dignity of piety, he quietly but clearly affirms the superior
wisdom and the humanity of the individual life guided by reason.[40]

It might seem that Oedipus's fate and his final renunciation of reason
constitute a devastating indictment of reason. By declaring at the end of
the play that "it is not noble to speak of what it is not noble to do,"
Oedipus suggests that it is not noble even to think about the ignoble

---

[40] For a helpful account of the obstacles to the life of reason, see Ruderman 1999,
especially 154–6, 159–60.

deeds he has done (1409–12). But Sophocles clearly disagrees with his Oedipus. For what is Sophocles' play if not a written speech about the deeds of Oedipus, noble and ignoble, and a timeless invitation to reflect on those deeds and on his fate? Sophocles clearly wants us to reason about the evils that Oedipus recoils from thinking about at the end of the play. If Oedipus had followed reason at the end of the play – if he had followed, so to speak, the humane rationalism of Sophocles – he would have benefited both his loved ones and himself and in this sense would have lived a nobler life.

2 Blind Faith and Enlightened
Statesmanship in *Oedipus at Colonus*

ALL'S WELL THAT ENDS WELL?

Sophocles' *Oedipus the Tyrant* seems to be a perfect tragedy because it inspires so effectively both pity and fear (see Aristotle *Poetics* 1452a32–33, 1453a5–22, 1455a16–18). The story moves us to pity, since Oedipus falls so suddenly from the greatest prosperity to the greatest misery and shame, and since he ultimately commits the very patricide and incest he has striven so mightily to avoid. But, more importantly, the story also inspires fear for our terrifyingly precarious condition as human beings. For if so fortunate a man can fall so far so suddenly, what confidence can we have in any good fortune, no matter how secure? And if the gods not only permit but impel so great a man to commit such horrible crimes, what hope can we have to live just or decent lives? Must we not conclude that the world we live in, governed as it is by indifferent fortune or cruel gods, is simply hostile to our hopes for virtue and happiness?

Yet Sophocles' story of Oedipus does not end with the terrifying *Oedipus the Tyrant* but rather with the hopeful tale of the apotheosis of Oedipus in *Oedipus at Colonus*. At the beginning of the play, Oedipus is the most accursed of men, shunned by men and gods for having committed the most monstrous crimes, condemned to a life of squalor, wandering from town to town as a helpless, blind beggar, accompanied only by his almost equally helpless daughter Antigone.[1] Yet by the end of the play, we see him protected and honored by Athens, triumphant

[1] See 1–4, 20, 140–1, 149–52, 220–36, 324–30, 345–52, 551–9, 740–52, 939–49, 1254–63; also 75–6.

48

over his enemies, and apparently rewarded by the gods with the greatest
of all rewards, everlasting well-being after death. Sophocles' tale of
the quintessentially tragic Oedipus, then, has a miraculously happy
ending.[2]

The stunning reversal of fortune that Oedipus undergoes in *Oedipus the
Tyrant* is itself reversed in *Oedipus at Colonus* (Whitman 1971, 196–7).
Oedipus the Tyrant ends with the chorus's reflections on the miserable
fragility of human life (1524–30). But *Oedipus at Colonus* ends with the
conclusion that Oedipus was rewarded by the gods after his death. First,
the chorus of Athenian elders prays that he be rewarded: "For since many
woes came [to you] without cause, may a just deity once again exalt you"
(1565–7). Then, according to a messenger, Antigone, the chorus, and
Theseus, Oedipus is so rewarded (1661–5; see 1705–8, 1722–3,
1751–3). Sophocles' tale of Oedipus apparently ends by affirming that
the gods – led by "Zeus, all-ruling of gods, all-seeing," with whom
"Justice" sits – protect the just, no matter how weak, and lift up the
righteous, no matter how far they have fallen. In this way, the play would
seem to vindicate our hopes for divine justice and happiness.[3]

---

[2] Interpretations of *Oedipus at Colonus* have generally tended to conclude that
Sophocles means simply to celebrate the "apotheosis" (Waldock 1966, 219;
Segal 1981, 406) and "transfiguration" (Grene 1967, 157) of the pious
Oedipus. As Knox explains, "The gods of Sophoclean tragedy, the most remote
and mysterious creation in all Greek literature, here show their respect for the
hero in unmistakable terms; they gave Ajax his burial, Antigone her revenge,
Electra her victory, Philoctetes his return to life – but to Oedipus, who suffered
most and longest, they give, in the death he longed for, immortal life and
power" (1964, 162). Consider also Wilson 1997, 153–4, 177–86.

[3] 1085–6, 1380–2; on the gods' providence, see 143, 275–91, 864–70,
1010–3, 1544–78. Bowra remarks, "more than any other Greek play it touches
the heart of Greek religion. . . At the end of the *Oedipus at Colonus* no unresolved
discords remain, no mysteries call for an answer . . . The justice of the gods is
vindicated in their treatment of Oedipus and of Attica" (1944, 307, 349, 351).
See also Reinhardt 1979, 221–2; Adams 1957, 164; Whitman 1971, 191,
212, 215–16; Segal 1981, 404; Beer 2004, 155, 164–5. I therefore disagree
with Kaufmann's claim that the play is Sophocles' "blackest" work (1968, 236).
But the play ends happily only for Oedipus and the Athenians, not his
children. See Winnington-Ingram 1980, 274–5; Segal 1981, 402; Mills
1997, 175.

THE VIRTUE OF BLINDNESS AND THE REJECTION
OF REASON

But what causes the gods to deem the man they had previously condemned worthy of such rewards? The first explanation that suggests itself
is that the gods take pity on "this wretched phantom of a man, Oedipus"
(109–10). Before, Oedipus was "renowned to all" as the hero who saved
Thebes from the monstrous Sphinx (*Oedipus the Tyrant* 8, 35–48). Now,
"everyone in Greece" knows him as the man who killed his father
and slept with his mother (*Oedipus at Colonus* 595–7, 203–36, 299–
301, 510–45). *Oedipus the Tyrant* opens with the illustrious ruler of
Thebes addressing his admiring subjects, "children of Cadmus," who
look to him to save them from a terrible plague, just as he saved them in
the past from a terrible monster (1–57). *Oedipus at Colonus* opens with
Oedipus addressing his daughter, "child of a blind old man," and asking
her for guidance as they wander from city to city, begging for food and
shelter (1–13). The Oedipus we see as the play opens is a man without a
city, without a home, and virtually without a family. He has fallen as low
as it is possible for a man to fall, much lower than he fell when he fled
Corinth as a youth. For Oedipus then was strong enough to kill five men
single-handedly and wise enough to solve the riddle of the Sphinx. Now,
he is unimaginably weak, unable to protect himself, and even ignorant of
where he is (see Knox 1964, 145; Segal 1981, 365–6).

The weakness of Oedipus is epitomized by his blindness. From
the opening scene to the scene in which Creon and his soldiers seize
Oedipus and his daughters, the play reminds us over and over again of
the pathetic weakness of a man who must live in perpetual darkness,
unable to walk or sit by himself or to defend himself and his loved
ones (1–32, 144–202, 299–300, 493–502, 800–886, 1096–
1109). If Oedipus were not blind, he would still be shunned, but he
would be able to take care of himself as he did after he left Corinth.[4]

---

[4] Many scholars stress the age of Oedipus rather than his blindness (e.g,
Winnington-Ingram 1980, 266). But since Antigone is still young after
Oedipus's death – in the *Antigone*, she is referred to four times as "maiden
[κορη]" (395, 769, 889, 1100) and seven times as "child [παις]" (378, 423,
561, 654, 693, 949, 987) – and since his uncle Creon is still alive, Oedipus

It is his blindness that renders him most clearly helpless and pitiable. His blindness undercuts the indignation that the audience might feel if we saw the man famous for having committed patricide and incest hale and hearty before us. In the course of the play, the chorus, Theseus, Polyneices, and even Creon express pity for Oedipus (254–5, 551–9, 1254–66, 740–52). Perhaps the gods take pity on him as well, as one who has suffered enough, and more than enough, for his crimes.

Yet pity alone would not suffice to explain the gods' change of heart towards Oedipus. Insofar as the gods reward him, they must believe he positively deserves a reward, indeed the great reward of everlasting well-being. More importantly, insofar as Oedipus's suffering is caused by his blindness, it is a suffering that he inflicted on himself (see 551–4, 866–7, 1197–1200). Even though he did not choose to commit incest and patricide, he did choose to blind himself and thereby chose the life of a helpless man. If the gods do finally reward Oedipus, they must to some extent reward him for blinding himself. But why should the gods reward a man for blinding himself?

To address this question, we must first ask another: is the blindness of Oedipus simply a sign of weakness? The inability to see is, on the simplest level, a terrible weakness. Oedipus does not know where he is, where he walks, where he sits. Yet, when Oedipus had sight, when he was the strong and wise ruler of Thebes, he was utterly ignorant of his native land, his parents, his crimes, and therefore, in crucial respects, ignorant of himself. He had eyes, but he could not see. And Teiresias, the blind prophet of Apollo, somehow knew these crucial facts about Oedipus. As Teiresias puts it in *Oedipus the Tyrant*: "You have sight but you do not see in what evil you are, nor where you dwell, nor with whom you share your home" (413–4).

One might conclude that Oedipus was ignorant simply because he lacked the information – who his parents truly were – that would have enabled him to figure out for himself, rationally, either how to avoid committing the crimes of incest and patricide in the first place or, later,

must not be that old in years in *Oedipus at Colonus*. Wilson remarks that Oedipus "accelerates time by prematurely blinding, and thus aging himself" (1997, 181; see also Zeitlin 1986, 129). For the dramatic importance of Oedipus's blindness, see Edmunds 1996, 39–48, 57–8, 63–9.

that he had committed them. But Teiresias suggests that Oedipus's ignorance has a deeper cause. When Teiresias tells him, "I say that it has escaped your notice that you are consorting with your dearest ones most shamefully, nor do you see where you are evil," Oedipus declares that Teiresias has no access to the "strength of truth" "since you are blind in your ears, your mind, and your eyes." But Teiresias responds: "You are wretched, making these reproaches which soon all will make to you" (366–73). Teiresias suggests here that it is Oedipus who is blind in his "mind," that it is he who is blind – albeit metaphorically blind – in his whole understanding of the "truth," of the true world, and therefore that he is much more profoundly blind than Teiresias, who is merely blind to the world that the senses reveal.

Teiresias points to the cause of Oedipus's "blindness" in their exchange over his success in solving the riddle of the Sphinx. Oedipus declares that the soothsayer of Apollo and representative of divine wisdom failed to solve the riddle of the Sphinx and that he, Oedipus, solved it through reason alone (390–8). He thereby suggests that there may be no need for divine guidance since unassisted reason is sufficient to safeguard humans from such monsters as the Sphinx. Indeed, as we noted in Chapter 1, Oedipus evidently ruled successfully for some fifteen years without ever consulting oracles or soothsayers. But Teiresias suggests that it is precisely Oedipus's confident belief in the sufficiency of human reason to guide our lives that has blinded his mind.

TEIRESIAS: This day will beget and destroy you.

OEDIPUS: How very much do you say all things in riddles and uncertainties.

TEIRESIAS: Are you not by nature best at discovering these very things?

OEDIPUS: You reproach me for such things in which you will find me great.

TEIRESIAS: Nevertheless, this very luck has destroyed you. (438–42)

Teiresias suggests here that Oedipus's confidence in reason, a confidence based on the mere "luck" that enabled him to solve the riddle of the Sphinx, has destroyed him because it has blinded him to the inner truth about the world: the fact that the world is ruled by gods whose assistance is indispensable to us. The capacity to see the visible world is at least potentially blinding because it tempts us to believe that we can understand the world and fend for ourselves by the natural light of reason alone, without the help of a higher power. Sight tempts us to the sin of rationalism. Conversely, to be blind, as is Teiresias, is illuminating, for it teaches us our all-too human helplessness and our desperate need for divine assistance, and therefore reveals to our minds the folly of rationalism and the truth of piety.

The blindness of Oedipus in *Oedipus at Colonus*, then, is not merely or primarily a sign of his weakness but of his wisdom. The blind Oedipus sees what the seeing tyrant had failed to see: the truth of the gods and his need for the gods. The heretofore proudly enlightened ruler is now emphatically pious. He affirms the justice of the gods (1380–2), declares his singular devotion to Apollo and Zeus (605–28, 642, 791–3), and makes no mention whatsoever of his triumph over the Sphinx (539–41). Oedipus now repeatedly addresses the gods and invokes the gods because, in his darkness, he beholds the gods and gives himself entirely to their guidance (44–5, 49–50, 83–110, 275–91, 421–4, 1010–3, 1124–5, 1370–96). As he tells his daughters at the end of his last scene in the play: "This way, thus, this way, go. For this way he brings me, Hermes the Escort and the goddess of the underworld. Light, no light, though once before you were mine, I suppose, now for the last time my body grasps you. For already I walk, to hide, finally, my life in Hades" (1547–52). Oedipus, who had boasted of his triumph over the Sphinx through reason alone, now blindly lets the gods lead him into Hades.[5]

Oedipus at Colonus resembles no one in Sophocles' Theban plays more than Teiresias. Like Teiresias, Oedipus is superlatively pious,

---

[5] I therefore disagree with Whitman's contention that "Oedipus is the same man" he was before (1971, 202).

speaks in riddles, and curses his enemies without restraint.[6] Most importantly, like Teiresias, he is blind, and his blindness seemingly enables him to grasp a deeper dimension to the world, inaccessible to the senses or to the inquisitive mind, but visible to the trusting and pious heart. Like Teiresias, Oedipus understands that the blind man is the pious man par excellence, because he is the man who can see past the outer appearance of the natural world and grasp its inner, divine truth.[7] It would thus seem that, as a result of discovering that he has killed his father and slept with his mother, Oedipus has whole-heartedly abandoned his rationalism and taken Teiresias as his model. Indeed, Oedipus's piety may surpass even that of Teiresias. For, unlike Teiresias, Oedipus blinds himself. He chooses to be blind. He consciously rejects the guidance of the senses and reason. Oedipus's blinding of himself symbolizes his attempt to reject reason altogether. By destroying his eyes, he attempts to destroy his mind and surrender himself entirely to the gods.

It would seem, then, that the gods reward Oedipus with the greatest of rewards, not because they pity his blindness, but because they recognize its virtue. They reward Oedipus precisely for his pious rejection of rationalism. On the surface, the *Oedipus at Colonus*, together with the *Oedipus the Tyrant*, presents Sophocles' celebration of piety over reason. For the plays seem to teach that, while Oedipus's attempt to lead his life according to reason ends in disaster and misery, his rejection of reason and his blind faith constitute the path to redemption and salvation.[8]

---

[6] Compare *Oedipus at Colonus* 72–4, 576–80 with *Oedipus the Tyrant* 438–42 and *Oedipus at Colonus* 864–70, 1370–96 with *Oedipus the Tyrant* 449–63 and *Antigone* 1064–86.

[7] See Knox 1964, 144; Segal 1981, 384; Calme 1996, 23; Rocco 1997, 43–4; Van Nortwick 1998, 94; Beer 2004, 167. It is true that, to solve the riddle of the Sphinx (whose content, as we have noted in the Introduction, never appears in Sophocles), Oedipus does use reason to look past the sensible world and the metaphors of the riddle, but he does so in order to grasp the rationally discernible truth of our mortality. See Diodorus Siculus 4.64.3–4 and also Vernant and Vidal-Naquet 1988, 468.

[8] In Calme's words: "The vision of mortal men who think they can see through words is replaced by the belief of the blind, whose mutilation puts them in contact with real visual knowledge, that of the gods" (1996, 23). As Segal

OEDIPUS'S RECOURSE TO REASON TO DEFEND
HIS HOPES

Yet, closer reflection on the *Oedipus at Colonus* points us beyond this pious and anti-rationalist reading of the play. For it is not clear from the play either that Oedipus truly is rewarded by the gods or that he succeeds in completely rejecting reason. In contrast to the *Ajax* (1–133), but like the other two Theban plays, we never see the gods on stage in this play. We evidently do hear thunder, and Oedipus claims that it is Zeus who is thundering in order to summon him to Hades. But Antigone and Theseus are at least initially skeptical, and Theseus suggests that the thunder may simply be a natural occurrence (1503–4; see 1460–1, 1472–6, 1500–17). Oedipus apparently persuades them that the thunder is divine by reporting to them that the Delphic oracle told him when he was young that his life would come to an end when he heard thunder (1510–17). But in addition to the vagueness of the report – thunder would seem to be a rather common phenomenon – in Oedipus's earlier version of that oracle, the signs he recounted indicating the end of his life would be "either an earthquake or some thunder or lightning from Zeus" (95). Perhaps it is for this reason that Antigone, who is familiar with Oedipus's earlier version, is not persuaded that the thunder she hears is a sign from the gods that her father must now die (1459, 1474).

Moreover, while a messenger reports to the chorus after Oedipus's death that he was summoned by the voice of a god and that his body was taken to Hades either by a god or by the earth itself, neither Theseus nor Antigone nor Ismene confirms the claim that a god called to Oedipus (1620–30, 1646–65). Furthermore, whereas the messenger admits that he was not present at Oedipus's death, Theseus, who alone was present, does not confirm that Oedipus's body vanished, but

puts it, "Inner vision replaces the moral blindness of the young Oedipus" (1981, 390). Consider also Knox: "the gods give Oedipus back his eyes, but they are the eyes of superhuman vision" (1964, 148) and Adams: "physical blindness is rehabilitated in supernatural sight" (1957, 176). Knox speaks as well of Oedipus at Colonus's "blind faith in the prophecy" of Apollo (1964, 150). See also Van Nortwick 1998, 94; Wohl 2002, 253.

is instead ambiguous regarding that death, suggesting, on the one hand, that Oedipus has died with "the grace of the underworld," but, on the other hand, that he has a grave, albeit a secret one, and therefore that his death was natural, not miraculous (1751–67).[9] To be sure, Oedipus is rewarded in the course of the play with refuge, with protection from Creon, and with honor. But it is Theseus and the Athenians, not the gods, who bestow these benefits. It is therefore not clear from Sophocles' account that Oedipus is rewarded by the gods.[10]

One might conclude from the obscurity of the play concerning the gods that Sophocles means to show that, precisely since the world and the gods are mysterious, humans must eschew all efforts to live by the light of reason and must rely purely on faith, on such "blind faith" as Oedipus displays, that the gods will care for them.[11] Yet Oedipus, notwithstanding his apparently wholesale rejection of reason in favor of a blind piety, has considerable recourse to at least ostensibly rational arguments in the course of the play. Indeed, much of the play focuses on arguments Oedipus sets forth to attempt to defend his hope that the gods will reward him. Those apologetics are provoked by the almost

[9] Since Oedipus is last seen near a road that plunges down into the earth – apparently down into a ravine or cavern – it is even possible that Oedipus leaps to his death and that his "tomb" is in the ravine or cavern. See 1590–7, 1647–66, and also 52–8. See Jebb 1955, 256–7.

[10] One might think, in the light of the *Antigone*, that the gods reward Oedipus posthumously by answering his prayer that his sons kill each other. Yet by presenting in the *Oedipus at Colonus* Antigone's persuasive argument to Polyneices (1414–46) that he should not attack Thebes, Sophocles invites the reader to wonder whether the fratricide of Oedipus's sons was not caused by a combination of Polyneices' foolishness and chance rather than divine will.

[11] Knox 1964, 150. Consider Segal 1981, 370: "Unlike the younger Oedipus, he is not the riddle solver, proud of his intellectual triumph over nature's mysteries. His knowledge in the Coloneus ... has become fully tragic knowledge, self-knowledge, and it comprises a potential harmony with the mystery of nature ..." See also 387–8; Grene 1967, 162–3; Winnington-Ingram, 1980, 268–72. Wilson claims that "Sophocles has elevated Oedipus to the level of a true prophet for just this reason. To oppose the late Oedipus, who can deliver oracles as a student of Apollo and Zeus, to the early Oedipus, who could only manage an often facile, invariably futile resistance to the gods" (1997, 172).

universal view, at the opening of the play, that Oedipus is hated by the gods. For even though he is praised, especially by the chorus at the end, in the course of the play Oedipus is sharply criticized, not only by Creon, but also by the chorus, Theseus, and Antigone (848–55, 944–6, 226–36, 582–92, 1175–1203; Winnington-Ingram 1980, 259). Now, one might suppose that, insofar as Oedipus has completely surrendered himself to the gods and cherishes a pure, blind faith that the gods favor him, he would not be troubled by such criticism. Yet Oedipus repeatedly resorts to arguments throughout the play in order to persuade the initially hostile Athenians that he deserves their support because he both deserves and enjoys the support of the gods (see 258–309, 445–548, 568–667, 722–1015).[12]

The fact that Oedipus makes such efforts to win the Athenians' assistance suggests that he does not simply count on the gods to give him the protection he needs from his enemies. More importantly, the fact that he makes arguments to demonstrate that he deserves, not punishments, but rewards, from the gods, suggests that Oedipus is seeking to persuade himself as well as the Athenians that he will be so rewarded. We see, then, that, however far Oedipus seems to have gone in renouncing reason by blinding himself and by embracing piety, he still must make use of his reason. He cannot blindly place his hope in the gods. He cannot simply assert to the Athenians or to himself that the gods support him. His hope must be defended by reasons, by an argument that convinces others and himself that he deserves divine rewards. Just as Oedipus used his reason to solve the riddle of the Sphinx and thereby saved Thebes from the monster, so must he use his reason to attempt to save himself and his hopes for divine rewards against the skepticism of others and his own doubts.

The case of Oedipus suggests that, precisely if we human beings hope that the gods will reward us, we cannot simply reject reason but must have recourse to it, in the form of apologetics of some kind or another, to defend our pious hopes against our own doubts. For, given our nature and our condition, it can never be self-evident to us what the will of the gods is. We must always wonder whether they are

---

[12] Consequently I disagree with Slatkin's claim that Oedipus simply argues to the chorus that "It is up to the gods to judge whether he is pious or not" (1986, 216).

well-disposed, ill-disposed, or indifferent, and consequently we must always harbor doubts that they will reward us. And such doubts impel us to try to show for ourselves, to our satisfaction, and hence to our minds, that we may be reasonably confident that the gods will reward us.

OEDIPUS'S ARGUMENT THAT HE DESERVES DIVINE FAVOR

Oedipus's attempt to persuade the chorus of Athenian elders that he deserves divine rewards is remarkably successful. As a consequence of his arguments, the elders declare not only that they feel pity for Oedipus (254–5), but that it is right to pity him since he "is deserving of pity" (461); urge their king Theseus to grant him refuge (629–30); accuse Creon of acting unjustly against Oedipus both now, in attempting to seize him, and before, in exiling him (824–5); defend Oedipus in his dispute with Polyneices (1346–7, 1397–8); and finally pray that the gods reward him (1565–7). Given this success, it is tempting to conclude that, at least according to Sophocles, Oedipus's confidence in the gods' favor is reasonable. But is the chorus right to be persuaded that the man who committed incest and patricide deserves the divine reward of everlasting well-being?

When the Athenian elders first discover who Oedipus is, they react with horror and disgust and assume that the gods share their reaction (232–6). When Antigone begs for mercy, the old men soften, but still assume that the gods will punish them if they do not drive Oedipus out (254–7). As the play opens, the Athenians take it for granted that the crimes of Oedipus render him abhorrent to gods and men. This conviction is shared by Oedipus's countrymen, the Thebans, his brother-in-law Creon, and even his own sons, who drove him into exile some time after his crimes were revealed, "never to return again, since I am a father-killer" (600–1; see 437–44, 599–600, 765–771, 1354–61).[13] It is

---

[13] Oedipus at first suggests that his sons merely acquiesced in the Thebans' decision to exile him (427–44). Later (765–71), Oedipus speaks as though it was Creon who exiled him. But Oedipus asserts to Theseus and Polyneices that his sons

true that, according to Ismene, oracles have recently revealed to the Thebans that Oedipus's physical presence near Thebes will confer on that city a mysterious, divine strength (385–94). This report suggests, as Ismene observes, that the gods, who for so long seemed to torment Oedipus, may now favor him (394). Yet, even after those oracles have been revealed, the Thebans refuse to allow Oedipus to dwell in or be buried within their land since his shedding of "kindred blood does not allow" it (407). Furthermore, when Creon comes to Athens to take Oedipus away, by force if necessary, he assumes that the Athenians will be glad to be rid of one who has committed such atrocious crimes (944–9).[14] Indeed, after discovering his crimes, Oedipus himself thought he deserved punishment: hence he blinded himself and repeatedly declared that he should be exiled or executed.[15] To begin with, then, all – with the notable exception of Theseus – agree that Oedipus's crimes deserve to be punished (Slatkin 1986, 213).

As the play unfolds, however, we quickly learn that Oedipus has become convinced that the gods are, in truth, his champions. When the Athenian elders demand that he leave their land lest the gods punish them for harboring such a criminal, Oedipus boldly declares that the gods will punish them for expelling him! "Therefore, strangers, I beseech you, in the name of the gods, just as you also caused me to stand up, so save me, and do not honor the gods but then refrain from giving the gods their due. But believe that they look upon the pious

---

drove him into exile themselves (599–601, 1354–6; see 429–30). Perhaps he means to suggest that their acquiescence in the Thebans' decision to exile him was tantamount to complicity in that decision, just as he later argues to Polyneices that his decision to exile his blind father was tantamount to patricide (1354–61).

[14] Nevertheless, since Creon only mentions Oedipus's crimes after he has first sought unsuccessfully to persuade Oedipus to come with him; after he has then seized Oedipus's daughters, tried to seize Oedipus himself, and quarreled with the chorus; and after Theseus has appeared and denounced Creon's violence, Creon may exaggerate the degree to which he expected the Athenians to view Oedipus with horror. Compare 728–60 with 939–59.

[15] 427–44, 765–71, 1195–1200; see *Oedipus the Tyrant* 1182–5, 1265–79, 1327–1415, 1432–41, 1515–21; *Oedipus at Colonus* 431–44, 765–71, 1130–8, 866–7, 1197–1200.

one of mortals and also look upon the impious ones, and that there has never yet existed an escape for the impious one of mortals" (275–81). Oedipus's confidence here that the gods will reward those who help him and punish those who harm him is astounding. In the first place, it would seem that his crimes would render him hateful to the gods. But furthermore, as Oedipus and his daughters observe, it would seem that the gods have cruelly mistreated him, by concealing from him the identity of his parents and by leading him to encounter and kill his father and then journey to Thebes, to wed his mother, notwithstanding his efforts to avoid doing so (962, 964–5, 252–4, 394). Oedipus and his daughters here depict the gods as either mysterious beings, who harm or benefit mortals for reasons that are not evident to human beings, or as capricious beings, who destroy human beings without reason, but who then may whimsically raise them up from misfortune. But in either case, how can Oedipus be confident that the gods are now on his side?

The basis of Oedipus's confidence that the gods favor him is his argument that he deserves their favor. He is sure that the gods will reward him, not primarily because he trusts in oracles, but rather because he is convinced that Justice, who, he believes, sits with Zeus, demands that he be rewarded (1380–2). It is Oedipus's faith in the justice of the gods and his argument that justice demands that he be rewarded that, together, form the basis of his confidence in the gods' favor.

There are three distinct parts of Oedipus's overall argument that he deserves the favor of the gods. Most clearly, Oedipus argues that he does not deserve to be blamed for patricide and incest because he committed these crimes unknowingly and hence involuntarily. Furthermore, he argues that he does not deserve to be punished for killing his father because he was driven to do so by his love of himself as a whole and his desire for self-preservation in particular, a desire to which all human beings, given their nature, must yield. Finally, he argues that he deserves divine favor because he has been the victim of terrible crimes deliberately committed by evil men, and justice demands that those criminals be punished most harshly after death, in Tartarus, and that he, their innocent victim, be rewarded, in Hades.

Each part of Oedipus's argument is evident in his first speech to the chorus. "And yet how am I evil in my nature, I who, having suffered,

2 Oedipus at Colonus

retaliated, so that even if I had acted wittingly, not even in that case would I have become evil? But as it is, knowing nothing, I came where I came, but those at whose hands I suffered were knowingly attempting to kill [me]" (270–4). Oedipus argues that, because he did not know that Laius and Jocasta were his parents, and hence did not knowingly commit incest and patricide, he cannot justly be held responsible for these crimes. This is an argument that Antigone alludes to in her speech to the chorus (238–40) and that Oedipus repeats a number of times throughout the play (521–3, 525–6, 548, 974–7). Indeed, because the crimes he committed were committed in ignorance, and hence involuntarily, Oedipus does not speak of them as crimes in this play but rather as, at most, errors or mistakes (437–44; but see 966–8). Since he cannot be justly held responsible for such involuntary actions, Oedipus suggests, he will not be punished by the gods, ruled as they are by Zeus, with whom sits "Justice" (see 1085–6, 1382).[16]

Oedipus, however, does not limit himself to making the argument, specific to his own peculiar case, that, given his ignorance of his parents, he cannot be justly blamed for committing patricide and incest. It is not altogether clear why he believes this argument is in need of a supplement. Perhaps Oedipus worries that it would still leave him vulnerable to the charge, made by Creon and even by Antigone, that it was his "evil spiritedness" (1197–8) that led him to kill Laius, that he was too quick to indulge in his ruinous anger (854–5), and hence that he was guilty at least of murder (see 849–55, 1187–1200; Jebb 1955, 171–2, 210). Accordingly, Oedipus also makes the much more far-reaching argument that he cannot be justly held responsible for committing patricide or murder because he was driven to do so by his need to defend himself – that is, by his love of life and of himself, a love he shares with all human beings.

By raising the question "And yet how am I evil in my nature, I who, having suffered, retaliated, so that even if I had acted wittingly, not even in that case would I have become evil?" (270–2), Oedipus boldly

---

[16] Reinhardt describes this argument as one that persuasively ascribes to Oedipus "the inward innocence of a man who is outwardly guilty" (1979, 201). See also Edmunds 1996, 136–7. But consider Grene 1967, 162–3; Wilson 1997, 144–53.

suggests that it would not have been evil for him to have killed his father wittingly if it were necessary to do so to preserve his own life (see 546). Later he asks Creon: "If someone immediately, here, standing beside you, were attempting to kill you, the just one, would you inquire if the one trying to slay you were your father, or would you make him pay right away? I think, if indeed you love to live, you would make the guilty one pay the price and you would not look around for what is just" (992–6). The love of life is so powerful that it simply overrides all moral considerations, Oedipus suggests, including the prohibition on patricide.

This would seem to be a singularly shocking argument, especially given the tremendous importance the ancient Greeks placed on reverence for one's parents (see Winnington-Ingram 1980, 262). In the *Crito*, for example, Plato presents the laws of Athens as arguing that it is "not pious to do violence either to mother or to father," apparently under any circumstances (51c2; see Aristophanes *Clouds* 1325–41, 1374–90, 1420, 1443–50). In the *Laws*, Plato's Athenian Stranger presents the argument that, since our parents are the creators of our being, since they are the ones who brought our "nature . . . into the light," "in this case alone, where a man is about to be killed by his parents, no law will permit killing one's father or mother to defend oneself against death." Rather, one must "endure, suffering everything, before doing such a thing" (869b7–c3). Indeed, in Sophocles' *Trachinian Women*, Hyllus refuses to commit patricide, even though his beloved father Heracles is suffering unbearable and incurable pain, even though his father commands him to do so, and even though Hyllus has sworn a solemn oath to Zeus to obey his father's commands (1157–1215). These passages suggest that, according to the Greeks, the debt we human beings owe to those who begot and bore us is so absolute and so profound, indeed so akin to the debt we owe to our divine creators, that our duty to them must override all of our desires, including our desire for life (*Laws* 930e3–932d8). Accordingly, Plato's Athenian Stranger suggests, those who kill their parents, even in self-defense, deserve to suffer "many deaths" and hence deserve to suffer terrible punishments in Hades (869b6–7; see 880e7–882a1; consider as well *Exodus* 21:15, 17).

Nevertheless, Oedipus denies that even this fundamental moral duty can override the love of oneself. He suggests that, given our nature, any human being must be excused even for having knowingly committed so terrible a crime as killing his father if he was led to do so by the desire to preserve himself. "For what noble (εσθλος) man is not dear to himself?" (*Oedipus at Colonus* 309). Oedipus suggests here that no man is so noble that he can overcome his self-love and sacrifice or transcend his self-interest. Therefore, human beings who are driven by the apparently compelling love of self cannot be justly held responsible for their actions. Accordingly, when Oedipus declares that neither incest nor patricide was "chosen by myself" (523), he may mean not only that he did not consciously choose to sleep with his mother and kill his father because he did not know who they were, but also that, so compelling is the desire for self-preservation in the human heart, he simply had no choice but to kill his father once he believed his own life was threatened.

One may take Oedipus's argument here one step further. Oedipus never explicitly uses his argument concerning self-preservation and self-love to excuse the crime of incest, but only argues that he does not deserve to be punished for that crime since he did not know who his mother was (see 266–74, 525–6, 978–87). However, it might be possible to argue that Oedipus was led to commit incest out of a desire, not for self-preservation, but to rule Thebes successfully, and hence out of self-love broadly understood. For even though Oedipus was offered rule over Thebes as a reward for having vanquished the Sphinx, as a young foreigner his rule might well have seemed illegitimate unless he had also married the widowed queen. It was presumably out of fear that his rule would be crippled by doubts about its legitimacy that the Thebans "bound" Oedipus to accept the "gift" of a wedding with Jocasta (525–6, 539–41). The thesis, then, that human beings, given their nature, are compelled to act, not only in order to preserve their lives but in order to secure what they believe to be their self-interest broadly understood, would seem to lead to the conclusion that Oedipus would not deserve to be punished for committing either incest or patricide, even if he had known the identity of his parents. And Oedipus himself does hint at such a broad interpretation of his thesis. "For what noble man is not dear to himself?" (309).[17]

---

[17] For expressions of this thesis concerning self-interest and justice that were quite possibly familiar to Sophocles and his Athenian audience, consider

Oedipus's arguments that he cannot justly be blamed for his crimes both because he committed them unwittingly and therefore involuntarily, and, above all, because he committed patricide out of self-defense and therefore involuntarily, lead to the conclusion that he does not deserve to be punished. For it would be manifestly unjust to blame him for committing crimes he could not know he was committing and could not avoid committing. But Oedipus's arguments do not lead to the conclusion that he positively deserves divine rewards. For why should he merit reward for simply following the evidently irresistible human impulse to defend one's life and pursue one's self-interest? Indeed, Oedipus's thesis here implies that, since human beings are compelled by their nature to follow what they believe to be in their self-interest, they cannot ever deserve to be punished or rewarded for their actions. Humans may be pitied for failing to see where their true interests lie. They may be admired for the intelligence with which they discern and pursue their self-interest. But, since they are not free to transcend their self-interest, they cannot reasonably be held morally responsible and hence deserving of reward or punishment for doing what they do.

Evidently because Oedipus senses this implication of his thesis, he also sets forth an argument that he positively deserves to be rewarded by the gods. This argument is based on his contention that, not only has he not been responsible for great injustice, but that he has been a victim of great injustice. Oedipus goes so far as to claim that "my deeds are more what I have suffered than what I have done" (266–7). Throughout the play, Oedipus draws attention to the evils he has suffered (521–3, 537, 595, 872–3, 891–2, 896). Indeed, in his very first words in the play he reminds Antigone – who is fully aware of his sufferings, since

Thucydides 1.75–76.2, 3.44–45, 4.61, 5.105. In these passages, Athenian envoys at Sparta, the Athenian Diodotus, the Syracusan statesman Hermocrates, and the Athenian ambassadors at Melos all contend that human beings are compelled by their nature to pursue what they perceive to be in their self-interest, regardless of the contrary demands of justice. As Whitman observes, "The plays of Sophocles are not the works of one who stood apart from his age" (1971, 240). For post-Sophoclean discussions of this thesis, see Plato *Meno* 77b2–78b8, *Laws* 860d1–861e1; Aristotle *Nicomachean Ethics* 1109b30–1114b25, 1135a15–1136b14, 1145b2–1152a36.

"on account of time I do not need to learn this" (22) – that he is "a blind old man," "a wanderer," who asks for little and receives still less, evidently from hard-hearted witnesses of his travails (1–8). Yet, as Theseus points out, others too have suffered evils. Theseus himself has endured as much as any man the hardships and dangers of being a stranger in a strange land (560–6). More broadly, the lot of all human beings is a hard one, vulnerable as we are to pain and sorrow (566–8). Accordingly, when Oedipus asserts, "I have suffered, Theseus, terrible evils upon evils," Theseus asks, "For what is your affliction, which is greater than what is in accordance with being human?" (595, 598). Why should Oedipus's suffering, however undeserved, lead him to believe that he deserves divine rewards?

In order to make the case that he deserves such rewards, Oedipus tries to argue not only that he has suffered terribly but that he has been the victim of great injustice, deliberately perpetrated by willfully evil men. Because he has suffered such wrong, if there is any justice in this world the gods must punish those who have wronged him so and must compensate him for what he has suffered (Bowra 1944, 314–15; Adams 1957, 161–2). But what exactly has he suffered? In the first place, Oedipus suffered deliberate injustice at the hands of his parents, who "were knowingly attempting to kill [me]" when they ordered him killed as a baby (274). Oedipus draws here an implicit contrast between his own crimes against his parents and theirs against him. His parents deserve to be blamed for their (attempted) crime because, as he points out, they knew he was their child and, he implies, they were not driven to kill him by any necessity but simply acted maliciously and wickedly. Similarly, Oedipus is victimized by Creon, who seizes his daughters, attempts to seize him, and then "voluntarily" speaks ill of him and Jocasta in front of the Athenians (985–6). Here, too, Oedipus suggests that Creon is an unjust and evil man who deserves to be blamed because he is freely choosing to inflict pain on Oedipus, out of sheer malice (1000–2, 761–83). Oedipus has also suffered exile from his own city. Finally, and most importantly, Oedipus has suffered at the hands of his own two sons, who deliberately and cruelly wronged their own father by driving him away from home and hearth, again, apparently, out of sheer malice: "When I, who sired them, was so dishonorably thrust out of my fatherland, they did not hinder this or defend me, but I was driven out by the two of them, I was sent out and proclaimed an exile . . . . [T]hen it was, after all that time, that the city drove me out of my land with violence, and they, sons of their father, who had the power to benefit their father, did not wish to act, but for want of a small word from them, I was driven out, an exile, a beggar, forever" (427–30, 440–4).

Accordingly, when Theseus asks him what distinguishes his suffering from that of other humans, Oedipus succinctly replies, "I was driven away from my land by my own seed" (599–600). Indeed, he goes so far as to accuse his son Polyneices of being a "murderer" (1361) of his own father, a would-be patricide, since "you yourself drove out your own father here and made me a man without a city. . . If I had not begotten these children to be my nurses, I would not exist, as far as you are concerned" (1356–7, 1365–6). By exiling their blind, helpless, father, his sons virtually condemned him to death, since it was a sheer accident that their sisters (and charitable strangers) kept their father alive. Oedipus is therefore not only innocent of patricide; he is himself a victim of willful and deliberate patricide. Oedipus himself is not evil, but his son Polyneices is a "most evil one," indeed "most evil of evil ones" (1354, 1384).

Oedipus has thus been the victim of truly horrible and outrageous crimes. Therefore the gods must compensate him for his suffering. It is because of his belief in his innocence and in the outrageously unjust character of what he has suffered that Oedipus is confident he is "sacred and pious" and will be rewarded by just gods who always care for "the pious one of mortals" (287, 278–81). As Aristotle remarks in the *Rhetoric*, "For anger inspires confidence, since it is not committing injustice but suffering injustice that makes us angry, and it is supposed that the divine helps those who have suffered injustice" (2.5.21–22; see also, for example, Thucydides 5.104, 7.77.1–4).

Oedipus's confidence that he deserves to be rewarded by the gods, then, rests fundamentally on two arguments. On the one hand, he does not deserve to be punished for his crimes because he committed them unknowingly and hence involuntarily and because he committed patricide in order to satisfy his compelling desire for self-preservation and hence involuntarily. On the other hand, he has been the innocent victim of willful, culpable, outrageous crimes committed freely and maliciously by his parents, his countrymen, and his sons. Yet these two arguments contradict one another. For, as Sophocles shows in the play, those who inflicted suffering on Oedipus did not do so maliciously, as Oedipus claims, but rather in order to defend themselves from harm, just as Oedipus killed his father in order to defend himself from harm. Oedipus himself alludes to the fact that Laius heard from an oracle that he would "die at the hands of his children" (969–73). But if the desire for self-preservation is so compelling that it excuses Oedipus's killing of his father in self-defense, does it not also excuse his father's attempt to kill him as a baby after he heard from an oracle that his child would grow up to kill him? Similarly, when Oedipus attempts to show that Creon is "evil," he explains that Creon seeks to abduct him in order to save Thebes "from evils" (784–6). But if the desire to defend himself from harm excuses Oedipus's killing of Laius, doesn't the desire to defend his city from harm excuse even Creon's brutal kidnapping of Oedipus and his daughters (see 387–409, 755–60, 848–52)? Moreover, doesn't the desire for self-preservation also excuse the decision of Creon, Oedipus's sons, and the Thebans to send Oedipus off into exile after his patricide and incest were revealed? Would it not have been reasonable for them to believe, as Oedipus himself at one point believed, and as the Athenians themselves initially believe, that the gods demanded that he be exiled for his crimes and that they would punish Thebes for refusing to exile him (see 407, 431–44, 599–601, 765–71, 849–52, 228–36, 254–7)?[18] Indeed, if, as Oedipus insists, it was not evil for him to kill his father in order to defend himself from harm, how can it be evil for Polyneices to send his father into exile in order to protect himself and his city from harm, especially if he thought that his sisters might care for him? And even if Oedipus argued that it was unreasonable for his son and the Thebans to believe that the gods would punish them for failing to exile him, would Oedipus still not have to concede, insofar as the Thebans exiled him in order to protect themselves from harm, that they must be excused since, however

---

[18] Scholars tend to be harshly critical of Creon. See Reinhardt 1979, 210–12; Whitman 1971, 207; Segal 1981, 378–81; Opstelten 1952, 116; Winnington-Ingram 1980, 251; Adams 1957, 171; Mills 1997, 181–2. But consider Bowra 1944, 335–6; Grene 1967, 161–3.

mistaken their concern, they were driven to act as they did by the same irresistible impulse of self-love that has driven him to act? "For what noble man is not dear to himself?" (309).

In order to show that he does not deserve to be punished for his crimes, Oedipus argues that we humans are compelled by our nature to follow what we perceive to be our self interest, regardless of what justice otherwise demands, and therefore cannot be held responsible for our actions. But in order to show that he deserves to be rewarded by the gods, Oedipus argues that he has been the innocent victim of men who have freely chosen to act unjustly, out of sheer malice, that they therefore deserve to be punished, and that he deserves to be compensated by the gods. Oedipus's confidence that he deserves to be rewarded by the gods rests therefore on a contradiction, and hence is unreasonable. By invoking the thesis that the desire for self-preservation is compelling to excuse his own crimes, but then ignoring that thesis when denouncing the crimes of others, Oedipus tries to have his cake and eat it too.

While Oedipus insists on arguing that the desire for self-preservation and the love of oneself is so compelling that it excuses his crimes, he refuses to recognize that it may excuse the crimes of others against him.[19] He refuses to follow his argument to its deepest conclusion because to do so would require him to conclude that it is impossible for him, or for any human being, to deserve the divine reward of everlasting well-being. For how can we human beings deserve such a reward if we are truly incapable of resisting or transcending our self-interest even in regard to the most sacred of laws, the laws that protect the family?

To begin with, Oedipus attempts to reject reason completely in the name of a blind faith that the gods will reward him with everlasting well-being. But the doubts of others and, most importantly, his own doubts, eventually impel him to seek reasons to justify his faith that the

[19] See Grene 1967, 163–5; Winnington-Ingram 1980, 258–9; Reinhardt 1979, 216–19. Consider as well Wilson 1997, 178. I therefore must disagree with Whitman's claim that Oedipus's treatment of Polyneices "rests on the same absolute standard he had espoused" (1980, 211; see also Segal 1981, 383).

gods are not his enemies but his champions. In the end, however, even though Oedipus has recourse to argument to defend his hope for divine favor, he ultimately balks at fully accepting his own argument lest it undermine that hope. Oedipus follows reason insofar, but only insofar, as it can support his hope for immortality.

THE PLEASURES OF ANGER AND THE REJECTION OF REASON

The clearest sign that Oedipus does not accept the thrust of his own argument regarding the power of self-love is his anger. According to his argument, it is unreasonable for humans or gods to be angry with him for having killed his father because he was compelled to do so out of his love for life and for himself, and it is unreasonable to be angry with someone for doing what he can not help doing. Indeed, he goes so far as to claim, "I suppose the soul of my father, being alive, would not speak against me" (998–9). Rather than rage and curse, the slain Laius would understand and forgive his son. But in the course of the play, Oedipus himself is extremely angry, with (at first) the chorus, his parents, Creon, Thebes, and, above all, with his own sons, for acting against him, for inflicting pain and suffering (though not death) upon him, in order to benefit themselves: "And did the most evil ones ... place tyranny before longing for me? ... But they have chosen, instead of him who begot them, to hold sway with the throne and the scepter and to be tyrant of the land" (418–19, 448–9; see 427–30). So bitter is Oedipus that, when his son Polyneices comes to ask for forgiveness for his neglect, he responds by accusing his son of patricide: "You, most evil one, who, holding scepter and throne, which now your blood-brother in Thebes holds, you yourself drove away your own father here and made me without a city, to bear also these clothes, which now beholding you shed tears over, because you have happened to go into the same labor of evils as I. These things must not be bewailed but must be borne by me, just as I should live, having remembered you, a murderer" (1354–61). Oedipus goes on to unleash what may be the angriest curse ever uttered by a father to his sons in all of Greek literature: "Go, spat out and unfathered by me, most evil of evil ones, having collected these curses, which I now call on you, you will not hold sway over your native land by spear, nor will you ever return to hollow Argos, but by kindred hand you will die and kill him, by whom you were driven out. Such things I curse, and call on a hated, paternal darkness of Tartarus, I call on these daemons, I call on Ares, who has cast among you the terrible hatred" (1383–92).[20] Here Oedipus prays not only for the death of both his sons but that they may become stained with the crime of fratricide, the crime of shedding "kindred blood," as he himself has been stained with the crimes of incest and patricide, and apparently damns them to an eternity of suffering in Tartarus.[21]

Given the glaring contradiction between his argument that he is not to be blamed but forgiven for his actual patricide and his argument that his sons are to be pitilessly blamed and punished eternally for their virtual, tacit, attempted patricide, one might wonder how it is possible for Oedipus to fail to recognize this contradiction. If he were genuinely concerned with justice, as his righteous indignation might seem to suggest, would he not feel the force of this contradiction at the heart of his belief that he deserves divine rewards? Would he not feel compelled to wrestle with this contradiction and reflect on it? What prevents him from recognizing it, and allows him not to see it, is his towering and willful anger, an anger that is ultimately more fundamental to him than a genuine concern for justice.[22] Indeed, so willfully angry is Oedipus with those who have harmed him that he refuses even to consider why they might have harmed him and whether they may not have been led to do so by such considerations as led him to kill his father.[23]

---

[20] In contrast, in the *Antigone*, when Haemon goes so far as to threaten to kill his father, Creon nonetheless refrains from cursing him (751–80).

[21] Reinhardt remarks: "There is no excuse for the savagery of his curses" (1979, 219). See also Grene 1967, 164–5; Winnington-Ingram 1980, 316. For defenses of this curse, see Bowra 1944, 327–31; Adams 1957, 175; Whitman 1971, 211–12; Segal 1981, 383–88; Mills 1997, 174–5.

[22] Winnington-Ingram describes Oedipus as "an ill-used man brimming over with thumos" (1980, 258; see 257–60).

[23] As Winnington-Ingram remarks, Oedipus "in his passion is blind" to the resemblance between his case and that of Polyneices (1980, 277).

But what is the cause of such willful anger? What might be the positive appeal of feeling such anger? Anger would seem to be a painful experience, since it is occasioned by either suffering pain oneself or seeing a loved one suffer pain. Yet anger means more specifically suffering pain in a way that gives you hope. For anger is not stirred up by pain accompanied by the belief that the pain you suffer is justly inflicted or caused by blind necessity. Anger is rather provoked by pain that you believe has been deliberately, maliciously, and unjustly inflicted upon you. And, as Aristotle points out in the passage cited earlier, that experience – that sense of righteous indignation – naturally gives rise to the heartening belief that justice demands that you be aided and that the unjust be punished, and hence that there be gods who favor you as you deserve and punish your enemies as they deserve (see *Rhetoric* 2.5.21–22).[24]

Within the play, Oedipus's confidence that the gods favor him is greatest when he is most angry at what he perceives to be injustice.[25] It is only after the Athenian elders have demanded that he leave and have thereby, in his judgment, violated their promise to shelter him, that he denounces their impiety, affirms that he is himself "sacred and pious," and declares that the gods will reward the pious but punish the impious (compare 203–27 with 258–91). It is only after Creon attempts to seize him that Oedipus confidently calls on the gods to punish Creon and his family (compare 761–847 with 863–70). But the height of Oedipus's confidence comes immediately after his interview with Polyneices. Just before that interview, Oedipus asks himself whether it is "righteous" for him to thank Theseus for rescuing his daughters by embracing and kissing him. Oedipus evidently fears that he may suffer from an indelible "stain" from his crimes, as Creon has argued, however involuntarily he may have committed those crimes according to his own argument (1130–8; see 944–9, Jebb 1955, 202–3). But immediately after that interview, Oedipus confidently declares that the

---

[24] As Ruderman explains, "the desire to vent our anger presupposes both a moral position (viz., injustice is freely and knowingly chosen by the wrongdoer) and a theological one (viz., the gods punish wrongdoers)" (1999, 155).

[25] In Winnington-Ingram's words: "his confidence always seems to grow with his anger" (1980, 256).

gods are now summoning him to eternal rewards in Hades (1457–61, 1472–6, 1505–12, 1536–52).

Oedipus evidently feels especially confident that the gods will reward him during the interview with Polyneices because he feels acutely the magnitude of the wrongs he has suffered. It is during this interview that Oedipus claims to have been the intended victim of the gravest of crimes – patricide – at the hands of his sons. Accordingly, his rage here is greater than it is at any moment in the play, even greater than it is when Creon seizes him and his daughters. For while he denounces Creon as "impious," "shameless," and "most evil," Oedipus denounces his son as "most evil of evil ones" and as a would-be patricide, disowns him, and calls down on him the curse that he both commit and suffer fratricide and that he be punished by the gods after death (823, 863, 866, 960, 1354, 1383, 1360–6, 1369–96). Oedipus feels so confident after this interview that he will be rewarded after death because he believes that, given the outrageous wrongs he has suffered, justice demands not only that his sons be punished but that he be rewarded.

Oedipus's tremendous anger blinds him to the unreasonableness of his confidence that he deserves rewards from the gods (Winnington-Ingram 1980, 277). Indeed, Oedipus relishes and embraces the feeling of anger precisely because it enables him to feel in his bones, regardless of the contradictory nature of his arguments, that justice demands that he be rewarded with everlasting well-being. Oedipus's anger specifically protects and supports his hope for immortality. Now, the hope for immortality would seem to be natural to human beings, since it would seem to arise naturally from our awareness that we are mortal and our longing for immortality. But anger reflects our passionate *rejection* of our mortality. In the case of Oedipus, anger transforms his hope into a confidence that he will be rewarded with immortality for it inspires in him the pious conviction that he deserves to be so rewarded. Yet, as Oedipus's own argument concerning the compelling power of self-interest suggests, and as the play as a whole suggests, reason teaches that, since we human beings are incapable of transcending our concern for ourselves, we are incapable of deserving the reward of immortality. To follow reason means to accept our mortal nature as a harsh truth of our condition, as a given of our world. But anger means the refusal to accept the world as it is. It means refusing to accept, as Oedipus refuses to accept, that human beings are necessarily self-interested and hence that his parents love life and that his sons seek to defend themselves against harm as surely as he does. It means refusing to accept that we are incapable of deserving the divine reward of immortality. It means refusing to accept, as Oedipus refuses to accept, not only the self-interested nature of human beings but their mortal nature as well.

More than his blindness, it is Oedipus's anger that reflects his pious rejection of reason. The case of Oedipus suggests that religious anti-rationalism is rooted in such essential features of our human nature as our awareness of our mortality, our hope for immortality, and, above all, our angry refusal to accept our mortality. In this way, the play suggests that religious anti-rationalism is an enduring feature of political life.

THE ENLIGHTENED STATESMANSHIP OF THESEUS

Yet, even if we grant that Oedipus's anger is unreasonable, we might still wonder, is it not also a source of towering strength? Does it not inspire Oedipus to forge ahead and struggle on, notwithstanding his seemingly hopeless condition at the beginning of the play? Moreover, the play does have a happy ending for Oedipus. Even if he is not clearly rewarded by the gods, he is certainly protected and honored by the Athenians. Is it not Oedipus's spiritedness, his tremendous capacity for indignation, his refusal to accept his plight, and his confidence in his righteousness, as well as his arguments, that account for his amazing success in winning over the Athenians and thwarting the Thebans? Might not the play suggest that, insofar as Oedipus's spiritedness enables this helpless blind man to gain allies, triumph over his enemies, and win lasting honor, it is, if not reasonable, a source of great strength, beneficial to him, and therefore admirable?[26]

---

[26] Consider Bowra: "His high temper, which before contributed to his undoing, is now an instrument of strength" (1944, 340). Kaufmann also speaks of Sophocles' celebration of Oedipus's "defiant strength" and "rocklike . . . confidence in his spiritual strength" (1968, 239). Wilson suggests that "the

But, while Oedipus's perseverance in the midst of terrible hardships
is indeed admirable, the play presents sharp criticisms of his spiritedness for causing, in large measure, those very hardships. As Creon
declares, "you indulged your anger, which always ruins you" (855;
see also 592, 1175–80). And in a surprising echo of Creon's charge,
Antigone denounces her father's spirited refusal to meet with his son:
"You begot him. Therefore, even if he has performed actions of the
most evil, impious sort, it is not righteous for you, father, to perform
evil actions against that one. But as for him, others have evil offspring
and a sharp spiritedness, but, once they are advised by the charms of
loved ones, their nature is charmed. Look away from these woes and
toward those of your father and mother that you have suffered. And
should you gaze on those woes, I know that you will recognize how
evil comes to be the end of an evil spiritedness. For you do not have
slight grounds for reflection, bereft as you are of your eyes, unseeing"
(1189–1200). It was, Antigone gently reminds her father, his "evil
spiritedness" that led him to kill Laius and to drive Jocasta to her
death.[27] It was, as Oedipus himself admits, his rage that led him to
blind himself, and thereby doomed him to the helpless condition we
find him in at the beginning of the play (431–44, 765–71). It was his
anger that doomed his daughters to be his nurses, rather than to be
cared for by him.[28]

Furthermore, it is not sufficient to say that Oedipus's spiritedness
leads to the happy outcome of *Oedipus at Colonus*. For a crucial role in

---

intensity of his conviction, and perhaps our own amazement that a man so
evidently beaten by life can still maintain such ferocity, pushes us on an
emotional, rather than an intellectual, level to accept his claims of heroic
stature" (1997, 153).

[27] Given Sophocles' portrayal of her loving but critical stance toward her father,
I cannot agree with those scholars who claim that Sophocles "presents an
Antigone who consistently manifests an 'Electra complex' of the classic
Freudian type, in that she remains trapped in a fixation on her father" and
exhibits an "extreme attachment" to him (Griffith 2005, 94, 100; see also
Johnson 1997).

[28] See Winnington-Ingram 1980, 259–60. Reinhardt notes that here
"Sophocles finally moves away from his hero" (1979, 216). Consider as well
Wilson 1997, 166, 176.

that outcome is played by Theseus, who grants Oedipus and his daughters sanctuary, defends them against Creon, and bestows the Athenians' honor on him. But Theseus too is a critic of Oedipus's spiritedness. When Oedipus decries his sons for trying to force him to return to Thebes, Theseus responds, "Fool! Spiritedness is not advantageous among evils" (592). Theseus criticizes Oedipus specifically here for quarreling unnecessarily with his sons even though he desperately needs their help. More broadly, Theseus suggests that, inasmuch as the human condition is one that is always beset by evils, it is always foolish to indulge in such anger (592, 598, consider 658–60).

Theseus is himself remarkably free of anger.[29] For example, Theseus stresses in his opening remarks to Oedipus that he too has suffered the dangers and hardships of the life of an exile (562–6; see Homer *Iliad* 1.260–8; Plutarch, *Theseus* 4–20). Yet, unlike Oedipus, Theseus expresses no anger whatsoever regarding his sufferings, but rather stresses the unavoidable character of such suffering and even how he profited from it by receiving an "education." Furthermore, Theseus never expresses the moral indignation over Oedipus's patricide and incest that the chorus initially feels and that Creon expects him to feel (compare 551–68 with 220–36, 254–7, 510–46, 939–50).[30] Even without hearing Oedipus's argument, he evidently accepts that those crimes were involuntary.[31] But Theseus also never expresses anger at Creon and Oedipus's sons, in contrast with Oedipus himself, as well as with the chorus (461–2, 1211–48, 1346–7, 1397–8, 1448–55). This is especially clear in Theseus's confrontation with Creon. Creon enters Athens with Theban soldiers, violently seizes Oedipus and his daughters, even though they have been granted refuge by the Athenian king, and brazenly insults the Athenians. The Athenian elders are understandably outraged (831, 842). Theseus would seem to have

---

[29] "Anger is not for him," says Reinhardt (1979, 213). He adds that this lack of anger distinguishes Theseus from both Creon and Oedipus and reminds one of Pericles (213).

[30] Indeed, Theseus himself was, according to Plutarch, at least indirectly responsible for the death of his own father (*Theseus* 22). In the judgment of Plutarch, Theseus can "hardly, I think . . . escape the accusation of patricide" (*Theseus and Romulus* 5.2). See Mills 1997, 14–18.

[31] See Adams 1957, 170; Slatkin 1986, 219; Winnington-Ingram 1980, 273.

every reason to be angry with Creon in the name of Athenian patriotism, as is the chorus. When Theseus appears on the scene, he remarks
to the chorus that he would treat Creon harshly, *if* he were angry. "As
for this one [Creon], if I dealt with him with the anger he deserves, I
would not let him go unwounded by my hand" (904–6). Yet when
Theseus turns to confront Creon directly, he criticizes him most emphatically—in the name of Thebes! "Yet Thebes did not educate you to
be evil. For they do not love to rear men who are outside of justice, but
they would not praise you, if they learned that you plunder my things
and the things of the gods, bringing away violently miserable mortals,
suppliants . . . . But you bring shame on a city that does not deserve it,
on your own city" (919–23, 928–30). Theseus grasps that, however
insulting Creon is toward Athens, he is a Theban patriot, a man devoted
to his city and desperately trying to protect it from harm (387–409,
755–60, 784–6, 848–52). Consequently, Theseus appeals to Creon's
Theban patriotism to persuade Creon and to shame him.[32] And
Theseus is at least somewhat effective, inasmuch as Creon seems less
angry and self-confident after Theseus has spoken (consider 939–59,
1018, 1036, but also 1037).

The causes of Theseus's freedom from spiritedness are his understanding that humans are naturally self-interested and his capacity
to view the world from the perspective of the self-interest of others.
For example, whereas Antigone condemns Oedipus's spiritedness as
harmful to others, Theseus stresses that it is harmful to Oedipus
himself (compare 1189–1203 with 589–92). Similarly, while Oedipus denounces Creon's actions as harmful and insulting to him and the
chorus denounces them as harmful and insulting to Athens, Theseus
denounces them as harmful and insulting to Creon's own beloved city
of Thebes. Theseus does not expect Creon to put Athens first, as the
chorus expects Creon to put Athens first and as Oedipus expects Creon
and Thebes, as well as his own sons and daughters, to put his interests
first. Theseus expects human beings to be self-interested, accepts that

---

[32] See Reinhardt 1979, 213–14. Reinhardt notes that Theseus's (and Sophocles')
praise of Thebes here is remarkable given that the play "must have been
written at a time when Thebes was the bitterest of all Athens' enemies" (214;
see also Whitman 1971, 209; Vernant and Vidal-Naquet 1988, 337–8).

they are necessarily so, and therefore does not blame them for being so. Instead he tries to understand what their interests might be in order to appeal to them.

Indeed, in his sympathetic understanding of other humans, in his capacity to place himself in the position of others and to view the world from their viewpoint, Theseus reminds us of no one more than the poet Sophocles himself, who must see the world through his characters' eyes in order to give them voice and bring them to life.[33] Theseus's understanding and acceptance of the compelling power of self-love highlight his fundamentally rational outlook. In contrast to the spirited Oedipus, Theseus never claims to be less self-interested than, and hence morally superior to, others. He never claims to deserve any rewards from the gods, much less the reward of everlasting well-being. Accordingly, however respectful Theseus may be of the piety of his subjects, he never evinces a pious hope for immortality. Just as Theseus is free of Oedipus's anger at the self-interested nature of human beings, so is he free of Oedipus's anger at our mortal nature.

The question naturally arises, what might Theseus's own self-interest be? On the surface, the Athenian king's offer of refuge and protection to Oedipus against Thebes would seem to be a simply noble, compassionate, and selfless act.[34] For the Athens we see in this play is, compared with its neighbors, a political and military midget. The play takes place at the dawn of Athenian history, when Theseus united such villages as Colonus into the city of Athens and established himself as king (see Jebb 1955, 77; Thucydides 2.15; Plutarch *Theseus* 24–5). Athens is of so little consequence at this time that Oedipus, who grew up in the royal household of Corinth and ruled over Thebes for some fifteen years, does not even know whether neighboring Athens is ruled by a king, and has never even heard of Theseus (66–9; see 947–9).

---

[33] As Opstelten puts it: "as far as this play goes, he was more closely akin to its Theseus than to its Oedipus" (1952, 114).

[34] Consider Walker: Theseus "accepts Oedipus simply and solely because he is a stranger in distress" (1995, 185; see 188); and Scodel: "Theseus receives Oedipus without any concern for what Oedipus can give him in return" (1984, 113). Mills speaks of "Theseus' unique nobility" (1997, 175). See also Bowra 1944, 332–3; Whitman 1971, 207; Beer 2004, 159.

Athens is so weak militarily that when Polyneices is ousted by his
brother from his throne and seeks aid in his plan to return to Thebes at
the head of an army, he goes to far-off Argos rather than nearby Athens
and does not even bother to invite Athens to join him (371–81). The
most vivid sign of Athens' political and military weakness in the play is
the contempt with which Creon treats the Athenians. He repeatedly
expresses scorn for their city, as the chorus laments (835–43, 857–63,
877–83; see 897–903). He seizes Ismene, Antigone, and Oedipus
without any fear of retaliation by Theseus and his subjects (813–9).
Moreover, when Theseus arrives and bloodlessly rescues Oedipus and
his daughters from Creon's men, the chorus speaks of this seemingly
minor police action as a glorious military victory (see 1044–73).
Athens here is militarily dwarfed by Argos, and especially Thebes.
Theseus's defiance of Thebes would thus seem to be risky. When Creon
threatens retaliation, his threat must be taken seriously (837, 1037).
Accordingly, it seems fitting that Oedipus bless Theseus for standing
up to Thebes: "May you have profit, Theseus, in thanks for your
nobility and your just forethought for us" (1042–3).

Yet Theseus's willingness to defend Oedipus is not as imprudent as
it first appears. Thebes does not retaliate against Athens because it is
devastated first by the war between Oedipus's two sons and then by the
strife between Creon and Antigone. Furthermore, Theseus evidently
knows that there is tension between Oedipus and his sons (588) and
strife between Polyneices and Eteocles, even before Oedipus arrives.
Theseus does not, for example, ever ask Oedipus why Polyneices is
dressed in Argive garb. Theseus also presumably knows that there is
a vast Argive army, headed for Thebes, camped outside his city
(1301–25). So he may surmise that, given such strife, Thebes will
not punish Athens for protecting Oedipus. Moreover, by protecting
Oedipus and his daughters against his sons and Creon, Theseus
encourages division within the Theban royal family at a time when
Thebes is threatened by foreign invasion. And by agreeing to let
Antigone and Ismene return to Thebes at the end of the play, Theseus
sets the stage for the further, and foreseeable, struggle within Thebes
that we witness in the *Antigone*. Theseus's treatment of Oedipus and his
family serves Athens' interest by fomenting strife within Thebes and
thereby weakening Athens' powerful neighbor.

But most importantly, Theseus benefits himself and his city by winning the protection of the gods in return for granting Oedipus sanctuary (Grene 1967, 161–3). Oedipus repeatedly promises the Athenians that they will profit from his presence in their city (68–72, 285–8, 448–60, 576–82, 607–28, 1518–55, 1586–1667). More specifically, Oedipus promises that, if Theseus gives him refuge, protection, and burial, then, when the Thebans attack Athens in the future, "At that time, my cold corpse, sleeping and covered, will drink their warm blood, if Zeus is still Zeus and Zeus's son Phoebus is sure" (621–3). Oedipus goes on to claim that he will defend Athens against Thebes for the rest of time as one empowered by Zeus and Apollo to become a protective deity, as long as he is honored by the Athenians (1518–55).

The chorus of Athenian elders is deeply impressed by this claim. For these elders are emphatically pious. They praise their city as one blessed by the gods and pray to the gods to continue to favor and protect it.[35] Even though Athens is a young, militarily and politically weak city in this play, it is already renowned as a superlatively pious city. Oedipus invokes this reputation when he appeals for refuge from the Athenians: "What is the benefit of renown or noble reputation if it flows in vain? They say that Athens is the most god-revering, that she alone is able to save the stranger who has suffered evil, and that she alone is able to defend him. Where are these things for me?" (258–63). The reputation of Athens for a pious hospitality toward suppliants explains not only why Oedipus and Antigone have sought refuge there, but also why Ismene, Creon, and Polyneices all assume that Oedipus is to be found in Athens.

Oedipus's promise that his presence will confer divine protection on Athens plays a decisive role in overcoming the chorus's initial hostility to him. Even though they initially demand that Oedipus leave their

---

[35] 668–721, 1044–98. For other illustrations of the Athenians' superlative piety, see 36–65, 75–80, 117–38, 143, 149–69, 254–7, 461–92, 887–9, 897–903, 907–36, 1179–80, 1556–78, 1604–66, 1692–5, 1764–7. Consider 258–62, 275–91, as well as 1456, 1462–71, 1477–85, 1491–9. See Walker 1995, 178; Mills 1997, 169–70, 177.

land after learning his identity, after he claims that through him the
gods will protect Athens, the elders respond: "You are deserving of
pity, Oedipus, you yourself and these children. And since you add to
this argument that you yourself will be the savior of this land, I want to
recommend expedient things to you" (461–4). After Oedipus repeats
this claim to Theseus, the chorus endorses it (630–1). The chorus
evidently hopes that the gods will protect its beloved city, and Oedipus
appeals to these pious hopes.

Yet, as we have seen, it is not at all clear that Theseus shares the
pious hopes of the Athenian elders. In the first place, he is skeptical
when Oedipus claims that he is being summoned to Hades by
thunder sent from Zeus. Furthermore, and more importantly, in
contrast with the pious Oedipus and the pious chorus, Theseus is free
of righteous indignation at the self-interestedness of others and free of
the pious hopes that accompany such indignation. Finally, Theseus
stands out within the galaxy of Sophoclean kings and tyrants in the
Theban plays as a statesman whose rule is independent of religious
authority and based on his wits alone. King Laius and Queen Jocasta
are so deferential to soothsayers and oracles that they agree to kill
their only child and remain childless (Oedipus the Tyrant 711–22,
1173–6). Creon, Polyneices, and Eteocles repeatedly consult and
heed those who claim to speak for the gods (555–7, 1422–31,
1438–45, 1515–20; Antigone 991–5; Oedipus at Colonus 385–420,
1291–1300). And, notwithstanding his own apparent rationalism as
ruler, Oedipus himself piously consults the oracle and soothsayer of
Apollo at moments of crisis (Oedipus the Tyrant, 68–77, 284–9,
787–97). But, in contrast to all of those rulers, Theseus is never said
to consult either oracles or soothsayers. Indeed, there is no one in
Athens whom Theseus permits to wield the independent authority
that Teiresias evidently wields in Thebes under the reigns of Laius,
Oedipus, Polyneices, Eteocles, and Creon. And in contrast to the
reigns of all of those rulers, each of whom suffers a disastrous fate,
Theseus's rule is an unqualified success. We see him at the end of this
play beloved by his subjects, blessed by Oedipus and his daughters,
and victorious over his adversaries. Theseus is a statesman guided
by compassion and reason, not spiritedness or piety. Through his
example – the only example in the Theban plays of a successful

statesman – Sophocles teaches the superiority of political rationalism over religious politics.[36]

Yet Theseus is not an enemy of piety, as is the Oedipus of *Oedipus the Tyrant* at times (390–8, 946–85) and as Creon in the *Antigone* momentarily becomes (1033–59). Theseus publicly prays to Poseidon and is publicly respectful of the piety of Oedipus and the chorus (*Oedipus at Colonus* 887–9, 1179–80, 1209–10, 1760–7). Although Theseus himself does not rely on the gods for assistance, he understands the importance of pious hopes for his people and pious fears for his enemies. Accordingly, he understands that, even if it is not true that protecting Oedipus can gain for Athens divine protection, protecting him can benefit Athens by enhancing her reputation for piety. Oedipus certainly does enhance that reputation. After Theseus saves him, Oedipus declares to Creon: "It escapes your notice that if some land knows how to revere gods with honors, this one excels in this" (1005–7). And after his daughters are rescued, Oedipus exclaims to Theseus and the Athenian elders: "For no one else of mortals, but you [singular], saved them. And may gods grant to you what I wish, to yourself and this land. Since I have found piety only among you [plural] of human beings as well as decency and honesty" (1123–7). Oedipus bolsters the beliefs of the Athenians in the sanctity of their city. He strengthens the pious confidence of the Athenians that their young city is not simply left by an indifferent world to fend for itself but is rather blessed by gods who will protect it. In this way, Oedipus truly benefits the Athenians. As Theseus evidently recognizes, such a pious patriotism, such a belief that one's nation is under God and favored by providence, is salutary and beneficial to any political community, even if that belief is not simply reasonable.[37]

---

[36] I therefore cannot agree with Wilson's claim that Theseus "displays no political skill, no tact whatsoever" (1997, 198) as well as with Zeitlin's characterization of him as "this kind and *simple* king" (1986, 141 – my emphasis). Though I agree with Whitman that Theseus is "the representative of truly Hellenic justice and civilization" in the play, I would at least qualify his claim that Theseus is "champion of the true Athenian religiosity" (1971, 223, 213; see also Mills 1997, 177, 183; Segal 1981, 377).

[37] Oedipus also evidently enhances the individual authority of Theseus within Athens, perhaps especially in relation with the council of the Aeropagus, to

Theseus's political rationalism is a mean between the anti-rationalist and wrathful piety exemplified by Oedipus at Colonus and the arrogant political rationalism of Oedipus the Tyrant. Theseus's rationalism is politic, cautious, and moderate, mindful of the power and utility of religion and therefore respectful of the religious passions and hopes of his subjects. Theseus bears witness to the possibility of a genuinely enlightened statesmanship, one that faces and accepts both human mortality and human piety.[38]

CONCLUSION

Nietzsche rightly recognizes in Oedipus at Colonus a representative of religious anti-rationalism, but he errs in concluding that Sophocles deems Oedipus's rejection of reason to be "wise" (1967, 42, 68–9). As we have seen, Sophocles' play seeks to demonstrate that the religious anti-rationalism exemplified by Oedipus is self-contradictory and, more importantly, self-destructive. The play reveals that Oedipus's piety is ultimately based, not on his "blind" or pure rejection of reason, nor on his ostensibly rational, but actually self-contradictory, argument that he deserves the reward of immortality, but rather on his longing for immortality and, above all, on his anger at his mortality. It is this pious anger – which leads Oedipus to harm both himself and his loved ones – that is criticized most emphatically in the play by Theseus, the true hero of the play, the representative of political rationalism and humane wisdom, the man who embodies "the humane greatness of Athens at its

which Creon seemingly appeals at 939–49. For Oedipus entrusts to Theseus alone the secret of where his sacred tomb, which will protect Athens, will lie, and Theseus alone will be able to hand down this secret to his hand-picked successor (1518–34). See 1629–57, 1754–67.

[38] Bowra (1944, 334–5), Knox (1964, 153), and Winnington-Ingram (1980, 273–4) praise Oedipus over Theseus. Although Wilson and Mills praise Theseus highly, they also suggest that Oedipus is ultimately superior because he is a "true prophet" (Wilson 1997, 171–2; see 178–9) and "associated with divinity" (Mills 1997, 166; see 168). But Reinhardt suggests that Theseus may be the true hero of the play (1979, 208).

best" (Knox 1964, 152),[39] but a figure whom Nietzsche's analysis of the play never even mentions.

Yet, while the play is critical of Oedipus, it is not at all dismissive of him, as is indicated by the fact that Theseus himself expresses compassion for Oedipus and does all that he can to help him. Oedipus is a grandly tragic figure, whose tremendous perseverance and towering strength of soul we naturally admire. He inspires pity without any admixture of contempt, for his flaws are rooted in our common humanity. We naturally pity Oedipus, since his hope for immortality is rooted in a longing and an anger that seem common to our nature as mortal beings who are aware of our mortality. We naturally fear suffering what Oedipus suffers, since we naturally share the passions and the mortal condition that cause his suffering. In pondering the tragic fate of Oedipus, we see all too clearly our own nature and our own condition.

The fact that the play does not simply dismiss Oedipus's religious anti-rationalism is precisely what distinguishes Sophocles' analysis of religious passion from that of Enlightenment liberalism. For while modern political rationalism has tended to believe that religious zeal will naturally fade as we human beings become freer to act in accordance with our nature and more enlightened concerning our natural condition, Sophocles shows that religious zeal is rooted in such enduring traits of human nature as our awareness of our mortality, our hope for immortality, and our angry refusal to accept our mortality. Accordingly, Sophocles advocates a sober and cautious political rationalism, one that recognizes and seeks to address the dangers of religious passion to political life, but also recognizes the permanence of religious passion within political life. Living as we do at a time when religious

---

[39] Consider also Bowra: "into this last play Sophocles has flung his unwithered love of his country" (1944, 347). Knox comments: "this play contains the most moving and beautiful ode in praise of Athens that was ever written" (1964, 144; see 154–6; Adams 1957, 172; Beer 2004, 160). See Reinhardt 1979, 197, 221; Whitman 1971, 192, 209–10, 239–40; Waldock 1966, 218–19, 227–8; Opstelten 1952, 111–12; Scodel 1984, 108; Walker 1995, 174, 179, 188–9; Mills 1997, 185. Segal describes Sophocles' account of Athens in this play: "Its civilizing achievement is no longer in its might and dominion but in its spiritual radiance, its privileged openness to divinity" (1981, 374).

passion poses a growing challenge to political rationalism, and when the heirs of modern political rationalism seem caught off guard by that challenge, the *Oedipus at Colonus* is especially timely. For through it, Sophocles warns against both the dangers of blind religious passion and the dangers of an excessively hopeful political rationalism that overestimates the power of reason and underestimates the power of religion in the human heart.

3 The Pious Heroism of Antigone

RIGHT OVER MIGHT?

The *Antigone* presents the always welcome tale of right triumphing over might. A solitary girl defies the edicts of a cruel, tyrannical king in order to bury the corpse of her brother.[1] When arrested, she bravely denounces the king to his face for his injustice and impiety. This denunciation proves to be so powerful that, in time, it is repeated by the king's own son, by a soothsayer, by the king's wife, by the elders of his realm, and eventually by the king himself. At the end of the play, the chorus of Theban elders concludes that King Creon did not see justice until it was too late and failed to recognize that "no one ought to be impious to the gods" (1270, 1349–50; see also 450–70, 692–700, 742–9, 940–3, 998–1032, 1064–90, 1301–21). The seemingly helpless girl finally triumphs completely, for the corpse of her brother is duly buried and the king suffers the devastating loss of his son, a loss foretold by the soothsayer Teiresias as a divine punishment, and one that renders Creon "a living . . . corpse" (1167). This stunning victory seems due, then, to gods who side with the weak but pious girl and who punish the mighty but impious king. On the surface, the *Antigone* celebrates piety in all its moral grandeur, for it reassures us that there are gods who ensure the triumph of the righteous, no matter how weak, and who visit destruction on the wicked, no matter how strong.[2]

---

[1] Ismene (60), Antigone (506), Teiresias (1056), and the first messenger (1169) refer to Creon as tyrant.

[2] Consider, for example, Reinhardt: "This is not right against right, idea against idea, but the divine, the all-embracing with which the young girl knows she is

The pious victory of Antigone is especially remarkable since hers is a most spectacularly impious family, one that is guilty of the most atrocious crimes against the family. Her brothers have just committed fratricide, her father has committed patricide, and she herself was born of her parents' incestuous union. It is no wonder that the chorus and even Antigone herself suspect that the gods may seek to punish her for the sins of her flesh and blood (583–603, 853–71; see also 471–2, 1–3, 49–57). Yet, through her heroic devotion to her family[3] – through her willingness to defy her king, her sister, and her city to bury the corpse of her brother, and through her willingness to sacrifice her marriage to the king's son, to sacrifice all the happiness, power, and prestige that such a marriage would have brought her, and to sacrifice her life itself – Antigone evidently redeems her family in the eyes of the gods. For the gods send their soothsayer Teiresias, the ancient adversary of her father, to intervene on behalf of both Antigone and her brother (1029–30), and they ultimately ensure the burial of Polyneices and avenge both her and her brother by punishing Creon and his family. Antigone, then, wins a victory, not only for herself, but also for her family. The unhappy history of the house of Laius ends with the glorious death of Antigone – Laius was killed by his son, Jocasta killed herself, and Eteocles and Polyneices slew each other. Even Oedipus, though ultimately honored and revered in Athens, died in exile, still infamous for his crimes, and with his enemy Creon still ruling over Thebes.[4] But Antigone dies

---

in harmony, against the human, which appears as limited, blind, self-pursuing, self-deceiving and distorted" (1979, 77).

[3] Jebb goes so far as to claim that "Nowhere else has the poetry of the ancient world embodied so lofty or so beautiful an ideal of woman's love and devotion" (1979, xxv).

[4] Jebb argues that Ismene's allusion to her father's death at 49–50 is "irreconcilable" with the account of *Oedipus at Colonus*. Ismene says: "Consider, sister, the father of us both, how he died, hateful and infamous." For this and other reasons, he argues that Antigone was composed earlier than the other two Theban plays (1979, xxix, xxvii–xxviii). Nevertheless, it is possible that Ismene means here that, while Oedipus won glory in Athens when he died, in his native Thebes, where the two sisters are right now, he remains "hateful and infamous." I agree with Jebb and also with Knox that each of Sophocles' plays is "an independent whole" and "complete in itself" (1979, xxx; Knox 1964, 2). As Knox observes, it was Sophocles who departed from the Aeschylean trilogy to

heroically, redeeming her family, avenged by the gods, and honored by her fellow Thebans.

Yet the impression that the play finally vindicates Antigone and, through her, the justice of the gods, is called into question by the anguished self-doubt that she suffers at the end of her life. Just before she is to be rescued by her fiancé Haemon and spared by a contrite Creon, she commits suicide. Shortly before, Antigone reveals herself to be in the grip of agonizing doubt regarding her own justice and piety: "What justice of divinities have I transgressed? Why should I, a wretched one, still look to the gods? Whom should I call to as an ally? Since, while I have been pious, I have acquired impiety. But if, then, these things [namely, Creon's condemnation and punishment of her] are noble in the eyes of the gods, we, having suffered, will recognize that we have erred" (921–6). The fact that she then proceeds to kill herself suggests either that she believes she deserves to be punished by the gods for impiety or that she feels forsaken by gods who are indifferent to her justice and piety. If, then, the play celebrates Antigone, why does she come to such a miserable end? If the play simply vindicates her faith in the gods and their justice, why does she herself lose faith in her final vindication? Is her piety simply too weak? Is her character less heroic than it at first seems? Or are her doubts regarding her own justice reasonable?

Furthermore, the play makes clear that, even though Creon suffers a terrible fate, he is not an impious tyrant but is both genuinely devoted to the city and pious. Creon forbids the burial of Polyneices because Polyneices led a foreign army in an attempt to conquer Thebes and killed his own brother, King Eteocles, in that attempt. These are facts that Antigone never disputes. Creon insists it was the gods who saved Thebes from destruction and that the gods wish him to honor the just Eteocles by burying him and to punish the evil Polyneices by leaving him unburied. For Polyneices "came as an exile and wished to burn with fire from top to bottom the land of his fathers and the gods of his

write single, independent plays (2–4). Nevertheless, I incline to the view that, given the unifying story, the common themes, and what Jebb himself calls "the finely-wrought links of allusion" among the Theban plays, they are properly studied together (1979, xxx). On the possible dates of the production of the plays, see Winnington-Ingram 1980, 341–3; Tyrrell and Bennett 1998, 3–4.

race, to taste the blood he shared with us, and to lead us into slavery"
(199–202). Accordingly, when the Theban elders later wonder, upon
hearing of Polyneices' mysterious burial, if the gods might have been
responsible, Creon responds: "Stop before you too fill me with rage, lest
you be revealed mindless as well as old. For you say things that are not to
be endured, saying that divinities take thought for this corpse. Did they
cover him to give him special honor, as though he were a benefactor, he
who came to burn their pillared temples, their dedicated offerings, and
their land and to scatter their laws? Do you see gods honoring the evil?"
(280–8; see also 511–22). Creon is evidently devoted to both Thebes
and the gods – and consequently the chorus supports him, even against
Antigone, throughout most of the play.[5] Even Teiresias acknowledges
that Creon has always been devoted to the gods and to the city (992–4).[6]
And though Creon does respond to Teiresias's command that he spare
Antigone and bury her brother by bitterly attacking him, he quickly
repents of his attack and obeys the soothsayer's command. The play, then,
also presents Creon as being, in his way, just and pious. Rather than
presenting a clear-cut conflict between godly right and godless might,
the play presents a conflict between two protagonists who, to begin with,
are convinced of their own piety and justice and convinced that there are
just gods who will vindicate them.[7] And both come to unhappy ends.
What is the cause of the downfall of these two pious figures? Are both
punished by the gods? Are neither?[8]

---

[5] Consider 100–61, 471–2, 681–2, 852–6, 872–5, 929–30, 955–87. These
passages call into question Goethe's claim that Creon "has everybody in the
play against him" (1984, 143).

[6] I therefore think Segal goes too far in his claim that Creon "begins as the
embodiment of the secular rationalism of the Sophistic Enlightenment"
(1981, 152; see also 160, 165–6, 174, 179, 186; 1966, 66, 81; Ehrenberg
1954, 54–61, 65–6).

[7] On this point, consider Hegel 1962, 73–4, 133, 178, 325. See also Knox
1964, 75, 91, 101–2; Vernant and Vidal-Naquet 1988, 41.

[8] As Segal puts its, "Yet three innocent people have died, one precisely because
of her piety toward the gods; and two are far from old age. Neither these losses
nor the intensity of Creon's suffering – to say nothing of Eurydice's – can be
assimilated into the comfortable moral explanation with which the chorus
ends" (1995, 137).

The fact that Teiresias predicts that the gods will punish Creon by killing his son and that Haemon immediately dies thereafter would seem to offer conclusive proof that there are, according to the play, just gods who punish the wicked, that they clearly punish Creon, and hence that they must side with Antigone, perhaps by conferring rewards upon her in an afterlife. Yet, notwithstanding the claims of the chorus and of Creon that Teiresias is perfectly wise, the play does not clearly present Teiresias as an infallible soothsayer (1091–7; see also 1059). He fails to predict at all the death of Antigone and, it seems, the death of Creon's wife Eurydice as well (though consider 1077–9). What is more, Teiresias's prediction regarding the timing of Haemon's death – which occurs on this very day – is rather open-ended: "Know that the sun will not have completed many courses before you yourself will give back one corpse from your insides as a repayment for the dead ones" (1064–7). Moreover, the prediction that Haemon will die before long as a result of a conflict with his father is not an entirely uncanny or unreasonable prediction, if, as is possible, Teiresias has heard of the public quarrel that has just occurred between father and son, in which Haemon has threatened to commit either patricide or suicide (751–2, 760–5).[9] It is also important to keep in mind that, according to the account given by the First Messenger, Haemon's death almost does not occur. When Haemon discovers that Antigone has committed suicide, he first tries to kill his father, and only then, when his father barely eludes his reach, does Haemon, in anger, kill himself (1220–39). Finally, while the chorus claims that Teiresias never speaks falsely (1091–4), we know from *Oedipus the Tyrant*, at least, that he is fallible, for he failed to solve the riddle of the Sphinx (390–8).

The intervention of Teiresias, then, does not prove definitively that, according to Sophocles in this play, the world is ruled by just gods and that it is they who punish Creon. The play invites the reader to consider the possibility that, as the First Messenger claims when announcing the death of Haemon, it is not the gods who rule the world but blind, indifferent, chance: "For fortune sets straight and fortune brings down both the fortunate one and the unfortunate one, always. And there is no

---

[9] Benardete remarks, "Nothing Teiresias said argues for a more than human source for its truth" (1999, 138).

soothsayer of the things established for mortals" (1158–60).[10] We are left to wonder why both Antigone and Creon are brought to ruin in the course of the play and what are the causes, human or divine, of their downfall. In order to explore these questions, let us examine the play more carefully. For while the play surely inspires awe before the power of piety, it also invites us to examine the nature and the problem of piety.

THE PIOUS HEROISM OF ANTIGONE

The story of the *Antigone* is the tale of a conflict between a king and a girl over a corpse. The new king of Thebes, Creon, seeks to punish the corpse of Polyneices by leaving it unburied, on the grounds that he was an enemy to his city, to its gods, and, as the killer of his brother, to his family. Antigone seeks to honor the corpse by burying it, on the grounds that Polyneices was her brother. The play draws our attention most emphatically to the action of Antigone because her decision to bury the corpse of her brother – notwithstanding the edict Creon that has just issued that anyone who buries the corpse will be publicly stoned to death – is, quite simply, astonishing.

Indeed, to begin with, no one, not even Creon, can believe that Antigone did this deed knowingly (see 376–83, 403, 406, 441–3, 446–7, 449). Creon and Ismene both wonder whether Antigone has not lost her mind (561–4, 98–9). Although it seems understandable that Antigone would wish to see her brother buried, it is amazing that she simply acts on her own and tries to bury the body herself – twice – in flagrant defiance of the king, rather than, for example, taking the less dangerous course of begging the king for pity, as Priam begs Achilles for pity in the final book of the *Iliad*; or of trying to persuade the king to be magnanimous toward his vanquished enemy, as, for example, Odysseus and Ajax's brother Teucer try to persuade Menelaus and Agamemnon to permit the burial of the corpse of Ajax in the *Ajax* (1047–1162, 1223–1373); or even of trying to persuade Creon to

---

[10] I think Winnington-Ingram is too quick to dismiss this character as an "ordinary man of little insight" (1980, 112, 127).

bury the corpse by appealing to his piety, as Teiresias does later in the play (see *Antigone* 992–1114).

Furthermore, Antigone defies Creon all by herself. She has no allies who might pressure Creon to relax his edict or to spare her, none who might overthrow him, and little hope of winning such allies among her fellow Thebans, since the man whose corpse she is burying has just led an Argive army to conquer and destroy Thebes, has killed the king of Thebes, and may well be responsible for the deaths of other Thebans, including relatives of the chorus (see 100–54, especially 117–26).[11] Creon takes it for granted that whoever attempted to bury Polyneices was part of a broad and powerful conspiracy – perhaps a fifth column within Thebes – with sufficient resources to bribe the soldiers guarding the corpse and, perhaps, to bribe the soothsayer Teiresias as well.[12] When Creon discovers that Antigone is the one who buried the corpse, he assumes that at least her sister must have helped her (484–96, 531–5, 561–2, 577–81, 769–71). But Antigone acts alone. She is even more alone than the heroes Achilles or Ajax when they oppose their fellow Greek warriors, inasmuch as they at least enjoy the support of their own Myrmidon or Salaminian soldiers.

Finally, and perhaps most importantly, Antigone's defiance of Creon is astonishing because she is a girl, a very young woman, about to be married, who is most widely referred to in the play as a "maiden [κορη]" or "child [παις]."[13] Everyone in the play assumes that only a man would

---

[11] One might object that Antigone has the very important ally of her fiancé Haemon, the king's son. Yet, according to our manuscripts, Antigone never refers to Haemon in the play, and hence, it would seem, never regards him as a potential ally in the play, perhaps assuming that he will be as absolutely loyal to his father as she is to her brother.

[12] 289–326. See 1033–63, as well as 221–2. See also Reinhardt 1979, 69–71; Knox 1964, 88.

[13] Antigone is referred to in the play four times as "maiden [κορη]" (395, 769, 889, 1100) and seven times as "child [παις]" (378, 423, 561, 654, 693, 949, 987). It is true that she is also referred to eleven times as "woman [γυνη]," but nine of these references are by Creon and may reflect his eagerness to dissuade the chorus and Haemon from pitying her (525, 579, 649, 651, 678, 680, 740, 746, 756; 61, 694). Consider, for example, Creon's remark to his son: "Do not now – ever – child, cast out your wits for the sake of the pleasure of a *woman*, since you know that this embrace becomes cold, when an

dare to challenge the king since, it is presumed, only a man would have the strength to confront Creon's soldiers or face the torture with which Creon threatens those who oppose him (248, 332–75, especially 347; consider as well 218–22, 268–77, 304–14, 432–40; 931–2). Ismene suggests that, since they are women and hence naturally weaker than men, they cannot win in an open, violent conflict with the mighty king (61–4). Yet Antigone does not use secrecy or deception, as Ismene advises, to overcome her natural debility (84–5). She does not use the indirect, subtle methods other heroines of Greek drama use to outwit and defeat their powerful male adversaries. She does not conspire against Creon, as Clytaemnestra conspires against Agamemnon, Electra against Aegisthus, Medea against Jason, or Praxagora against the democratic assembly of men in Athens. Alone in Greek literature, among mortal women, Antigone openly and publicly challenges her enemies. She fights like a man. Indeed, she is more defiant of Creon than any man in the play, except for the aged soothsayer Teiresias, who, unlike Antigone, knows he commands the respect of the Thebans (992–4, 1090–5). The guards cower before the king, the venerable elders are frightened of him, the common people of Thebes dare not speak their mind to him, and even Haemon is, at least initially, diplomatic and flattering toward his father. But Antigone is fearless (compare, for example, 218–44, 259–77, 329–31, 635–8, 683–6, 690–1 with 432–6, 441–8). Creon himself compares her to "the mightiest iron," attributes to her "mighty" deeds, and fears that, unless she is punished, she will prove to be more manly than he is (473–6, 484–5; see also 525, 677–80).[14]

---

evil *woman* shares your bed and your home" (648–51 – emphases added). The chorus and the guard only refer to Antigone as "maiden" (395, 1100) or "child" (378, 423, 949, 987), never as "woman." Haemon refers to Antigone once as a child and once as a woman, when he tells his father: "It is possible for me to hear these things under darkness, that the city mourns for this very child, since she is dying most undeservedly of all women and most evilly, for the most glorious deeds" (692–5). Even Creon refers to Antigone twice as "maiden" (769, 889) and twice as "child" (561, 654). For Antigone's imminent marriage to Haemon, see, for example, 568, 627–30, 1223–5).

[14] Tyrrell and Bennett go so far as to suggest that the play implicitly compares Antigone to an Amazon warrior woman (1998, 42, 72, 103, 109).

The word that Creon and the chorus use to characterize Antigone's act is not, however, manliness or courage (ἀνδρεία) but daring (τόλμα–248, 449; see also 370–1, 913–5). The word daring in the play seems to denote a fearless willingness to transgress or transcend all limits. In order to grasp the significance of Antigone's daring, let us consider the chorus's famous second ode, whose theme is daring, and which suggests that daring, together with thoughtfulness (περιφραδής–347), is the central characteristic of human nature (see Jebb 1979, 100, xii). For while the chorus in *Antigone* generally represents the conventional, and fluctuating, perspective of the Theban elders, the second and fourth choral odes in particular present insights that transcend that perspective.[15]

After the chorus hears that someone has buried the corpse of Poly- neices in defiance of the edict of the king, it sings an ode on the singularly terrible or uncanny (δεινός) character of man (ἄνθρωπος).[16] The ode suggests that man is the most remarkable and dangerous being of all because, alone among the natural beings, he does not simply follow nature but dares to challenge the limits of his natural condition. This daring takes three forms. First, man seeks to master the natural world by, for example, building ships to cross the sea, inventing instruments to extract food from the earth, ensnaring and taming animals for his use, and curing diseases (332–53, 363–4). Further- more, man strives to overcome the harshness of his natural condition by altering his own nature. For man teaches himself speech and thought, he civilizes himself by making himself a law-abiding, urbane, political animal, and he thereby creates civilized life out of anarchy (354–70).

---

[15] As Ehrenberg observes, "Although we can perhaps understand this song as the expression of a weak and frightened chorus of ordinary old men, it gains its full significance only when we realize that the poet, by way of his famous 'irony,' made the chorus say things of a far wider and deeper meaning" (1954, 65; see also Reinhardt 1979, 252).

[16] For a valuable account of the word δεινός, see Nussbaum 1986, 52–3, as well as Knox 1964, 23–4. Heidegger's famous analysis of this ode centers on a discussion of the word δεινός, a word that "encompasses the extreme limits and the abrupt abysses of [man's] being" (1980, 149; see 148–65). According to his account, man is δεινός above all because he is "one who uses power, who not only disposes of power but is violent insofar as the use of power is the basic trait not only of his action but also of his being-there" (149–50).

Yet, finally, he strives to overcome the limits imposed on him by human society, to violate the laws and destroy cities, and even to transgress the "justice sworn by the gods" (369; 365–71). Daring, then, is a profoundly ambiguous human trait, because it leads humans toward good or evil, betterment or misery, civilization or anarchy.

The ode suggests that the two defining characteristics of human beings are daring and thoughtfulness. Yet the relation between these two characteristics seems paradoxical. On the one hand, what makes daring possible is the surpassing inventiveness of human beings. Only humans can devise means to navigate, farm, hunt, heal, legislate, and rebel. On the other hand, the ode might seem to suggest that daring is a sign of human folly rather than reason. For the conclusion of the ode stresses the absolute limits of human daring: "He is resourceful in every way. He faces nothing that is to come without resource. Against Hades alone will he bring forth no escape. But escapes against incurable diseases he has contrived. Possessing a certain wise, artful capacity to devise, beyond hope, he reaches sometimes toward evil, at other times toward good. When he strings together laws of the earth and justice sworn by the gods, the city is high. But without any city is he who is not noble, on account of daring" (360–71). At first glance, the ode seems to stress most emphatically that what limits man is death. It would seem to be the immovable restraint, the final limit, on man. Man strives to cure diseases, to feed, shelter, and protect himself in order to preserve himself, in order to avoid death. And yet he must finally die, because death is inescapable, and therefore all of man's striving to overcome the limits on his existence proves, in the end, to be futile. But must man die? Upon closer examination, the ode is tantalizingly unclear on this question. For the word the ode uses is not "death" but "Hades" (361). Perhaps what is inescapable is not death – that is, extinction – but Hades – that is, a place we will go to when we pass away. But then, is there an escape from death after all, through winning some kind of immortality? Might it not be possible to escape death and win a kind of well-being from the gods in Hades, above all by meeting the demands of divine justice?[17]

---

[17] I am inclined to disagree with Segal's claim that this ode "reflects much of the optimistic rationalism of Sophocles' time" (1966, 71; see also 1981, 155). Segal contends that the ode "with its rationalistic confidence, is the only ode in

The ode suggests that man is the being who strives to overcome his limits because, unlike the other beings, he is a reflective being. Because he is thoughtful, he is aware of death. But because he is thoughtful, he wonders whether death truly is the end of his existence or perhaps a path to another, possibly higher life. Above all, this awareness of death gives rise to the longing for a deathless existence, a longing to escape all the limits imposed on us by our nature, including our mortality. The ode suggests, then, that daring is at heart a reflection of the human longing for immortality, a longing later described by the chorus as erotic (781–90; see also 90, 220). We dare to transgress the limits of our seemingly mortal nature because we long for immortality.[18]

Daring is, according to the ode, a broadly human characteristic. For example, by devising his edict to refuse burial to traitors, Creon dares to reform the traditional laws concerning the dead in order to overcome

the play without mythical allusions" (165). Yet he goes on to discuss the ode's reference to "Ga, 'imperishable, timeless, highest of gods' (338–9)" (169). Moreover, he states: "'Hades is the only thing that man cannot escape,' said the chorus in the Ode on Man (361–2). This sentence haunts the tragic action of the play" (178).

[18] Heidegger understands the choral ode as one that portrays man as a fundamentally "violent, creative" being who imposes order on the world around him, and as one that celebrates such creative violence (1980, 163; see also 152–3, 161). "In the unique need of their being-there" the Greeks "alone responded solely with violence, thus not doing away with the need but augmenting it; and in this way they won for themselves the fundamental condition of true human greatness" (164). But Heidegger's treatment of the ode entirely apart from the rest of the play, especially apart from the fourth choral ode on eros, leads him to overlook the second choral ode's identification of human daring, not only with an impulse to impose order, but also with a passionate, erotic, hopeful, and sometimes anarchic longing for immortality. Moreover, Heidegger mistranslates the word "Hades" as "death" in 361: "All violence shatters against one thing. That is death [Das ist der Tod – 1998, 121]. It is an end beyond all consummation, a limit beyond all limits" (1980, 158; see 147). But precisely through its use of the word "Hades," the ode, like the play, points to a fundamental question of human life: is death truly the limit of our existence? This error leads Heidegger to slight the importance of pious hope as well as longing in the account of the human condition set forth by the ode. See too Nussbaum 1986, 73.

the anarchy that has hitherto plagued Thebes.[19] Yet, inasmuch as the chorus concludes the ode by emphasizing that daring leads human beings to rebel against the limits imposed both by nature and by human society, and hence to place themselves outside the political community (ἀπολις–370), it is Antigone who exhibits most vividly the daring spoken of in the choral ode.[20] By burying her treasonous brother's corpse, Antigone dares to step beyond the laws of her king. Moreover, by stepping outside the private sphere of the household to challenge publicly the authority of her king and uncle, Antigone dares to step beyond the restraints on women, especially young women, imposed by convention and tradition. Indeed, following Ismene, we may say that, by directly and openly challenging the full might of Creon – by choosing to fight, so to speak, like a man – Antigone dares to step beyond her female nature and so defies nature itself, as well as convention.[21]

What seems in the first instance to inspire such a supernatural daring in Antigone to act, all alone, against all odds, against convention and nature both, is her conviction that she is in the right. From the beginning, she is absolutely convinced that it is just for her to bury her brother's corpse and that it is simply outrageous for the king or the city to stand in her way. For Antigone, justice self-evidently means devotion to one's family. Although she never denies that Polyneices was a

---

[19] On this point, see Saxonhouse (1992, 66).

[20] See Segal 1981, 153. Creon and the chorus seem to use the word "daring" primarily to express their amazement at Antigone's fearless willingness to transgress her king's edict. When he wishes simply to condemn Antigone for her lawlessness, Creon uses the word "hubris [ἀπολις]" (compare 449 with 480–3; see also 309).

[21] See Saxonhouse 1985, 29; 1992, 69–70, 76. Segal contends that the "conflict between Creon and Antigone is not only between city and house, but also between man and woman," that Creon represents both "masculine rationality" and "male-centered political rationalism," and, together with Teiresias, embodies "patriarchal authority," whereas Antigone stands, with Eurydice, for "female procreative power" and "emotionality" (1981, 183–4, 200–1, 194–5, 186; see also 1966, 69–70; 1995, 125–7, 134–6). Yet this thesis, while somewhat plausible regarding Creon in particular, leads Segal to downplay crucial features of the play: the public and heroic character of Antigone's defiance of Creon, the conflict between Antigone and Ismene, the piety of Creon, and the elements of rationalism in both Ismene and Antigone.

deadly enemy of Thebes, her city and his, she never mentions his treason, or the Thebans' victory over him, as worthy of any consideration whatsoever. What is important about Polyneices is simply that he was Antigone's blood brother, offspring of her own mother and father (45–6; see also 466–8, 502–4, 511, 513, 517, 911–2). Only members of her family are "loved ones" (9–10, 73; see also 461–4). The most important common bond among human beings is the bond of flesh and blood (consider 37–8; Knox 1964, 79–82). The family is the principal human community and consequently the principal arena for just deeds (see line 1 of *Antigone*). By pleasing her family, she pleases "those whom I ought to please most" (89).[22]

So confident is Antigone that it is just to bury her brother's corpse that she does not even bother to explain to her sister Ismene why she thinks Creon's edict is wrong.

"For does Creon not, regarding the grave of our two brothers, prefer one in honor and dishonor the other? Eteocles, as they say, with a just use of justice and law, he has hidden beneath the earth, honored by the corpses below. But the corpse of Polyneices, having died miserably, they say, he has proclaimed to the townsmen that no one may hide in a grave or lament, but they must leave him unwept for, unburied, sweet for birds, a treasure to behold for their food. These things they say that the good Creon proclaimed to you and to me – I say even to me! – and he comes here to proclaim these things clearly to those who do not know, and the affair is not without consequences. For whoever should do any of

---

[22] Consequently, while I certainly recognize the prominence of the themes of incest and eros in the Theban plays, I ultimately find unpersuasive the Freudian/ Lacanian thesis of Griffith and others that Antigone displays an incestuous, "single-minded fixation," first for her father and then for her brother, and that she never even claims to be devoted to her family as a whole (2005, 94–7; see also Anzieu 1966; Johnson 1997). For a somewhat harsh critique, consider Vernant, who goes so far as to warn that, when "*philia* and *eros*, family attachment and sexual desire . . . are confused together and one called a 'substitute' for the other, the text [of *Antigone*] is not made clearer; on the contrary, the play is ruined" (Vernant and Vidal-Naquet 1988, 102). It should be noted that, whereas Lacan contends that Antigone is "borne along by a passion" for Polyneices, he stops short of claiming that this passion is incestuous (1997, 254; see 254–6, 265, 276–9, 282–3; see also Griffith 2005, 129).

these things, murder is set forth by public stoning in the city. There you have it, and you will soon show if you are by nature noble or if you are an evil daughter of noble parents" (21–37). Antigone's scathing sarcasm here – her references to the "justice" of the "good" Creon – reflect her visceral belief that arguments against Creon are superfluous inasmuch as any claim that his edict is just is self-evidently absurd.[23]

Antigone's strength here seems, at first sight, a purely moral strength. In this young girl with no physical strength at all, with no guile or calculation, no interest in gaining advantage through conspiracy, deception, diplomacy, or even persuasion, indeed with no apparent self-interest at all, we seem to witness at its purest the strength of Justice herself (see 451, as well as 538). Antigone comes to sight as being wholly dedicated to justice, selflessly willing to sacrifice her life "to benefit the dead" (559–60), and hence "by nature noble" (38).

The opening of the play highlights Antigone's heroism by contrasting her with her unheroic sister Ismene. Ismene most obviously lacks the courage of her sister, for she refuses to defy the tyrannical Creon and bury her brother. Moreover, Ismene argues against Antigone's noble and just intentions on the prudential, self-interested grounds of self-preservation. In contrast to her noble sister, Ismene seems all too quick to abandon her brother and to settle for survival at all costs, even if that means neglecting her duties to her family and the gods. Indeed, even by the standard of prudence, Ismene falls short, inasmuch as she fails to dissuade her sister, and Antigone does ultimately succeed in ensuring that her brother is buried.

Nevertheless, it is important to recognize that Ismene proves to be both sensible and even, in certain respects, quite loyal to her sister. She is, for example, the first person who dares to point out to Creon that, by killing Antigone, he will be killing his son's fiancée (568–71, 574). Moreover, according to all the manuscripts, Ismene is the first and only character who urges Haemon to come to Antigone's defense (572).[24] Through these interventions, Ismene almost saves Antigone's life (see 771–80, 1206–25). Furthermore, however ignoble and ineffective

---

[23] For other examples of Antigone's sharp sarcasm in this scene, see also 74, 95–6; consider as well 469–70.

[24] See Saxonhouse 1992, 70; Benardete 1999, 74; Winnington-Ingram 1980, 93.

Ismene's argument against defying Creon may be, it must be remembered that, later on in the play, Antigone herself expresses far-reaching doubts concerning the wisdom of her own defiance. Finally, and most importantly, through her seemingly ignoble argument, Ismene prompts Antigone to reveal the true nature of her nobility. Let us now consider the argument of Ismene more carefully.

After recounting the sufferings of their family, Ismene explains: "Now that, in our turn, the two of us, have been left alone, consider in what way most evilly we shall perish if by violence we transgress the vote of the law or the might of tyrants. But you need to keep this in mind, that we are women by nature, so that against men we will not battle and, then, that because we are ruled by the stronger, we are to heed both these things and things yet more painful. I, then, begging those below the earth to forgive me, since I am forced to do these things, I will obey those who hold office. For to do excessive things makes no sense at all" (58–68). Ismene here does not challenge Antigone's contention that Creon's edict is unjust. But she argues that, in this case at least, justice must yield to the natural necessity of the weak to bow to the strong. Ismene argues as follows. Because our family is dead and, more importantly, because it is "hateful and infamous" in the eyes of our fellow citizens (including, perhaps, Teiresias, she supposes) – having committed the base and unjust deeds of incest, suicide, and fratricide – we two are left all alone, without family to support us and without any reasonable expectation of support from anyone else. But we need allies in order to defy successfully the tyrannical might of Creon, since we are women and he is stronger, not only because he is a man, but also because he is a ruler, with guards and soldiers at his command. To violate the edict of Creon without the strength to succeed makes no sense, since all that we will achieve is our own destruction.

Ismene here challenges not only the prudence but also the nobility and justice of the action Antigone is contemplating. For she argues here not only that Antigone's plan to attempt to bury her brother is dangerous, but that it is "excessive [περισσος]" (68; see also 780). It is excessive because Antigone is incapable of executing her plan. She will not succeed in burying her brother. If she buries the body, Creon will simply order it unburied. It is therefore, as she later says twice, an "impossible" thing to bury Polyneices successfully (90, 92; see also 79). In this way, Ismene asks, how can this act be noble or just if it is futile, if it fails to benefit

either themselves or their brother? Antigone had challenged Ismene to
show that she is by nature noble. But Ismene answers that, in this case at
least, one cannot be noble by nature unless one is strong by nature, unless
one has the capacity to complete one's noble deed. And since neither of
them is sufficiently strong, neither can act nobly or justly in this case.
Ismene argues, then, that Antigone must face natural necessity, accept the
limits placed by nature on her nobility and justice, and leave the corpse of
their brother unburied, to be eaten by the birds.

Antigone responds to Ismene's argument by affirming, for the first
time in the play, her belief in an afterlife in which the gods reward the
noble and the just: "That one I shall bury. It is noble for me, doing this,
to die. I will lie, dear, together with him who is dear, having committed
a pious crime.[25] Since there is more time during which I ought to satisfy
those below than those here. For there I will lie forever. But if you are
resolved, dishonor the things honored by the gods" (71–7). Antigone
insists here that it is not self-destructive for her to attempt to bury her
brother. For even though she admits she will be executed by the naturally
stronger Creon, there are supernatural beings – the gods – who will
reward her for her noble and just deed with an eternal well-being after
death. Here, we see that the basis of Antigone's daring and strength is
not only her justice but also her piety, and specifically, her belief in an
afterlife in which justice is rewarded. She is not selflessly but wisely
devoted to justice, for she knows, she insists, that her justice will bring
her an everlasting well-being. Antigone concedes that the unjust triumph in this world and hence that she will be foiled and killed by Creon,
but she is convinced that there are gods who will reward her justice and
nobility in another, nether world. As she later declares, she is convinced
that Justice herself is a goddess (451). She is convinced that, notwithstanding Ismene's argument, she is not truly alone and she is not truly
weak, even though she is by nature weaker than her enemies. For she has
the supernatural gods on her side. Indeed, Antigone is convinced that she
has no reason to fear the death threat of the naturally stronger Creon
because she herself is not by nature mortal, but immortal.

---

[25] Benardete suggests translating this arresting phrase ['οσια πανουργ ησασ]:
   "having stopped at nothing in the performance of holy things" (1999, 12).
   Consider as well Knox 1964, 93.

Antigone responds to her sister's argument in favor of yielding to natural necessity by denying that there is such a necessity. First, she denies that as a woman who is by nature weaker than a man she must yield to the naturally stronger, for the gods will more than make up for her weakness as long as she honors them by acting justly and nobly. But furthermore, and more importantly, Antigone denies that, as one who is by nature a mortal, human being, she must yield to those with the power to kill her, because she denies that she is mortal. As long as she satisfies the gods, she will enjoy immortal happiness. Antigone defends the wisdom of attempting to bury her brother by denying natural necessity and especially the natural necessity of mortality (see 469–70). Antigone most obviously rebels against the human laws and conventions of her city. But her deepest rebellion is against the sway not of Creon or Thebes but of nature itself.

The characteristic act of Antigone's heroism, the act that most clearly reveals the nature of her heroism, and the denial of human mortality, which is the basis of that heroism, is her insistence on burying the corpse of her brother. The insistence on disposing of the dead in one fashion or another seems to be a universal human phenomenon (see, for example, Herodotus 3.38). It was clearly important to the Greeks, as can be seen from their literature and their deeds. In the *Iliad*, for example, the Achaean warriors fight desperately to protect the corpse of Patroclus in order to keep it for burial, and the Trojan King Priam exposes himself to death and disgrace in order to recover the corpse of his son Hector for burial. In Sophocles' *Ajax*, Teucer runs great risks in order to ensure that the corpse of his half-brother Ajax will be buried. In Euripides' *Suppliants*, Theseus and the Athenians go so far as to wage war on Thebes in order to recover the corpses of non-Athenian, Argive soldiers for burial. Perhaps most spectacularly, the Athenians put to death the admirals who had just led them to one of their city's greatest naval victories – at Arginusae – because they had chosen not to recover for burial the corpses of the Athenians sailors during a dangerous storm after their victory.[26] Antigone and eventually Creon himself allude to eternal, divine "laws" that require the

[26] Xenophon *Hellenica* 1.6.24–1.7.35; Diodorus Siculus 13.31. See Fustel de Coulanges 1900, 11–12; Montaigne 1958, 12–13.

burial of the dead (449–70, 1108–10). These divine laws are referred to as well, for example, by the gods in the *Iliad* (16.453–7, 667–75), by Teucer and Odysseus in the *Ajax* (1129–32, 1342–5), and by Theseus and his mother in Euripides' *Suppliants* (18–19, 307–13, 524–63).

To be sure, there were Greeks who did not place such importance on the burial of the dead, as required by divine law. Most notably, the philosopher Socrates, on the day of his death, expresses utter indifference as to how, or even whether, he should be buried, on the grounds that, once he is dead, he will no longer exist in any way in his body. His body will simply become a lifeless thing (Plato *Phaedo* 115c2–116a1). Socrates goes so far as to suggest that the belief that the dead somehow live on in their corpses is an "evil" of the soul (115e4–6). Socrates also tried to prevent the Athenians from executing their victorious admirals who left the bodies of the dead sailors at sea in order to save the sailors who were still alive (Xenophon *Hellenica* 1.7.9–15; Plato *Apology of Socrates* 32a5-c4). Indeed, Fustel de Coulanges suggests that the admirals were themselves "students of the philosophers" (1900, 11). But it is also true that, like the admirals, Socrates was condemned to death and executed by his fellow citizens for impiety, and that all philosophers were, according to Socrates, believed to be atheists (Plato, *Apology of Socrates* 23c7-d7; see also *Laws* 966d9–967d2). The example of Socrates, then, only underscores the great importance the Greeks as a whole – the unphilosophic, pious Greeks – placed on the burial of the dead.

But why is it so important for human beings to bury their dead? Antigone suggests that, unburied, the corpse of her brother will be food for the birds (*Antigone* 29–30; see also Creon's statement at 198–206 and Haemon's at 696–8). The premise of Antigone's desire to bury her brother would seem to be that, contrary to the Socratic view, her brother is somehow still present, somehow still alive, in the corpse, even after he has died. What is so horrible about the spectacle of birds eating her brother's corpse is that they will be devouring and destroying her still living brother and not merely a lifeless corpse that was once his. Later, Haemon claims that the common people of Thebes admire Antigone because "she is one who would not leave her own brother, who fell in bloody conflict, unburied, to *perish* because of dogs who eat raw flesh or some bird" (696–8 – emphasis added). Haemon suggests that, in the common view, a dead human being has not truly perished and hence is not truly dead unless its corpse is destroyed, for example, by hungry dogs. What is so important about burying the corpse is that one thereby saves the dead from death and hence that one somehow allows the dead to live on after death. Viewed in this light, one buries the dead in order to benefit the dead, by conferring a kind of immortality on them (see 559–60).

Yet, one might still ask, even if burial prevents the corpse from being food for birds, will it not still be food for other living creatures – worms, for example – once the corpse is buried (consider Herodotus 3.16)? The play invites us to ask this question because it presents such a vivid account of how corpses naturally decay. One of the guards of Polyneices' corpse explains that, after returning to the corpse from informing Creon that someone had sprinkled dust on it, he and his fellow guards fulfilled the king's orders to exhume the body. "Once we brushed off all the dust laid on the corpse and stripped naked the damp body, we sat at the top of the rocky hill, away from the wind, fleeing the smell of the body upon us . . . These things were so for some time, until, in the midst of the sky, stood the shining circle of the sun and the heat was scorching" (409–12, 415–17). Through this description of touching and smelling the damp, stinking body, Sophocles indicates with stern clarity the fate of even the corpse that escapes being torn to pieces by dogs and birds and also, it would seem, the fate of the corpse that is buried. This description suggests that what makes an unburied corpse so terrible for us who remain alive is that, by seeing – and smelling – it, we witness a body, which was just alive and which may still seem alive, quickly and surely rot and decay. We see this body become visibly, evidently dead. And we are tempted, by the overpowering evidence of our senses, to conclude that the dead human being truly is no more. To fail to bury a corpse, to treat a corpse as a mere thing – to be used to feed animals, for example, or even to be left, as a fallen leaf, to wither away on the ground – is to affirm, in perhaps the most vivid manner possible, the mortality of human beings.

To bury a corpse, then, is to escape the vivid, sensual apprehension of the deadness of the dead, and hence of our own mortality as well. Viewed in this light, we bury the dead in order to benefit not only the dead but also ourselves, by hiding from ourselves the full, sensible

manifestation of our natural, human mortality, and so enabling ourselves to affirm, notwithstanding the abstract awareness of the decay of
dead human bodies, that human beings truly do, somehow, live on after
death. To bury the dead, then, is to deny that we are by nature mortal
beings. Accordingly, Antigone's passionate insistence on burying the
corpse of her brother reflects her passionate longing and hope for immortality.

The key to understanding Antigone's uncanny, heroic daring is her
piety. She dares to defy her king all by herself because she is convinced
that she is not all by herself but is rather supported by gods. She dares
to risk death to bury the corpse of her brother because she is convinced
that, by doing so, she will not truly die but will rather enjoy the divine
reward of eternal well-being. She dares to step beyond her female nature
and even her mortal nature by defying the death threats of those who
are naturally stronger because she denies the sway of nature and places
her hopes in supernatural beings who enable the weak to overcome the
strong, women to overcome men, and mortals to win the divine reward
of immortality in another, nether world, after death. In Antigone, then,
we witness above all the seemingly supernatural strength and daring of
piety itself. For it is the pious hopes, convictions, and longings of this
solitary, seemingly helpless young girl that give her the strength to
defy, against all odds, her king, her city, and even nature itself.[27]

We may view Antigone as a Greek version of the Bible's pious hero,
David. Like David, the young girl bravely opposes a mighty adversary,
against overwhelming odds, convinced that the gods stand behind her
(see, for example, *I Samuel* 17:45–7). Indeed Antigone appears even
more daring and pious than David. For she is not only a youngster, like
David, but a girl, challenging a male king in a man's world, without
any weapon in hand at all, without even the moral support of her fellow
citizens or her surviving sibling. In Machiavellian language, she is a
wholly unarmed princess. Antigone truly faces her Goliath alone,
armed only by her faith in the gods. Hers is a pure heroism of faith.

---

[27] Consequently I must disagree with Segal's contention that "In the great fifth-
century debate between nature and convention, *physis* and *nomos*, Antigone stands
on the side of nature" (1981, 155). For a helpful account of Antigone's com-
plicated understanding of, and relation to, nature, see Saxonhouse 1992, 66–76.

Yet it is precisely her faith that buckles and collapses at the end. In the end, Antigone is not destroyed by the superior physical strength of her enemies. On the verge of being rescued from imprisonment by Haemon and released altogether by a contrite and frightened Creon, Antigone loses all hope that the gods will save her, and kills herself.

What undermines the piety of this pious heroine is not threats but arguments, arguments that challenge her wisdom, justice, and piety. Antigone appears in three scenes in the play, two of which are dominated by debates: one with Ismene about the wisdom of burying their brother and then one with Creon about the justice and piety of burying her brother. In her final scene Antigone expresses grave doubts about her justice and piety. In the play, then, Antigone's faith is put to the test by reasoned arguments. While her faith is evidently not shaken by the challenge of Ismene, it is weakened and ultimately, it seems, destroyed by the challenge of Creon.

JUSTICE AND SELF-INTEREST: THE CHALLENGE OF ISMENE

Antigone replies to her sister's argument that it is foolishly self-destructive for her to bury Polyneices by suggesting that, inasmuch as there are gods who reward the just with eternal well-being and punish the unjust with eternal suffering, Ismene is the one who is foolish. By committing the evil deed of leaving her brother unburied, she is provoking the wrath of the gods. Indeed, Antigone repeatedly suggests that Ismene will be punished by the gods after death (76–7, 83, 89, 93–7; consider also 46, 542–3, 553). Antigone later goes so far as to suggest that she herself buried her brother's corpse, partly because she feared lest the gods punish her for failing to do so (458–60). Yet Ismene, who is so mindful of the fearsome power of her earthly king Creon, is not troubled by Antigone's allusions to divine punishments in an afterlife.

What is the basis of Ismene's confidence that she will not be punished by the gods after death? Ismene suggests that the gods and the souls beneath the earth will forgive her for failing to bury her brother, since she is forced to yield to Creon (58–68, 78–9). She implies that,

precisely inasmuch as the gods are just – as Antigone herself believes
(450–2, 93–4) – they will not punish her for doing what she is
compelled to do, for what she cannot help but do, because it would be
unjust to punish involuntary injustice.[28]

Yet Ismene is certainly not physically forced to obey Creon. She
could choose to disobey him and face execution, as her sister does.
Ismene evidently means here that she is compelled by the fear of her
own death to obey Creon. In other words, Ismene follows here the thesis
set forth by her father in *Oedipus at Colonus* that no man is so noble that
he can ever overcome his love of life or, more broadly, sacrifice his self-
interest (see especially 992–6, but also 270–2, 309, 546). Ismene
ostensibly argues that it is impossible to bury her brother in the teeth of
Creon's opposition (78–9, 90). But the play shows that this is not true.
Her brother's corpse is ultimately buried. Furthermore, Ismene herself
must know that it is not simply impossible to bury the corpse. Once she
sees that Antigone is determined to bury Polyneices, Ismene tries to
help her to do so successfully. She tries to persuade Antigone to bury
the corpse in secret, she later on tries to persuade Creon to spare Antigone, and she also tries to stir up Haemon to induce his father to spare
Antigone (84–5, 563–72). So Ismene must believe that there is a
possibility, however remote, that, through secrecy and persuasion, she
and her sister might bury the corpse successfully without suffering
execution. The fundamental issue is how important is the burial of the
corpse? How reasonable is it to risk one's life in order to bury a corpse?
The corpse of Polyneices is finally buried, but the price paid is high: the
deaths of Antigone, Haemon, and Eurydice and the virtual death of
Creon. Is this price worth paying? Ismene evidently thinks it is not. In
this respect, at least, her perspective seems philosophic or Socratic. She
characterizes Antigone's passionate desire to bury her brother's lifeless
corpse by observing: "You have a warm heart for cold things" (88).

In her own view, Ismene is compelled by her desire for self-preservation and, more generally, by her concern for her own well-being to

---

[28] As Knox puts it, "as Ismene sees it, there is no choice at all" in this matter
(1964, 64). Consider as well 563–4, where Ismene suggests to Creon that
Antigone may not be responsible for her actions, and hence may not deserve to
be punished, inasmuch as she has acted mindlessly.

obey Creon rather than sacrificing her life for the sake of a cold, lifeless body. As a rational being concerned for her well-being, she cannot knowingly and voluntarily sacrifice what she believes to be her self-interest. And it would be unjust for the gods to blame or punish her for doing what she cannot help doing, for yielding, as she must, to the sheer necessity of acting in what she believes to be her true interest. Indeed, insofar as all human beings are compelled by their nature as rational beings to pursue their own good as they understand it, regardless of the demands of justice otherwise, it would seem that it is impossible for human beings as such to deserve punishments or rewards in an afterlife. It would seem, then, to be on the basis of her belief in the compelling nature of self-interest that Ismene is confident before the threat of divine punishment after death.

But what of Antigone? Isn't she noble precisely because she is willing to sacrifice her life, and all her expectations of happiness from life, for the sake of her beloved brother? She herself suggests that she is "by nature noble," and hence a worthy offspring of "noble" parents, because she is willing to sacrifice her life "to die nobly" and "to benefit the dead" (37–8, 96–7, 559–60; see also 555). As Haemon later says, Antigone, of all women, is most deserving of a golden honor, from gods and men, because "She is one who would not leave her own brother, who fell in bloody conflict, unburied, to perish because of dogs who eat raw flesh or some bird" (696–8). Doesn't the example of Antigone refute Ismene's thesis by showing that it is possible consciously to choose to sacrifice one's self-interest for the sake of what is right and hence possible for human beings to deserve rewards and punishments from gods who are just?[29]

[29] Hegel suggests that Antigone's love for her brother is "without the slightest implication of anything blameworthy or egotistical," and consequently calls her "the noblest of figures that ever appeared on earth" (1962, 147, 360; see also 268–70). Jebb too declares that "Sophocles has preferred to portray Antigone as raised above every selfish thought, even the dearest" – namely, the thought of "earthly happiness." He insists that "her "sole reward was to be in the action itself" (1979, xxiv, xxv). Yet Jebb also remarks that she turns "for comfort to the faith that beyond the grave, the purest form of human affection would reunite her to those whom she had lost" and thereby acknowledges that she does hope for a reward after death (xxiv). In the same vein, he compares her

Yet, as we have seen, Antigone herself insists that, by nobly sacrificing her life to bury her brother's body, she is acting in her self-interest (71–7). Antigone insists that her nobility is not mindless, as Ismene contends, but wise and even, as she later says twice, a "gain" [κερδος], since, by nobly sacrificing her life for her brother, she will earn the just reward of eternal well-being from the gods (see 461–4). It would seem, then, that the case of Antigone does not refute Ismene's thesis that human beings are incapable of rising above their concern for themselves, since they are compelled by their nature as rational beings to care above all for their own well-being.

Ismene's thesis would seem to pose a fundamental challenge to the pious beliefs and hopes that underlie Antigone's heroism. Antigone is confident that the gods will reward her because she is confident that, by sacrificing her very life for the sake of her brother, and hence by nobly sacrificing herself for the sake of justice, she demonstrates that she deserves the reward of eternal happiness from gods who are just (see especially 450–60). But if, when all is said and done, it is to Antigone's advantage to sacrifice her life for the sake of her brother, if by doing so she will receive the reward of eternal happiness, in what sense is her "sacrifice" a genuine sacrifice? In what sense is it noble? If, by burying her brother in defiance of Creon, Antigone is simply pursuing her own good as she understands it, how can she reasonably claim to be morally superior to her sister who, by yielding to Creon, is pursuing her own good as she understands it? On what grounds, then, can Antigone reasonably hope that the gods will reward her with everlasting happiness?

Antigone might defend herself by arguing that, even though she believes that she will be rewarded by the gods for burying her brother, her *primary* goal is to benefit her brother and, more broadly, to benefit her family (see especially 559–60). It is, she might say, because she is primarily devoted to her family and not to herself, that the gods will favor her over the merely self-interested Ismene (see 37–8, 71–7, 80–1, 89, 93–7). Yet, if her primary goal were to benefit her brother, she would strive at all costs to bury him successfully. Now, if she believes her brother can be benefited only if he is buried and stays

to "a Christian martyr under the Roman Empire" (xxi). For an account of her self-interestedness, consider Tyrrell and Bennett 1998, 71.

buried, it would be futile simply to bury him once since Creon can always order him unburied.[30] Precisely if she believes that her brother can only be benefited by being buried and staying buried, then, Antigone should try to persuade the king to change his edict and enlist the aid, for example, of the chorus, Haemon, or Teiresias. Yet, whereas Ismene appeals to the chorus and Haemon to help her sister, and Haemon and Teiresias attempt to change Creon's mind, Antigone never makes any effort to persuade the king to leave her brother buried once she has buried him. How eager, then, is she to benefit her brother?

Perhaps Antigone believes that it is sufficient to perform a ritual burial of the corpse, to sprinkle dust over it while praying, in order to confer on her brother immortal well-being (but see 423–33; consider Benardete 1999, 14–15).[31] Such a ritual (or virtual) burial would require that Antigone reach the body secretly, undetected, in order to evade the guards and perform it successfully. Yet, when Ismene urges her to follow this very course of action – "But then at least do not announce this deed beforehand to anyone, bury him secretly, and I will do the same" – Antigone declares to Ismene that she will hate her if she does not tell *all, beforehand* that she will bury the body: "Oh, shout it out! You will be much more hateful if you keep silent, if you do not proclaim these things to everyone" (84–7). Antigone here expresses utter indifference as to whether or not she successfully buries the corpse of their brother. What is evidently most important to her is that she sacrifice her life in the attempt to bury the corpse. Her noble death will, in her words, be a "gain," for by dying she will dwell in Hades for ever, welcomed by her family there as well as the gods (461–6, 71–7, 89). Antigone's primary goal, then, is to die in such a way as to win immortal well-being in Hades. But in order to gain for herself the divine reward of immortality, she must perform a deed that is, at least

---

[30] According to the guard, when Antigone finds the corpse once again unburied, she is upset and tries to bury it again (423–33). But once she is caught, and has every reason to believe that Creon will unbury the corpse again, she never even tries to persuade him or anyone else to leave it buried or to rebury it (see, for example, 450–70, 497–500, 806–16).

[31] For a suggestion that it was the gods, not Antigone, who first sprinkled the dust on Polyneices, see Segal 1981, 159–60; Tyrrell and Bennett 1998, 56–60, 64–6.

in her eyes, a spectacularly just deed, the most glorious deed she can imagine: to bury her brother in defiance of the deadly edict of the king (37–8, 502–6, 692–9).

It would seem that the example of Antigone supports Ismene's thesis that we human beings are naturally incapable of transcending our concern for ourselves, that consequently we are naturally incapable of deserving either rewards or punishments from the gods in an afterlife, and hence that immortality is simply unavailable for such beings as ourselves. Yet Antigone is not at all shaken by this far-reaching challenge from Ismene. Not only does Antigone proceed to bury Polyneices, but, when brought before Creon, she proclaims her conviction, without any trace of self-doubt, that the gods support her and will reward her (450–70). Antigone seems absolutely confident that the just gods support her and will provide her with the "gain" of a better life, free of evil and pain, after death. She is evidently not at all disturbed by the suggestion of Ismene that, insofar as she is acting nobly primarily for the sake of divine rewards, she is not truly acting nobly and hence cannot deserve those rewards. Antigone does not seem troubled by the apparent contradiction between her claim that, by dying for her brother she is acting nobly, to benefit the dead, and her claim that, through her death, she is acting in her own self-interest, in order to gain for herself the reward of everlasting happiness (compare, for example, 37–8, 95–7, and 559–60 with 71–7 and 450–70).

What seems to resolve this apparent contradiction between nobility and self-interest in Antigone's mind is her understanding of the family as a natural and sacred community.[32] By burying her brother, Antigone is acting for the sake of her family (74–7, 89, 559–60). But the family is not merely a collection of individuals who are dear to one another. It is rather a community that binds its members together body and soul (9–10). In the first place, Antigone and her siblings are "born of the same womb," the common womb of their mother; are sired by the same father; and share "the same blood" (511–13, 466–8; see also 1066). But furthermore, the fact that the family shares a common physical nature produces, according to Antigone, a reasonable expectation that they share a common moral nature – for example, a noble soul.

[32] See Winnington-Ingram 1980, 132–4.

Antigone declares to her sister: "You will soon show if you are noble [or well-born–ευγενης] by nature and birth [πεφυκας] or if you are an evil daughter of noble parents" (37–8). In the natural course of things – though not always, she admits – children inherit the moral as well as the physical nature of the parents (consider as well 471–2). The family, then, is a natural community, a physical and moral community, of bodies and souls.

Moreover, the family is a community that links its members to the past and to the future, from generation to generation, and therefore is in some sense an immortal community, even if there is no afterlife. But for Antigone, the family is quite literally an immortal community, since family members – who are loyal to one another and do not betray the family as, in Antigone's eyes, Ismene does – will dwell together, after death, forever (71–6, 897–9; see 93–4, 536–60). The family is not only or merely a natural entity but also, and above all, a sacred entity, for it is honored by the gods and is supported by eternal laws that are enforced by Zeus, Justice, and the other gods (76–7, 450–70). The family is an entity larger than the sum of its parts. It is a true community, which demands sacrifices from its members but which also benefits its members by enabling them to live on beyond their natural individual lives, both on earth and in the afterlife, and thereby enables humans to escape, in some sense, from seemingly inescapable death (361).

By devoting herself to her family, Antigone is devoting herself to something larger than herself and making sacrifices for something beyond herself. In this sense, she is indeed acting nobly and selflessly. Yet, by devoting herself to the good of her family, she is devoting herself to the good of a community – a community of flesh and blood and soul – that includes her own good. She is devoting herself to a truly common good, a good that is common to all members of the community. It is in this unselfish sense that she is acting also in her own self-interest. Indeed, her vision of eternal happiness is one in which she will be together, in eternal communion, with her family. What gives Antigone confidence in her own justice and nobility and hence in her worthiness of divine rewards is her belief that the family is a true community that is both larger than herself but that also encompasses her own good.

Now, Ismene does gently raise questions about Antigone's vision of the family. By referring to the crimes and conflicts that have torn their family apart — their father's blinding of himself, their parents' incest, their mother's suicide, and their brothers' fratricide — Ismene tacitly calls into question whether the family truly is a community such as Antigone conceives, rather than a group of individual mortal beings related by blood, linked by common experiences, but who may or may not be kindred souls, who may or may not love one another, and whose interests may bring them into conflict with one another (49–57; compare also 61–2 with 37–8). In this way, Ismene implicitly calls into question the wisdom of devoting oneself to the family as a sacred community rather than to one's own well-being. But Ismene never explicitly and directly challenges the justice of Antigone's devotion to the family and therefore never touches the center of Antigone's confidence in her own righteousness. It is precisely the justice of Antigone's devotion to the family, however, that is challenged most forcefully by Creon.

As the play shows, Ismene is in certain respects wiser than her heroic sister. Antigone rebuffs her sister's arguments against burying their brother, but in the end she loses faith that her action was just or pious, kills herself in despair, and through her death destroys the lives of Haemon, Eurydice, and Creon. It is the sensible Ismene, not the noble Antigone, who survives the events of the play.

Yet it is not at all clear that Ismene's survival is enviable, as Antigone points out, for it is not clear what is left to her besides survival (553). Ismene seems at first to believe that survival, even under the harsh rule of Creon, even at the cost of leaving her dead brother unburied and her sister — her last remaining family member — to be executed, is preferable to joining Antigone in defying the king. Ismene seems content to devote herself to her own self-preservation rather than to anything that might seem larger or higher. For example, she is the only character in the play, with the exception of the Second Messenger (who has only fourteen lines), who never directly mentions the gods. Furthermore, in contrast to both Antigone (23–4, 94, 451, 459, 538, 921, 928) and Creon (208, 292, 662, 667, 671, 742, 1059) as well as the chorus (369, 791, 854, 1270) and Haemon (743), Ismene never speaks of justice. Ismene seems at first simply to devote herself to her own self-interest and to identify her self-interest entirely with her self-preservation.[33] In this respect, Ismene is wholly unphilosophic and especially unlike Socrates, who chose to die rather than abandon the philosophic life.

Yet Ismene herself in the end recognizes that a life dedicated simply to self-preservation is insufficient for happiness, that it is hollow and shallow. When Creon discovers that Antigone buried her brother and then has her arrested, Ismene is suddenly eager to share responsibility for the deed, to be "a shipmate" of her sister's suffering, and to be executed with her (541). As she explains, "What life is livable for me, alone, without her?" (566). In this way, Ismene renounces her previous arguments and belatedly, and much to her sister's indignation, declares her eagerness to sacrifice her life and to partake of her sister's fate in Hades (554). While Ismene initially dismisses her sister's longing for eternal well-being as an erotic love for impossible things, she too longs for something more than mere life (90). She too feels the longing for something beyond mere life that is naturally awakened by the aware-ness of our mortality. She too feels the longing that the second choral ode suggests is essential to our humanity: the longing for Hades, for immortality. But Ismene does not feel that longing as powerfully as Antigone, she does not take that longing as seriously, she does not reflect on that longing as deeply, and therefore she lacks the full humanity – the depth, grandeur, and insight – of her sister (consider 460–1). It is not surprising that it is Antigone, not Ismene, who stirs the heart and inspires the love of the noble Haemon.

JUSTICE AND THE FAMILY: THE CHALLENGE OF CREON

It is tempting to dismiss Creon's argument for punishing Polyneices' corpse since, at first glance that punishment seems simply cruel and seems to reflect a wantonly cruel nature. By forbidding the burial of Polyneices and exposing his corpse to dogs and birds, Creon forbids

---

[33] In the words of Lane and Lane, "Obedience – and hence survival – are the ultimate values for Ismene" (1986, 167). But consider Mogyoródi's sugges-tion that "her motives are rather confused" (1996, 363–4).

those who loved him from expressing their grief while at the same time exacerbating that grief (26–30, 198–206, 696–8, and especially 407–31). When a guard reports that someone has secretly buried Polyneices, Creon threatens to torture all the guards unless they arrest the culprit (304–14, 324–6; see also 259–77, 327–31). When Antigone admits to having buried her brother, Creon pitilessly condemns her, as well as her sister, to death (473–98, 577–81). When Haemon, Antigone's fiancé and Creon's own son, pleads for her life, Creon vows that he will execute her before his son's very eyes (760–1). Finally, when Creon begins to fear that the gods may punish him for shedding the blood of his niece, he decides to shut Antigone up in a cave, with the apparent expectation that she will starve to death (773–80, 883–90). Even if Creon does not derive pleasure from cruelly inflicting pain on his subjects, he seems all too eager to base his rule on fear rather than love.

By the end, Creon seems to be the villain of the play, even in his own eyes. Once he is commanded by Teiresias to bury Polyneices, Creon, after at first balking, relents and laments that he has not followed the established religious laws by allowing Antigone to bury the corpse of her brother. In this way, Creon concedes that Antigone was right to affirm that the gods – including Justice herself – demand that families be allowed to bury their dead, even if they are enemies of the city, and hence that devotion to the family take precedence over devotion to the city (1108–14, 450–70). Furthermore, by accepting the blame of the chorus and of his wife for the suicide of his son Haemon and by blaming himself for the suicide of his wife Eurydice, Creon seems to condemn himself specifically as an enemy of the family and hence of the gods. He apparently shares the chorus's conclusion that, by issuing the edict forbidding Polyneices' burial and by punishing Antigone for defying that edict, he has been both unjust and impious (see 1261–1350).

Yet it is important to remember that throughout most of the play the chorus supports both Creon's edict against the corpse of Polyneices and his punishment of Antigone. At the beginning of the play, they celebrate their victory over Polyneices and accept Creon's edict punishing his corpse (100–54, 211–14). It is true that, after they hear that the corpse has been mysteriously buried, they wonder whether a god might have buried it and hence wonder whether the gods may not disapprove of Creon's edict (278–9). Nevertheless, after Creon's defense of his edict, they proceed – in the absence of the king – to denounce sharply the "evil" and "ignoble" human being who violated the edict (365–75; see 385–6). When Antigone denounces Creon's edict as a violation of divine law and justice, the chorus denounces her as "savage" (471–2). The chorus praises, at least initially, Creon's argument to Haemon for executing Antigone (681–2). And even after the chorus expresses sympathy both for Haemon's defense of Antigone and for her suffering, they still criticize her, to her face, as an enemy of the goddess Justice (724–5, 801–5, 853–6). It is possible that the chorus denounces Antigone in Creon's presence because, as Antigone and Haemon contend, they fear the wrath of their king (504–7, 509, 688–700; see also 724–5). Nevertheless, the fact that the chorus also denounces the violation of Creon's edict in the second choral ode, when they are alone, and the fact that Antigone interprets the chorus's final criticisms of her as sincere suggests that the chorus is largely persuaded by Creon's defense of his edict throughout most of the play (385–6, 800–82). Moreover, Antigone herself takes the argument Creon makes seriously. While Ismene's argument challenging the wisdom of her burial of Polyneices does not shake her resolve, Creon's argument challenging her justice and piety seems to arouse in her far-reaching doubts concerning the justice and piety of her actions. For it is only after her debate with Creon that Antigone's self-confidence begins to falter and eventually collapse. In order to see why, let us examine Creon's argument for the justice of his edict.[34]

Creon's argument for punishing the corpse of Polyneices is based on the claim that this measure will strengthen the city, and on the thesis that justice means devotion above all, not to the family, but to the city. Creon is surely aware that this thesis is at odds with the traditional

[34] Notwithstanding his boundless admiration for Antigone – "that noblest of figures that ever appeared on earth" – even Hegel points out, that "Creon is not a tyrant, but really a moral power" (Hegel 1962, 360, 325). But see, on the other hand, Goethe 1984, 141–4, as well as Winnington-Ingram 1980, 120–7; Meier 1993, 196; Tyrrell and Bennett 1998, for example, 50–62; Carter 2007, 110–14. Lacan remarks that Creon is "like all executioners and tyrants, a human character. Only the martyrs [namely, Antigone] know neither pity nor fear" (1997, 267). Earlier he contends that Antigone is "inhuman" (263).

understanding of the divine law, according to which justice demands that family members be permitted to bury their dead relatives regardless of their loyalty or disloyalty to the city (see 1113–14). But Creon evidently believes that, since justice cannot consist of devotion to one's family over one's city, and since the gods must be just, the traditional understanding of the divine law must be mistaken (see 280–9; 511–22).

The beginning point for Creon's argument concerning justice is the nearly fatal political crisis Thebes has just gone through, a crisis caused by the fratricidal struggle for power between Oedipus's sons, Polyneices and Eteocles. Creon prefaces the announcement of his edict by describing the political situation in Thebes to the chorus: "The gods, having shaken the affairs of the city with much tossing, have safely set them straight again. But I have sent for you, out of all, by messengers, because I know well that you always revered the might of Laius's throne, and also because, when Oedipus set the city straight and, once he perished, you still remained steadfastly loyal in your spirit to their children. Since those children, by a double fate, on a single day, perished, struck and smitten each, polluted each by a hand of their own flesh, I myself hold all might and the throne, in accordance with my kinship with the dead" (162–74). Creon indicates here that the principal cause of the turmoil that almost destroyed Thebes was familial strife. Creon observes that the Theban elders, the civic leaders of the city, were always devoted to Laius's rule, then to his son Oedipus's rule, and most recently to Oedipus's children's rule. In this way, the Theban political community has always been united through its loyalty to one family, the royal house of Laius. However, now that that house has been divided, and the two sons of Oedipus have warred on each other, there is, as Creon indicates, a danger that the chorus has itself been divided between those members loyal to Eteocles and those loyal to Polyneices. The problem Thebes confronts now is one of civil strife rooted in the strife within the family of Laius.

Hitherto, the Thebans have evidently believed, as Antigone still believes, that the family as such is a natural unity or whole. Accordingly, they have based their own political unity on devotion to a family. As long as the house of Laius was united, Thebes was united by its devotion to that family. But the fratricidal strife within that family indicates that the unity of Thebes must be based on something other than the loyalty to a family. Indeed, the whole history of the royal family from Laius to the present, which Creon alludes to here, would seem to demonstrate that the family as such can never be a reliable source of unity. The attempted infanticide of Laius, the patricide of Oedipus, and the fratricides of Eteocles and Polyneices seem to show that the family is not a truly natural community, that it has no clearly shared common good, inasmuch as members of that community will, for example, kill one another, their own flesh and blood, for the sake of attaining or protecting political power.

Accordingly, rather than arguing that the Thebans should now be loyal to the new royal house of Creon, and that they should, for example, pledge their loyalty to his son Haemon, Creon goes on to argue for loyalty to the entire city and for the importance of never favoring oneself or one's family over the city. "And whoever believes that a loved one is greater than his own country, this one, I say, is nothing. For I – let Zeus who always sees all know – I would not keep silent if I saw ruin approach the townsmen rather than salvation. Nor would I ever deem loved by me a man who is an enemy of the land, since I recognize that this land is what preserves us and it is by sailing on this land when she is upright that we can beget loved ones" (182–90). Creon here argues that the city, unlike the family, provides a clear, shared, and truly common good to all the citizens. For it resembles a ship, a ship of state, upon whom all citizens clearly depend for their very self-preservation. Creon does not explicitly attack the family here in the name of the city, but stresses rather that the very existence, the very safety, of families, and of individuals as well, depends on the safety of the city or country. To sink the ship of state for the sake of preserving a passenger one loves makes no sense, since, if the ship sinks, the beloved passenger will perish as well. There is, then, a common good for all citizens that encompasses their individual good and the good of the families – namely, the survival and the stability of the city.

Creon acknowledges that the city, like the family, can be torn apart by greed or ambition (see 288–303, 672–6). Indeed, in his view, a self-forgetting, patriotic love of one's city seems even less reliable a passion than love of one's family. But the city, unlike the family, can appeal to a natural human passion powerful enough to hold in check such greed or ambition – namely the individual desire for self-preservation. By providing security to the citizens, the city can satisfy their powerful desire to stay alive. And by demonstrating its awesome might to the greedy and ambitious, the city can arouse in them an overpowering and salutary fear of death. For even though "Gain has often destroyed men because of the hopes it raises" (221–2), the city checks such destructive hopes by inspiring a sobering fear of death. As Creon later remarks, "For even the rash flee, when they see Hades at last approach their life" (580–1).

The key to securing the city from danger is a firm ordering of both the city and the family. As Creon later explains to his son: "There is no greater evil than anarchy. This destroys cities and overturns households. This shatters the spear of an ally and routs him. But of those who act rightly, obedience to rulers saves most bodies" (672–6). The division or faction that destroys cities thereby destroys families as well. Moreover, disorder within a family – as the recent example of Oedipus's sons shows – can spread disorder to the city. Therefore, to preserve the city, which preserves us all, a forbidding and fearsome order must be maintained both throughout the city and within the family. Accordingly, Creon stresses, citizens must obey rulers, sons must heed fathers, the young must respect the old, and women must be ruled by men (see 218–22, 289–314, 324–6, 473–89, 525, 578–9, 632–80, 726–48). If these conventional hierarchies are not strictly respected and maintained, chaos will ensue and ultimately sink the ship of state. The passion, then, that the city should rely on for its stability is fear, and ultimately the fear of death. If citizens seek above all to preserve themselves, they will uphold order and thereby preserve the city. On the other hand, those who cherish some goal higher than mere life – those who, for example, seek power and wealth and violate the laws to achieve such goals – threaten the whole city with destruction. We see, then, that although Creon may well be temperamentally a harsh and cruel man, there is an argument for his harshness and cruelty in terms of the common good: by inspiring fear, Creon's rule avoids anarchy, maintains peace, and hence benefits the city. [35]

---

[35] Nussbaum faults Creon for his "simple" and "impoverished conception of the city" and of justice, and for failing to recognize that the city is a "complex whole" (1986, 60; see 54–63). But while she rightly points out that the play

Creon now turns to announce his edict. "Eteocles, who died doing battle on behalf of his city, having bested all with his spear, you shall cover in a grave and shall perform all the rites of purification that go to the best of the dead below. But as for his blood-brother, I mean Polyneices, an exile, who wished by fire to burn, from top to bottom, the land of his fathers and the gods of his kin, and wished to taste of the blood that he shares, and to lead the rest into slavery, it has been proclaimed to the city that this man no one shall honor with a grave or lament, but you shall leave him unburied, and see his body eaten by dogs and birds, tortured. Such is my spirit, and not ever by me shall the evil have honor before the just. But whoever is well-minded toward this city, shall have honor from me in life and death alike" (194–210).

Creon justifies his seemingly cruel edict by claiming that it will strengthen the city (191). First, the edict assures those who defend the city and risk their lives for it, as Eteocles did, that they will be honored by their grateful city after death and that they will receive the greatest rewards in an afterlife. The edict thus appeals to the citizens' desire for posthumous honor and immortal well-being, as well as to their desire for self-preservation, as a basis for their devotion to the city. However, Creon emphasizes the punishment of Polyneices more than the reward for Eteocles. The edict appeals then, above all to fear. It seeks to deter those citizens who may be tempted, out of ambition or greed or loyalty to Polyneices, to challenge Creon's rule, and plunge Thebes into anarchy, by appealing to their fear of death. For even though Polyneices is already dead, the effect of seeing his body torn and devoured by animals would seem to impress on those who behold this spectacle that Polyneices truly has been annihilated, that he truly is no more, since he will be deprived of the burial that would confer a kind of immortality on him, either in the afterlife or through posthumous honor. By punishing Polyneices in this way, Creon hopes to teach the potential enemies of the city a horrifying lesson they will never forget, a lesson in mortality. By showing them that the city can destroy them in every way, he hopes to teach them the importance of obeying the city that

ultimately criticizes his argument that justice means the devotion to one's city over one's family, she does not give due weight to Creon's thoughtful analysis of the problem of deadly anarchy, which forms the basis of his argument.

preserves them. Through this edict, Creon hopes to save Thebes from anarchy, and hence destruction, by appealing to the love of honor of its defenders and especially by inspiring terror in its potential enemies.[36]

Creon adroitly stresses here that Polyneices was an enemy of the family as well as of the city (198–206). Indeed, Creon emphasizes that the Thebans or, the Cadmeians, as he elsewhere calls them, share the same blood, and thereby suggests that Thebes constitutes the true, larger family of its citizens (508). In this way, Creon suggests to the chorus that by honoring Eteocles with burial, and especially by disgracing the corpse of Polyneices, he is upholding the demands of familial piety as well as those of patriotism. Nevertheless, Creon's edict clearly violates the established understanding of the divine law, according to which families must be allowed to bury their dead regardless of their disloyalty to the city (see 450–70, 1008–1114; but consider 211–14).[37] It would seem to be precisely because he recognizes the revolutionary character of his edict that Creon does not consult with Teiresias, as he has been wont to do in the past, before issuing it (992–5). By honoring Eteocles, Creon is honoring a fratricide, one who has committed a grave crime against the family and who is consequently, as Creon freely admits, polluted (170–4). Therefore the standard of justice that he applies in this case is not devotion to the family but devotion to the city, for Eteocles' fratricide is evidently eclipsed by his service to the city.

Now, Antigone challenges this elevation of the city over the family in the name of the gods. She explains her violation of Creon's edict by declaring to him and to the chorus: "For not at all to me did Zeus proclaim these things, nor did Justice, who dwells with the gods below – they who ordain these laws among human beings. Nor did I suppose that your proclamations had such strength that a mortal being would be able to outrun the unwritten and unshakeable laws of the gods. For they are not of the present or of yesterday; they live forever, and no one knows when they appeared. I was not about to pay the penalty among the gods for these things because I feared the spirit of any man. For that I would

---

[36] I therefore cannot agree with Knox's statement that "Creon's deepest motive for his action was hatred" (1964, 116).

[37] Regarding the question of how far Creon here departs from the traditional understanding of divine law, see Nussbaum 1986, 55, 437–8.

die, I knew full well – how should I not? – even if you did not proclaim it. If before my time I shall die, I count it a gain. For whoever lives among many evils [or many evil ones], as I do, how would dying not bring a gain? So for me, at least, to meet such a doom is no pain at all. But if I had endured the dead one, who came out of my mother, to be an unburied corpse, then in those circumstances I would have felt pain. In these, however, I do not feel pain. If in your opinion I have done foolish things, perhaps it is from a fool that I draw the charge of folly" (450–70).

Antigone contends here that it is only the gods' laws that are truly binding on human beings. For only the gods' laws are truly just, only they are eternal, and only they are enforced with the threat of divine punishment. Since the laws of political communities are devised and enforced by mere mortals, they may be justly and reasonably ignored if they conflict with the divine laws. Now Antigone insists that Creon's edict violates divine law by forbidding her from burying her brother. Indeed she suggests that the gods would punish her if she did not violate Creon's edict and bury her brother. Antigone suggests that the gods are fundamentally indifferent to the political community and that they do not support the punishment of such traitors as Polyneices, but that they care most deeply about the family, for they themselves punish, after death, those who not only betray the family but who simply fail, by omission, to fulfill their duties to their family. In Antigone's eyes, the city is simply a mortal entity, but the family is eternal. As Antigone has suggested to Ismene, the family continues to exist after death, forever, in an afterlife, and the gods reward with an everlasting happiness in the company of their family those who are devoted to the family (71–7, 80–1, 89, 93–7). Antigone suggests that, in the gods' eyes, it is not the city but the family that is truly sacred. Therefore humans should devote themselves to what is, in the eyes of the gods, the true community, the eternal community, of kindred flesh and blood.

Antigone's invocation of the afterlife here challenges Creon's whole argument for the importance of devoting oneself to the city. For in the light of eternity, in the light of divine rewards and punishments after death, how important is the self-preservation that the ship of state offers the loyal citizen and the death with which it threatens the disloyal one? Antigone argues that, since death is inevitable, and since there is an afterlife in which the just gods reward and punish human beings, it would be foolish to fear the threats or punishments of any merely mortal ruler. Rather, she suggests, one should strive to be worthy of the posthumous rewards of the gods. And the way to deserve such rewards is through devotion, even at the cost of one's life, to the community the gods themselves honor most – the family.

Creon, however, is not shaken here by this challenge. He seems wholly convinced that Antigone's violation of his edict is unjust and therefore that the gods cannot support her in her rebellion. For Antigone's belief that justice means devotion to the family over the city must, in Creon's view, destroy the city – and neither justice nor the gods can support the destruction of the city. As Creon insists earlier in the play, the gods cannot possibly regard as a good deed the destruction of a city that has always worshipped them (284–8; see also 194–206). He insists, then, that justice must consist in devotion to the city and hence that the gods must support him. To be sure, Creon does express some uncertainty about the gods' benevolence toward the city early in the play (162–3), and his failure to consult with Teiresias does suggest that he doubts the soothsayer would simply endorse his elevation of the city over the family. Nevertheless, at this point in the play at least, Creon is so insistent that the gods too believe that justice demands that devotion to the city take precedence over devotion to blood that he declares to the chorus: "Whether she is of my sister or nearer in blood than everyone who worships Zeus of my hearth, this girl and her blood-sister will not escape a most evil doom" (486–9).

The core of Creon's challenge to Antigone is his argument that the family is not a genuine whole or unity and therefore that it is simply impossible to be consistently devoted to the family. This challenge emerges in the following exchange:

ANTIGONE: There is nothing base in revering [or being pious toward] those who are from the same womb.

CREON: Was he not also one of the same blood who died on the other side?

ANTIGONE: Of the same blood, from one mother and the same father.

CREON: How is it that you honor with gratitude the one
              who is, for that [other brother], impious?

ANTIGONE: He will not bear witness to these things, the
              corpse who died.

CREON: If you honor him equally to the impious one?

ANTIGONE: For not some slave, but a brother perished.

CREON: But destroying this land, which the other defended.

ANTIGONE: Nevertheless, Hades longs for these laws.

CREON: But no good man longs to obtain the same as
              the evil.

ANTIGONE: Who knows if these things are pure below?
              (511–21)

Creon challenges Antigone's belief that justice means devotion to the
family by asking her a simple question: by honoring your brother
Polyneices with burial, are you not honoring the murderer of your other
brother? Now, Antigone could argue that by burying Polyneices, she is
not honoring one brother above the other but is simply making sure
that each receives the minimal honor due to any brother. But Antigone
herself believes that, if justice means devotion to the family, justice
demands the punishment of those who are disloyal to their family.
Hence she affirms that the disloyal Ismene will be hated by the souls of
their dead family and punished by the gods, and dreads that she herself
would be punished if she were not loyal to her brother (93–4, 76–7,
83, 542–3, 553; 46, 450–60). Yet, Creon asks, has not Polyneices
exhibited flagrant disloyalty to his family by killing his own brother?
How, then, can she believe that it is just to honor him? And how can
she believe that either the souls of Eteocles and her other dead family
members or the gods would approve of her honoring this fratricide with a
burial? Antigone can only reply by asking, "Who knows if these things

are pure below?" (521). Yet she thereby leaves entirely open the question of whether or not the dead and the gods approve of her action. But if she is so uncertain, how can she be confident of the justice and piety of her actions?

Creon contends that Antigone's own definition of justice self-destructs. If justice means devotion to the family, it is impossible for her to be just in this case, since each brother is guilty of a crime against the family. The premise of Antigone's whole understanding of justice and piety is that the family constitutes a true unity, a natural, permanent, and sacred whole. Antigone declares that justice means devotion to the family, that it means honoring, pleasing, and benefiting those blood relatives who are dead (76–7, 89, 559–60). Creon, on the other hand, perhaps especially impressed by the fratricidal conflict between Antigone's brothers, stresses that the family is not a true community but rather an arena of conflict, actual or potential. In addition to speaking of the conflict between the brothers Polyneices and Eteocles, Creon cites the conflict between himself and his niece Antigone – a conflict that he, in contrast to Antigone, portrays as a family conflict (164–74, 512–20, 486–9). He, as well as the chorus, may also allude to the conflict between Oedipus and his father Laius, as well as to the bitter conflict between Oedipus and both his sons (164–9, 471–2, 853–6; see also *Oedipus at Colonus*, especially 335–460, 593–601, 1156–1178, 1249–1396). Creon seems to suggest that the family is not a genuine whole but rather a collection of individuals who, though related by blood, may or may not care for one another or feel devoted to one another and whose interests always stand in actual or potential conflict. Therefore it is impossible to be devoted to the family as such. One can be devoted only to particular members of one's family. And by taking the side of one member, one is always, at least potentially, opposing another. For example, by honoring her brother Polyneices, Antigone is dishonoring and displeasing her brother Eteocles, not to mention her father Oedipus and her uncle Creon. Justice, then, cannot consist of devotion to one's family since the family is not a true community or whole.

The Theban plays as a whole suggest that Creon is right to call into question the natural unity of the family. In *Oedipus the Tyrant*, we learn of the attempt by Laius and Jocasta to kill their child, of Oedipus's killing of his father, and of his attempt to kill his mother. In *Oedipus at Colonus*, we learn that Oedipus's sons drove him into exile and proceeded to wage war on one another, and we see Oedipus bitterly curse his sons, pray that they commit the crime of fratricide against another, and pray that they be damned for eternity after death (1348–96). But, more than any other extant play of Sophocles, the *Antigone* calls into question the natural unity of the family. The play opens against the backdrop of two brothers deliberately killing one another. The opening scene then presents two sisters in bitter conflict with one another, and ends with one of them expressing her hatred for the other (86–7, 93–4; but see 98–9). We later see Creon condemn his nieces to death (486–9). We then witness Creon's son, Haemon, threaten to kill his father, and later hear of Haemon's conscious attempt to kill his father, an act of deliberate, attempted patricide unique in classical Greek literature.[38] Finally, we hear of Creon's wife, Eurydice, killing herself while cursing her husband as a killer of children (1301–5, 1312–13, 1315–16). It is impossible to read this play without a deep sense both of the dignity of the family and also of its natural fragility. One of the most obvious lessons of the play would seem to be that the ties of flesh

---

[38] Jebb (1979, 162–3) insists that Haemon "has no thought of threatening his father's life" at 751 and dismisses Haemon's actual attempt to kill his father as "a sudden impulse followed by remorse." See also 223 and Benardete 1999, 139. But the First Messenger describes the scene as follows: "In the furthest part of the tomb, we saw her [Antigone] hanging by her neck, in a noose of thread from linen she had fastened on herself. But he [Haemon] had thrown himself beside her, embracing her waist and bewailing loudly the destruction of his marriage bed, with one gone below, and the deeds of his father and his ill-fated bride. But as he [Creon] saw him, he approached the sullen one, wailing and shrieking out loud: 'Wretched one, what sort of deed have you done? What did you have in mind? In what calamity have you been destroyed? Come out, child, as a suppliant I beg you.' But at him, with savage eyes, the child glared, spat in his face, and, saying nothing, he drew his double-edged sword. But because his father rushed away in flight, he missed. Then the ill-fated one, enraged with himself, leaned against his blade and drove it halfway in, into his ribs. And on his wet arm, still conscious, he embraced the maiden. And, breathing, he cast out a river, upon her white cheek, of bloody drops" (1220–39). It is clear from the text that Haemon tries to kill his father, and only kills himself because he is angry with himself for having failed to commit patricide. See Segal 1981, 159; 1995, 131; Tyrrell and Bennett 1998, 141–2.

and blood are woefully weak, since having the same blood coursing through their veins evidently does not restrain human beings from hating and killing one another.

Antigone herself has of course been aware that divisions exist within her notoriously divided family, but she has evidently refused to face the implications of those divisions for her understanding of justice. For example, although Ismene twice mentions the fact that their brothers killed one another, Antigone never mentions this fact in the course of the play (compare 11–14 and 49–57 with, for example, 1–10 and 21–30). Furthermore, after her bitter quarrel with Ismene, Antigone deems her sister outside the community of the family and therefore conceives of their quarrel as one wholly external to her family. Indeed, later on, Antigone goes so far as to describe herself as the last living member of the royal house of Laius, thereby forgetting or dismissing Ismene entirely (940–3; see also 69–70, 93–4, 538–9, 542–3, 546–7, 549, 557, 559–60, 876–82, 895–6; but consider 891–4). In these ways, Antigone struggles to maintain her vision of the family as a whole, larger than herself or any of its members, and devotion to which ennobles her, renders her just, and thereby renders her worthy of everlasting happiness. Nevertheless, Creon's forceful challenge to that vision – a challenge underscored by the immediately ensuing public quarrel with her sister – evidently undermines Antigone's confidence that she has acted justly and therewith her hope that the gods will reward her. For in her final scene in the play, Antigone is overwhelmed by doubt concerning her own justice and piety.

THE WEAKNESS OF FAMILIAL PIETY: THE FALL OF ANTIGONE

The Antigone we see in her last scene in the play is a changed woman. Heretofore she has expressed utter indifference toward the city, has dismissed the citizens as cowardly, and has argued that the laws of the city lack authority over her (see, for example, 9–10, 78–81, 504–7, 450–60; see also 821). Now, for the first time, she addresses the city and her fellow citizens and asks for their sympathy (806–16, 839–51, 937–43). Previously, she had acted in the name of the eternal laws of the gods. Now she acts in the name of a law that she herself has discovered or devised (compare 450–60 with 904–15). Up to now, Antigone has insisted that her death would be a gain for her, since she would be with her family forever in an afterlife (71–6, 89, 93–7, 460–70, 553, 555; see also 1–6). Now, for the first time, she laments her death and specifically laments the fact that she will never know the joys of marriage and children (see 806–16, 876–82, 933–4, and especially 916–20; compare also 461–2 with 895–6).

The explanation for this change lies in Antigone's loss of confidence in her own justice and her consequent loss of confidence in winning for herself divine rewards after death. She compares herself to Niobe, a heroine who, along with her father Tantalus, was harshly punished by the gods (823–33; Homer *Iliad* 24.602–17; see *Odyssey* 11.582–92). She asks why she should look to the gods for help. And she regards it as an open question as to whether or not she is just and hence whether she will be rewarded or punished by the gods after death (921–8). Because Antigone now doubts that she is just, she also doubts that the gods are on her side, she is overwhelmed by her solitude, and she looks to her fellow human beings for sympathy, if not support.

Why has Antigone suddenly lost confidence in her justice? Evidently, Creon's challenge to Antigone's belief in the fundamental unity of the family leads her to wonder whether justice can truly consist of devotion to the family. For now, she discusses her family in terms of the individuals who constitute it rather than as a collective unit. For the first time in the play, Antigone speaks in some detail of her father and her mother, as well as of her brothers, though not at all of her sister (compare 1–6, 74–5, 89, and 559–60 with 857–66 and 897–915). And by focusing on the individuals of her family, rather than on the abstract entity "family," she inevitably focuses on the conflicts within her family and so alludes to her father's patricide, the incest between her parents, and her mother's suicide (857–66). Moreover, and perhaps most shockingly, she blames her brother Polyneices for her imminent death (870–1; see also 902–3). She seems to suggest that, by going to Argos, marrying an Argive princess, raising an army, and attacking Thebes, he sacrificed his sister for the sake of his quest for power. In this way, Antigone seems to embrace the view suggested by Creon that the family is not a true community but an arena of conflict, that devotion to the family as such is impossible and therefore cannot be just, and hence that her attempted devotion will not be rewarded by the gods.

Antigone does make one final attempt to justify her burial of Polyneices and thereby to justify her hopes for divine rewards after death. Moreover, she begins her last speech by addressing her ancestral gods as well as the city of Thebes. Finally, in her last words in the play, she declares to the chorus: "Look on me, you who rule over Thebes, the only one left of the royal family, such things do I suffer from such men, for having revered piety" (940–3). It might seem then, that Antigone ultimately dies confident that she has acted justly and piously and so will be duly rewarded by the gods after death.

Yet when she is imprisoned by Creon in a tomb-like cave with some food, and left to pray to the gods for salvation and to see whether or not they will save her, Antigone quickly kills herself (773–80, 1220–5). It seems that she dies in despair, without hope that the gods will save her from death or that a noble, pious death will bring her happiness in the hereafter. Her suicide suggests that, in the end, she cannot believe that she deserves the gods' assistance.

In order to understand why her faith in her justice collapses so quickly, let us consider more carefully the last argument she makes to justify her burial of her brother.

"Tomb, bridal chamber, deeply dug dwelling, eternal watchman, where I am going to those who are my own, that great number of those who have perished, whom Persephone has received among the dead. I, the last of them and most evil by far, I go down, before the portion of my life has passed. Yet I go greatly cherishing the hope that I will arrive there loved by my father, loved as well by you, mother, and loved by you, my brother. Since, when you died, with my own hands I washed and adorned you and poured libations on your tombs. And now, Polyneices, for preparing your body, such is the reward that I win. Yet those who think well will think that I did well by honoring you. For, had I been by nature a mother of children, or if my husband were dead and wasting away, I never would have taken up this labor with violence against my fellow citizens. What law do I invoke when I say these things? If a husband had died, I might have had another, and a child from another man, if I were bereaved of the first. But once my mother and father were hidden in Hades, no brother would ever sprout forth.

Through such a law, then, I honored you above all, but seemed to Creon to err in these things and to dare terrible things, dear brother. And now, taking me by the hand, he is leading me this way, unwed, without a marriage hymn, without my share of marriage and the nurture of children, but thus forsaken by loved ones, ill-fated, I go down, into the deeply dug chamber of the dead, alive. What justice of divinities have I transgressed? Why should I, a wretched one, still look to the gods? Whom should I call to as an ally? Since, while I have been pious, I have acquired impiety. But if, then, these things [namely, Creon's condemnation and punishment of her] are noble in the eyes of the gods, we, having suffered, will recognize that we have erred. But if these men [namely, Creon and the guards] are the ones who err, may they suffer no greater evil than I, even though they act without justice" (891–928).

Antigone begins by arguing that she has reason to hope that she will be welcomed in the afterlife by her father, her mother, and her brother Eteocles, and presumably by the gods, because she has fulfilled her duty to all her family by honoring each of them with a burial. In this way, Antigone invokes the divine law she had referred to earlier, which commands humans to be devoted to the family and to honor their dead kin with burial (450–70). Yet this argument evidently does not prove that she has been devoted to her family, for the objection of Creon remains: by honoring her brother Polyneices, she is honoring her brother Eteocles' murderer and hence honoring one who dishonored her family most emphatically. How then can she be confident that Eteocles and her parents will welcome her? How can she be confident that they will not condemn her for disloyalty to the family as harshly as she has condemned her sister? In this case, at least, it seems impossible to fulfill the divine law, since it is impossible for her to honor one member of her family without dishonoring another. The divine law appears to be fundamentally defective. It assumes that the family is a natural whole or unity, to which one can be consistently devoted. But the case of Polyneices and Eteocles shows that the family is not a natural whole or unity. Therefore Antigone cannot justify her burial of her brother and her hopes of earning rewards after death by invoking the divine law that commands humans to be devoted to the family.

Yet, rather than abandoning all hope for divine rewards after death and hence all hope for immortality, Antigone tries to justify her burial of her brother and her hope for divine rewards by invoking a new "law," one that she herself discovers, or devises, by her own lights. Like Creon, Antigone is led by the moral inadequacies of the divine law to seek on her own a new law, one that will reflect a new understanding of justice. Antigone now reasons that she never would have battled with her fellow citizens, that she never would have risked her life, in order to bury a dead husband or a child. For she could have found another man to take the place of her dead husband and she could have conceived and given birth to another child to replace her dead child. But since the death of her parents, it is impossible for Antigone to have a new brother to take the place of the dead Polyneices. His loss is irretrievable. According to this law, then, she acted justly by sacrificing her hopes for marital and familial happiness in this life in order to bury her brother.

The most striking feature of the law Antigone sets forth here is its relaxation of the demand to risk one's life for the sake of one's dead kin and the greater weight it places on the pursuit of one's own happiness in this life. Whereas the divine law evidently commands humans to sacrifice their lives, if necessary, to bury their family members, and warns them that if they do not they will be punished in the afterlife, this new law commands humans to sacrifice their lives only to bury those family members who have died and cannot be replaced (see 450–70; see also 45–6, 71–7). If your husband dies, Antigone's law says, do not risk your life to bury him, but replace him, presumably because it is possible for you to recover from his death and live happily. But if an irreplaceable member of your family dies, your loss is irremediable, and therefore it makes sense to risk all to honor that member.

Antigone seems to try, through this new law, to temper the duty to bury one's dead loved ones with devotion to one's own happiness in this life. As Antigone's doubts grow concerning the possibility of truly devoting herself to her family and thereby earning divine rewards after death, her concern for happiness in this life grows as well. As Antigone's doubts grow concerning the possibility of fulfilling her duty to her family, her concern for duty declines and her concern for her own well-being, in the here and now, is liberated. Indeed, the law she sets forth here seems to subordinate the devotion to family to the concern for one's individual self and one's individual happiness. For the law declares: Do not sacrifice your life for the sake of your loved ones unless *you* have suffered a loss *you* cannot replace. In other words, the law seems to counsel: Do not risk your life unless you have lost all hope for happiness in this life and your life is no longer worth living. Thus understood, the "law" would seem to be a counsel of prudence rather than a true moral law. [39]

Yet Antigone persists in speaking the language of law and justice rather than that of prudence and self-interest. Moreover, the law she sets forth here does not consistently make concern for one's happiness its priority. Antigone claims that, according to this law, she does well by sacrificing her life for her brother, since she can never have another

---

[39] I suggest that it is precisely Antigone's questioning here of her previously unqualified belief in divine law, duty, and nobility that has led numerous commentators to insist that these lines must be spurious. Consider, for example, Goethe: "There is a passage in *Antigone* which I always look upon as a blemish, and I would give a great deal for an apt philologist to prove that it is interpolated and spurious. After the heroine has explained the noble motives for her action, and displayed the elevated purity of her soul, she at last, when she is led to death, brings forward a motive that is quite unworthy and almost borders on the comic . . . . This is, at least, the bare sense of this passage, which in my opinion, when placed in the mouth of a heroine going to her death, disturbs the tragic tone and appears to me very far-fetched – to savour too much of dialectical calculation" (1984, 144). Jebb similarly asserts, "I confess that, after long thought, I cannot bring myself to believe that" Sophocles wrote these lines (1979, 182). But Jebb also admits that all of our manuscripts contain lines 904–20 and that Aristotle cites lines from this passage in *Rhetoric* 3.16.9. Winnington-Ingram, who admits to having changed his view "again and again," maintains that the passage is spurious because of her "contorted argument," and therefore concludes that Antigone at the end is "indignant rather than perplexed" (1980, 145–6). Reinhardt accepts the authenticity of the lines but denies that Antigone here questions the divine law. Indeed he goes so far as to assert that "the opposing sides in this drama, personified in Antigone and Creon, have no conflict within themselves" (1979, 65; see also 83–4, 251–2). Ormand contends that the "lines are consistent . . . with the values that Antigone expresses throughout the drama" (1999, 96; see also Foley 1996, 54–8). Tyrrell and Bennett, while accepting the lines, also deny that she doubts herself and even claim that, by committing suicide, she defiantly "seizes control of her body" (1998, 112–19, 143–4). Knox recognizes that she questions herself here but then insists that she remains self-confident, and reasonably so: "She is rightly confident of the gratitude of those beloved dead she goes to join" (1964, 113; 103–7).

brother. Now the fact that she cannot ever have another brother would naturally make Polyneices' death more grievous to her. But why should she not still seek happiness in this life, through marriage with the worthy Haemon and companionship with her remaining – and similarly irreplaceable – sister, Ismene? Why should she sacrifice her pursuit of happiness in this life simply because she can never have another brother? Why does she not follow the line of thinking implicit in her revision of the divine law to its ultimate conclusion and make the pursuit of her own happiness in this life her central, explicit concern?

What prevents Antigone from taking this step is her persistent attachment to her hope for immortality. She clings to the hope that, by sacrificing herself for her family, she will be rewarded by the gods for her nobility and justice. Now Antigone is shaken here in her belief in her own justice and in her hopes for immortality. Accordingly, she steps away from the divine law, and feels more powerfully than before a desire for happiness in this life. But she still clings to the belief that, by burying the corpse of her brother Polyneices, she is exhibiting her devotion to an entity larger than her individual self or any individual self – the family – and is thereby rendering herself worthy of divine rewards after death. In this light, the family appears to be a means through which she may feel superior to mere self-interest and may thereby hope to achieve the self-interested goal of personal immortality.

Antigone here points, however, to another, different way by which one may possibly satisfy one's desire for personal immortality through the family: the procreation of children. For the first time in the play, she evinces a desire, albeit a wistful desire, for marriage and offspring (see 916–20 as well as 806–12, 876–82). As Antigone's hopes regarding divine rewards in an afterlife fade, her longing for marriage and children in this life grows. Now, the passion for immortality, so powerful in Antigone, would seem to find its most widespread and tangible expression in what Aristotle calls "the natural impulse to leave behind another that is like oneself" (*Politics* 1252a29–30). By leaving behind one that is like oneself, one may cherish the hope that a part of oneself – another self – will live on after one has passed away. When Antigone refers to herself in her last lines in the play as "the only one left of the royal family" (941), she may mean to lament specifically that her family has no future because she has borne no children and therefore will leave nothing of herself once she is dead.

It is true that the story of Antigone's family in particular – the killing by Oedipus of his father, the exile of Oedipus by his sons – would seem to call into question the reasonableness of the belief that parents live on through their offspring after death. Nevertheless, through the scenes surrounding her death, Sophocles invites us to wonder whether Antigone's longing for happiness and immortality would not have found a healthier and more fruitful outcome through married life with Haemon than through dying for her dead brother in the hope of enjoying immortal well-being in Hades.[40] In the scene that precedes Antigone's final scene, we see that Haemon is so in love with Antigone that he publicly defies his father the king and thereby risks the loss of his father's affection and his own princely status. At this point, we hear the choral ode on the awesome, frightening, but also beautiful power of Eros (781–99). We then see Antigone express her wish for marriage and children in her last scene. Finally, we see again that Haemon is so in love with Antigone that he comes to her rescue, in defiance of his father's edict. Would the pious heroine not have found happiness with such a noble lover? Would she not have found satisfaction in marrying the prince of Thebes and ruling the city as part of a renewed "royal family" (941)?

Yet Haemon arrives to rescue his beloved only to find that Antigone has killed herself. Notwithstanding her lament at the end of her life that she will never know the joys of marriage and children, the focus of Antigone's hopes and longings is never happiness with Haemon, whose name she never even mentions in the play, but divine rewards after death. Accordingly, when she loses all conviction that she deserves the reward of everlasting happiness, she despairs of all happiness and takes her own life.

The first irrevocable act in the play is the suicide of Antigone. Until that moment, there is still hope that all that has been done may be undone and hence that she will be spared by a repentant Creon, see her

---

[40] Saxonhouse goes so far as to suggest that the opposition between Antigone and Creon "brings on the suffering that would not have occurred had either yielded to the powers of *eros*" (1992, 73).

brother buried, marry Haemon, and live happily with her loving husband, eventually even becoming queen of Thebes. She kills herself on the verge of being rescued by Haemon and hence on the verge, it would seem, of leading the life of marriage and family that she herself wishes for by the end of the play. One might argue that Antigone loses such happiness primarily because she lacks sufficient faith in the gods. After all, don't they send Teiresias to Creon and prompt him to bury her brother and spare her? Yet the fact that it is Haemon who comes to save her first suggests that Antigone's principal error is her lack of faith in human providence rather than divine providence.

Antigone first risks her life for the corpse of her brother because she believes that she will thereby win the divine reward of immortal happiness, and then kills herself when she loses hope of deserving such a reward. She is led by her desire to be pious and ultimately by her desire for a superhuman happiness after death to separate herself from, and even blind herself to, the love of Haemon. She thereby deprives herself of the possibility of a human happiness. Her self-interested desire for immortal happiness leads her to lose all hope for happiness in the here and now. Her deepest failing is not her loss of faith in her own justice or in her own worthiness of divine rewards or in the gods, but her lack of faith in human love, in the love of others for her. It is the pious reverence for the gods and the pious longing for immortality of this pious heroine that cause her ruin.

THE POWER OF FAMILIAL PIETY: THE FALL OF CREON

The demise of Antigone might seem to vindicate Creon. After all, Antigone dies persuaded by Creon that it is at least doubtful that justice consists of devotion to one's family, and hence doubtful that the divine law commanding devotion to one's family is truly divine. Yet the suicide of Antigone seals the doom of Creon. Her death is followed rapidly by the suicides of his son and his wife, deaths that shatter the spirit of the Theban king.[41] More importantly, Creon abandons his

---

[41] Of the six suicides that take place within the seven extant plays of Sophocles, three are reported within the space of just over a hundred lines at the end

understanding of justice as devotion to the city over the family at the end of the play, and returns to the divine law that commands devotion to one's family. While Antigone comes to question her attachment to the divine law in the course of the play, Creon returns to the divine law and condemns himself by it. Antigone kills herself out of despair of the gods; Creon condemns himself out of fear of the gods.

Creon's return to the divine law, however, precedes rather than follows the deaths of his son and wife. Those deaths occur after Creon has buried the corpse of Polyneices and has resolved to free Antigone from all punishment. It is not grief over the deaths of his loved ones that prompts him to return to the divine law and its elevation of the family over the city. Indeed, the death of his other son, Megareus, evidently did not inspire any change of heart in Creon at all (1301–5). As long as Creon is confident that justice means devotion to the city rather than to the family, he is not shaken by deaths within his family. What, then, causes him to lose his confidence in his own understanding of justice?

Creon begins to abandon his understanding of justice and to return to the divine law even before Teiresias declares that he must bury Polyneices or suffer punishment from the gods. The first indication of Creon's return is in the aftermath of his debate with Haemon. Before that debate, Creon had resolved to execute Antigone and also Ismene. After that debate, Creon resolves to spare Ismene entirely. As for Antigone, Creon explains to the chorus: "I will bring her where the path is bereft of mortals and I will hide her, alive, in a rocky cavern there. I will set before her just enough food for expiation, so that the whole city may escape pollution. There, calling on Hades, whom alone of gods she reveres, perhaps she will succeed in escaping death or, at least in that last moment, she will recognize that it is an excessive labor to revere Hades" (773–80). Creon declines to execute Antigone directly because to shed the blood of his own niece would bring pollution (μίασμα [776]) upon him, just as Polyneices and Eteocles brought pollution (172) upon themselves by shedding their brother's blood. In this way, Creon acknowledges that justice entails, at least, devotion

of the *Antigone* (1175–1283). The other three are those of Jocasta, Ajax, and Deianira (Knox 1964, 42).

even to those family members who have violated the laws of the city. He also expresses concern that the gods may punish him and his city for shedding the blood of his niece. Finally, he acknowledges the possibility that the gods will intervene to save her from death as a reward for having buried her brother as required by divine law and hence, presumably, the possibility that they may punish him for having attempted to thwart her. Accordingly, when Teiresias later demands that Creon bury Polyneices as required by divine law and free Antigone, it is not altogether surprising that Creon yields fairly quickly. For his dispute with Haemon has already prompted him to embrace the belief that justice and piety require devotion to family members who are disloyal to the city, and to wonder whether the gods may not deem Antigone's burial of her brother wholly just and pious.[42]

How does the debate with Haemon undermine Creon's conviction that justice means devotion to the city over the family? Until this scene, Creon has appeared adamant in this belief. In his first speech – in the immediate aftermath of the battle in defense of Thebes – in which he announces his edict on Polyneices, he has declared: "Nor would I ever deem loved by me a man who is an enemy of the land, since I recognize that this land is what preserves us and it is by sailing on this land when she is upright that we can beget loved ones" (187–90). Upon discovering that his niece Antigone is the one who buried the corpse of Polyneices, he has insisted that he will execute her: "Whether she is of my sister or nearer in blood than everyone who worships Zeus of my hearth, this girl and her blood-sister will not escape a most evil doom" (486–9). Finally, in response to Ismene's question, "But will you kill the bride of your own child?" he has replied, "For there are other fields for him to plough," and, again, "I abhor evil wives for my sons" (568–9, 571). Until this scene, Creon has seemed determined to punish with

---

[42] I must therefore disagree with Meier's claim claims that "no one, not even the son or the seer, manages to influence Creon" (1993, 200). I agree with Nussbaum that Creon's love for Haemon forces him to reject his understanding of justice, but I disagree that he "begins to feel the force" of that love only during the confrontation with Teiresias (1986, 62). Knox recognizes that Creon "changes his mind" after his confrontation with Haemon, but claims that he does so because he is "influenced by Haemon's emphatic claim that the people of Thebes praise Antigone's action" (1964, 72).

death those disloyal to the city, even the children of his sister and the wife-to-be of his son, and has even suggested that he would similarly punish one "nearer in blood." Creon, then, until this point, has seemed immovable in his conviction that devotion to the city must wholly eclipse devotion to the family.

However, when Creon actually comes face to face with one even "nearer in blood" than his nieces – his own son Haemon – he appeals to his son's filial loyalty as well as to his concern for the well-being of Thebes. Indeed, Creon appeals first to his son's love for him as his father. He first asks: "Child, can it be that you come here to rave to your father, after hearing the final resolution concerning your bride-to-be? Or are we loved by you, whatever we may do?" (632–4). Then, when Haemon reassures him of his love, Creon sets forth a vision of the family strikingly different from what he has said until now. "For, thus, child, you ought to be able in your heart to stand behind your father's judgment in all things. Indeed it is for the sake of this that men pray to have obedient offspring born in their homes: that they may retaliate against their father's enemy with evils and honor his loved one equally to what their father would do. Whoever begets children who are of no benefit, what would you say about this one except that, to him, labors were born and much laughter for his enemies? Do not now, or ever, child, cast out your wits on account of pleasure and for the sake of a woman, but know that cold this becomes to embrace, an evil woman sharing one's bed in one's home. For what would be a greater wound than an evil loved one?" (639–52).

Creon depicts the family here as a community based on love. Sons should benefit their fathers by punishing their enemies and protecting their loved ones. In return, sons benefit both from the judgment and the love of their fathers and of the rest of their family. Creon suggests here that the family is a more genuine community than the city. For the city is based on fear: the citizens' fear that they and their loved ones will sink with the ship of state if the city is destroyed, and the citizens' fear of their rulers, who must punish most terribly those who threaten the city with destruction. But the family, as Creon describes it here, is based on the positive desire to belong to such a community and to enjoy the love, the guidance, and the protection of one's kin. The only "punishment" Creon mentions here for a disloyal or disobedient son is inflicted, not by the father, but by the son himself, who must suffer the greatest evil: a cold, loveless life with an evil "loved one." Creon seems to suggest here that happiness is to be found primarily within one's family and that one should devote oneself to one's city above all because the security of one's family depends on the city.[43] The question arises, however, if one is devoted to one's city for the sake of one's family, does it make sense to sacrifice one's family for the sake of one's city?

The family, Creon hints, is also more of a sacred community than the city. For even though the gods are, in his view, angry with those who threaten the city, Creon never suggests that men pray, or should pray, to the gods to protect the city (see 282–9). Indeed, his very first lines in the play indicate that the gods are not reliable protectors of the city: "The gods, having shaken the affairs of the city with much tossing, have safely set them straight again" (162–3). But Creon does cite approvingly the fact that men pray to the gods for obedient sons and hence for a strong and united family (641–7). Creon, then, argues that Haemon should accept the execution of his bride, in the first place, because she is an enemy of his father and hence threatens to divide and destroy his family, the loving and sacred community to which he belongs and in which alone he may find happiness.

Creon proceeds to argue that Haemon should also accept his fiancée's death because it is necessary to the well-being of Thebes. Creon stresses here that, if he were to spare Antigone after she has violated his laws, he would seem to be a weak ruler, the citizens would lose their fear of him, and chaos would ensue. "There is no greater evil than anarchy. This destroys cities and overturns households. This shatters the spear of an ally and routs him. But of those who act rightly, obedience to rulers saves most bodies. So we must defend those who are orderly, and we must never be worsted by a woman. For it is better, if indeed one must fall, to fall at the hands of a man, and we would not be called less than women" (672–80). Creon here returns to his earlier argument that the city alone can save us and our loved ones from death, that the city's ruler must be strong and fearsome in order to protect the city from destruction, and hence that, as a ruler, he must punish remorselessly

---

[43] Zeitlin goes so far as to suggest that Creon "insists on the absolute unity of the family" (1986, 124). Consider as well Ormand 1999, 80–6.

those like Polyneices and Antigone who defy the laws of the city and thereby threaten to plunge the city into anarchy.

Haemon responds to his father by arguing that, precisely insofar as Creon is a fearsome ruler, he runs the risk of ignoring potentially dangerous currents in public opinion. For his subjects are too afraid to reveal to him what they truly think and feel. Haemon then asserts that the Thebans, in secret, are overwhelmingly on the side of Antigone. "It is possible for me to hear these things in the dark, that the city mourns for this child and that most undeservingly of all women and most evilly she is dying for having done the most glorious deeds. She is one who would not leave her own brother, who fell in bloody conflict, unburied, to perish because of dogs who eat raw flesh or some birds. Does she not deserve to receive a golden honor? Such is the dark talk that is going around in silence" (692–700). Haemon argues here that Creon should yield to the popular sentiment in favor of Antigone, not because it is just but because it is powerful. For if he does not yield, he will "be destroyed" (714–21). Haemon implies that, unless Creon gives in to Antigone, the citizens will revolt, kill him, and plunge Thebes into the very anarchy that he seeks to avoid. In this way, Haemon argues that his father should give in for the sake of the city's well-being as well as for his own sake.

Yet Haemon's argument here is unconvincing. There is simply no evidence in the play that the people of Thebes are so devoted to Antigone that they will rebel against Creon's rule to save her or avenge her death. The chorus of Theban elders expresses sympathy for what Haemons says here and also for Antigone in her last scene, but they also suggest that she has acted unjustly (724–5, 800–5; 853–6, 872–5). Antigone herself certainly feels as though she is dying unloved by all (839–52, 876–82, 923). Furthermore, Haemon's argument seems inconsistent in its portrayal of the Thebans. If they are too frightened of Creon to criticize him, will they not be too frightened to revolt against him (see 220)? Finally, Haemon offers only his own testimony to the popular support for Antigone. But is Haemon not under the sway of Eros and therefore a wholly unreliable witness in the case of his beloved bride-to-be?[44]

---

[44] See 568–70, 626–30, 781–99, 1220–5. Aristotle, in the *Rhetoric*, suggests that Haemon here simply attributes his own views to the common people of Thebes in order to make his defense of Antigone more credible (3.17.16–7). I

Indeed, is Haemon not merely repeating here his beloved Antigone's own earlier assertion that her actions have been most glorious and that the Thebans are hiding their overwhelming support for her because they fear Creon (compare 692–9 with 502–9)?

Whether or not the Thebans support Antigone, but in secret, out of fear of Creon, it is increasingly clear in this scene that Haemon himself openly and fearlessly supports Antigone in defiance of his father and king. When Creon calls his son "all-evil" for publicly quarreling with his own father, Haemon drops all pretense of concern about the public's support for Antigone and publicly declares in his own name that his father is both unjust and impious: "For I see you mistakenly doing unjust things" and "For you are not pious but tread on the honors of gods" (742–3, 745). Through this public accusation of injustice and impiety, Haemon suggests that his father deserves to be challenged by his son, overthrown by the Thebans, and punished by the gods. And when Creon insists that Antigone will be executed, Haemon responds: "Then this one will die and, dying, will destroy another" (751). In this way, Haemon appears to threaten to kill his own father and king, a threat he later attempts to carry out (1220–39).

Creon's first response to Haemon's accusation of injustice and impiety and threat to kill his father and king is to announce his intention to execute Antigone before his son's eyes, either in order to punish him or in order to terrify him into submission with an act of sensational cruelty. Yet, after Haemon departs, Creon immediately begins to yield, as his son had argued he should. He spares Ismene altogether and he imprisons Antigone rather than executing her directly, lest he be deemed polluted by the gods for shedding the blood of his niece. Why does Creon yield, even in part, to his son, given that he is not persuaded by his son's arguments, given his own belief that yielding will plunge Thebes into a destructive anarchy, and given that his son has just publicly accused him of injustice and impiety and has apparently threatened to kill him?

therefore cannot agree with the claim that the city of Thebes speaks to Creon "in the person of Haemon" (Knox 1964, 108, 114; see also Reinhardt 1979, 85; Meier 1993, 196, 200; Carter 2007, 110).

In order to understand why Creon begins to abandon his belief here that justice means devotion to the city over the family, one must consider what that belief would demand of him here. Haemon has publicly attacked his king as an unjust and impious ruler and has apparently threatened to kill him. By doing so, he has threatened the well-being of Thebes at least as much as Polyneices, who killed his brother the king, and certainly more than Antigone, who attempted to bury her brother in defiance of the king. Must the king not punish such dangerous lawlessness? Just as Creon was willing to punish his own niece with death in order to demonstrate his justice and strength and thereby save the city from a deadly anarchy, must he not punish his own son, even with death? The logic of Creon's own understanding of justice would seem to require him to execute his son for threatening to commit regicide.

Yet Creon recoils before such a conclusion. While he is perfectly capable of sacrificing his nieces, the daughters of his sister, one of whom is the bride-to-be of his son, for the sake of the city, he cannot bring himself to sacrifice his son Haemon. But why not? As we have seen, Creon has a vision of the family as a community based on love, in which fathers pray to the gods for obedient and loving sons who will protect the entire family. All his hopes for happiness appear to lie within his family. Yet, according to Eurydice, Creon has already sacrificed one son, Megareus, for the sake of the city (1301–5). Why, then, does Creon shrink from sacrificing his other son as well?

The key difference between Megareus and Haemon, in Creon's eyes, is highlighted by the chorus: "Here is Haemon, latest and last of your offspring" (626–7). The loss of any child must always be hard, but the loss of one's last remaining child is worse, insofar as it signifies the end of one's lineage, of one's flesh and blood, and therefore, in some sense, of one's self (consider 905–12). As is stressed throughout the play, fathers instinctively view their children as extensions of themselves. Haemon says to Creon, in his first words in the play, "Father, I am yours" (635). Teiresias later describes Haemon as coming from Creon's "inward parts (σπλαγχνων)" (1066). When the First Messenger announces, "Haemon has perished; with his very own hand (αυτοχειρ) his blood was slain," the chorus asks whether it was his father or "his own hand" (οικειας χερας) that killed him (1175–6; see also 55–7). In this way, the elders instinctively identify father and son together, as the same kin (εμφυλιους), in Creon's later words (1263–4), as the same flesh and blood.[45] Accordingly, by begetting a son, a father extends his own self, even beyond his lifetime.

With this thought in mind, let us reconsider the remark of Creon we cited earlier: "Indeed it is for the sake of this that men pray to have obedient offspring born in their homes: that they may retaliate against their father's enemy with evils and honor his loved one equally to what their father would do" (641–4). Creon suggests here that men pray for sons who will act as they themselves would act – "equally to what their father would do" – while their fathers are still alive, to be sure, but also once they are dead. Fathers pray for sons because through their sons they hope, in some sense, to live on, through an extension of their own selves, through their other selves. Similarly, fathers are, as Haemon observes, delighted by the "flourishing glory" of their children, in part because they share in that glory and hope to live on through that glory once they are gone (701–4). They themselves "flourish," as the First Messenger points out, with the birth of fine children because, through their children, they hope to continue to flourish even past their death (1164). As long as one has a child, the limit of one's self has been extended indefinitely past one's demise. For one's child lives on, as may one's child's children, and so on into the future. Having children, then, is a way for fathers and mothers to escape from inescapable Hades, to escape from mortality (361).

For Creon to kill his last remaining son would, in his view, be tantamount to annihilating himself, even more so than if he were simply to kill himself. One who kills himself, or dies in some other way, may still comfort himself with the thought that his child will live on. But to lose one's child, one's last child, is to lose all hope for the future. Hence Eurydice's suicide now, after the death of Haemon, but not after the death of Megareus, makes a certain sense. For the limit of

---

[45] As Nussbaum points out, Haemon's very "name means 'blood' (as the punning account of his death brings out, 1175)" (1986, 62). In Knox's words, Creon "must face the problem in the person of his own flesh and blood, Haemon, whose very name emphasizes the blood relationship between them" (1964, 88). See also Vernant and Vidal-Naquet 1988, 319.

her existence has been irrevocably fixed by the death of her last remaining child.

The *Antigone* raises far-reaching questions about the reasonableness of regarding one's family, and especially one's children, as an extension of oneself. Haemon, for example, is not only strikingly different from his father in his character, but even attempts to kill him. Nevertheless, the play also points to the family as a most powerful expression of the human longing – eros – for immortality. Indeed, the chorus responds to the bitter dispute between Haemon and Creon by singing an ode to Eros. Ostensibly, the chorus is commenting on the "unvanquished" power of eros to inspire a loving and obedient son to challenge and defy his father and king (781). But the words of the ode spotlight the intimate connection between eros and mortality. For while the ode notes that the immortal gods themselves cannot escape from the sway of eros, it focuses on the power of eros over humans, who "last but a day" (790). In this way, the ode suggests that eros is the longing of mortal human beings for immortality. Eros is the response of mortal man to his helplessness before death (see 90, 220, 361).[46]

---

[46] There are six appearances of the word ερως and related words in the play. Ismene says to Antigone, "You are in love [ερας] with impossible things" (90). The chorus assures Creon that, "There is no one so foolish as to be in love [ερα] with being dead" (220). The chorus remarks, in its third ode, that hope can be "a deception for light-minded loves [ερωτων]" (617). There is the choral ode on love where Ερως is mentioned twice in one line (781). Finally, Creon declares at the end of the play that he wishes to die and then says: "But these things I love [ερω] I have prayed for" (1336). Taken together, these references suggest that eros means not only being in love with another human being but, more broadly, longing and hoping for something apparently beyond our reach such as, for example, being deathless or immortal. It seems to me that Griffith overlooks this broad meaning of the term eros in the play when he claims that Antigone's "'love' is for her father, and her brother, and extends no farther" (2005, 95–6). Similarly, Nussbaum overlooks the broad meaning of eros in the play when she suggests that neither Antigone nor Creon is erotic. See, for example, 1986, 64: "Antigone is as far from *eros* as Creon." Consider as well Saxonhhouse 1992, 71–2, but see, on the other hand, Segal 1981, 197–9. It should be noted that Ismene states specifically that Antigone is, in a sense, erotic (90) and the chorus may suggest as much as well at 617. Creon too attributes eros to himself at the end of the play (1336).

In this light, Creon's inability to sacrifice his last remaining son for the city reflects the invincible power of eros. By killing Haemon, he would destroy his hopes of living on through him after death and thereby thwart his own longing for immortality. This Creon evidently cannot do. And just as he recoils from shedding the blood of his own son, his own flesh and blood, so does he recoil from shedding the blood of his nieces, who are also his own flesh and blood.

Creon's quarrel with his son reawakens his reverence for the family. Creon expresses outrage at Haemon and calls him "all evil" and "polluted," not for openly quarreling with his king but for quarreling with his father (742, 746). The outrageous behavior of his son reminds Creon of his deep-seated belief – one that had been overshadowed in his heart by the political crisis provoked by Polyneices' invasion and near-destruction of Thebes – that it is all-evil and impious to be insolent to your father and, more generally, that it is evil and impious to be disloyal to your own flesh and blood. But would he not himself also run the risk of pollution and impiety by punishing his own nieces, the daughters of his sister, his own flesh and blood? Indeed, if disloyalty to one's family is "all-evil," is not loyalty to one's family, even one's treasonous family members, all good? Might not Antigone, then, be deserving of honor rather than punishment?

Creon's original argument that justice means devotion to one's city over one's family was based on his thesis concerning the natural disunity of the family. As we have seen, that thesis draws considerable support from the play as a whole. That thesis undermines Antigone's confident belief in her own justice and piety and fills her with doubt and despair. But, ultimately, Creon cannot truly embrace that thesis himself. He cannot apply that thesis to his own family. When he sees his own son defy him and threaten to kill him, Creon retreats to the belief that the family is a sacred community, disloyalty to which is the greatest of evils.

Creon's concern for the city is rooted in his fear of instability and perhaps ultimately in his fear of death. But his concern for his family is rooted in his hopes for happiness in a community knit together by love – a happiness in this life that is the answer to his prayers, that is blessed by the immortal gods – and in his hopes for living on through his offspring after death. Creon's concern for his family, then, is ultimately rooted in his longing for immortality.

At the end of his dispute with Haemon, Creon agrees to spare Ismene altogether, and Antigone in part, in order to escape the pollution of shedding the blood of his own kin. Creon would rather risk plunging the city into destructive anarchy than provoke the wrath of the gods. To be sure, Creon claims here that he seeks to ensure that "the whole city may escape pollution" (776; see also 889). But it is hard to see why the city would be polluted if its king were to shed the blood of his own family. No one ever suggests that Thebes was polluted when king Eteocles shed the blood of his brother (141–6, 170–2). It would seem that only Creon would be polluted by killing his niece and hence that only he would be punished. By the end of his quarrel with Haemon, then, Creon's concern for the well-being of the city has been eclipsed by his fear that the gods may punish him for having acted disloyally toward his family.[47]

It is therefore not surprising that, when the soothsayer Teiresias demands that Creon bury Polyneices lest he be punished by the gods, and implies that he should release Antigone as well, Creon gives in fairly quickly. Indeed, Creon has always been reverent toward Teiresias and toward the gods, the soothsayer reports. And Creon evidently remains reverent toward the soothsayer, for he is immediately terrified when Teiresias warns him of the danger of divine punishment (991–7; see also 1058). It is true that Creon angrily accuses Teiresias of injustice and greed when he first demands the burial of Polyneices. But it is also true that Teiresias is somewhat peremptory in his demand and his explanation of why Creon should yield – birds are "screaming in evil and unintelligible agony," sacrifices are not burning properly, and "all" the city's altars and hearths are covered with Polyneices' flesh – may understandably strain credulity, especially since Teiresias is blind and relies entirely on his one slave for his entire report (1001–2, 1016, 1011–16). Moreover, even in the midst of his attacks on Teiresias, Creon concedes that the soothsayer is wise (1059). Finally, once Teiresias warns in detail that Creon will lose his son and will himself be punished and destroyed by the Furies, the avenging demons of Hades and the gods, Creon is overwhelmed by the pious fear that first began to emerge after

---

[47] I therefore cannot agree with Segal's claim that Creon exhibits "rationalism" here (1981, 174).

his quarrel with Haemon, and he gives in completely (1064–79, 1095–7, 1113–4, and also 1199–1282; see 773–80, 885–90). He buries the dead Polyneices and then goes to release the imprisoned Antigone. Indeed, when Creon discovers that Antigone is dead, and his own son attempts to kill him, and then successfully kills himself, Creon is so convinced of his own guilt in having violated the divine law, acted unjustly to the family, and angered the gods – and perhaps also impressed by Teiresias's prediction that, before long, the gods would punish him by killing his son – that he blames *himself* for his son's attempted patricide (1177–8, 1261–76, 1339–41; consider as well 1206–20; but see also 1064–7, 762–5). After his wife curses him as a killer of children and then kills herself, Creon condemns his own actions against the family in the strongest possible terms, as unjust and impious, while expressing no concern at all for the well-being of the city (1283–1353). After his quarrel with his son, then, Creon's return to traditional, familial piety is rapid and complete.

Yet it is precisely Creon's return to traditional, familial piety that destroys him. Once he resolves to yield entirely to Teiresias, Creon apparently decides, at the urging of the chorus, first to free the living Antigone and then to bury the dead Polyneices (1099–1112). However, after affirming the importance of following divine law – "For I fear it may be best to complete one's life preserving the established laws" (1113–15) – Creon evidently changes his mind and decides first to bury the dead Polyneices and then to free the living Antigone (1196–1282). This decision is disastrous, for he arrives too late to save Antigone. Had he arrived in time, the suicides of Antigone, Haemon, and Eurydice would not have taken place, Antigone and Haemon presumably would have gotten married, and Creon presumably would have continued to rule, albeit chastened by his experiences. Why, then, did Creon decide to bury the dead corpse before going to release the living girl? It would seem that he did so out of his devotion to the divine law and his fear of the gods' wrath. For it is the divine law, it is piety itself, that emphasizes the importance of honoring the dead more than the living and the importance of the next life over this life.[48] Teiresias, for

---

[48] Lacan notes that Creon "begins with the corpse" because he wants "to come to terms with his conscience" (1997, 266).

example, had insisted that Creon bury the corpse of Polyneices, had not referred at all to Antigone initially, and later had only vaguely hinted that Creon should free Antigone (1015–20, 1029–30, 1064–71).[49] Similarly, Antigone herself had insisted that, by sacrificing her life to bury the corpse of Polyneices, she was fulfilling the divine laws of Zeus and Justice (450–70). Creon's actions here are exactly in the spirit of Teiresias and Antigone. And they lead to his destruction. Like Antigone, Creon places greater importance on the corpse than on the living. And like Antigone, he is destroyed. The play, then, bears witness not only to the tremendous power, but also to the destructive power, of piety.

Nonetheless, even though Creon is destroyed by his return to the divine law, it was clearly a mistake for him to defy the divine law by forbidding the burial of the corpse of Polyneices. Creon believed that, by terrifying the citizens with the cruel spectacle of the traitor's rotting corpse, he could inflame their fear of death and deter any of them from fomenting strife within the city. But this attempt to impress on the Thebans that they are mortal, and hence must faithfully obey their mighty ruler, backfires. It provokes a pious reaction in Antigone, in Teiresias, and ultimately, if not initially, in the rest of the city as well – a zealous insistence that death is not the end, that we are not limited by our natural mortality, and that there are supernatural gods who have it in their power to confer immortality upon us and to reward and punish us well beyond this life (consider 278–9, 1091–1107). And so powerful is this pious longing for immortality in the human heart that it finally engulfs Creon as well. The play suggests that rulers must never underestimate the power of the pious longing and hope for immortality and that they must generally accommodate such passion rather than defy it. Prudence dictates that Creon should have permitted the burial of Polyneices, even though he was a traitor.

More broadly, the play suggests that it is futile to hope, as Creon did, that the political community can ever be secured against the threat of anarchy. Precisely given the power of pious sentiment, anarchy is, in some measure, inevitable. For piety, while inevitable in the city, always threatens to undermine the city. Indeed, as the scene between Creon

---

[49] I consequently disagree with Segal's assertion that Teiresias urges Creon to save Antigone first (1981, 176).

and Haemon demonstrates, piety threatens to undermine the family as well. The belief that the gods reward and punish us in this life, as well as in the next, and hence that they are the true rulers of human beings, inevitably weakens the authority of all human rulers. Accordingly, Antigone invokes the gods to justify her defiance of her king and uncle Creon, and Haemon invokes the gods to justify his defiance of his king and father Creon. Indeed, the fact that Haemon proceeds to threaten and then attempt to kill his father suggests just how far piety may undermine the family. For when Creon states that it is "all-evil" of his son to fight with his father, Haemon responds that it is just to fight with an unjust and impious father (742–5). But if it is just to fight with an impious father, might it not be just to kill such a father (746–52, 1220–39)? More broadly, the belief in the gods empowers the naturally weak to rise up against the strong. It inspires subjects to rebel against rulers, women against men, sons against fathers, the blind against those with sight. While the play, then, stresses the need to accommodate piety, it also highlights the explosively anarchic power of piety.

CONCLUSION

On the surface, the *Antigone* vindicates piety. Creon is punished for having violated the divine law and, though Antigone dies in her attempt to uphold that law, her death is avenged. Upon closer examination, however, the play reveals that both Creon and Antigone are destroyed by their piety. Creon fails to rescue Antigone because he places more importance on burying the dead than on saving the living. Antigone kills herself before she is rescued because she places insufficient trust in the human love of Haemon. A certain misanthropy implicit in piety – a certain diminution of human beings in the light of the superhuman gods – deprives each of them of a human happiness still within their grasp.

Yet, of the two, it is only Antigone who truly comes to wrestle with the question of piety and justice in the course of the play. By the end of the play, she begins at least to face the questions of whether her actions were just, pious, and wise, whether justice truly means devotion to the family, whether she was right to sacrifice earthly happiness for the sake of happiness in an afterlife, and whether it is wise or even possible to live primarily for others. Creon never exposes himself to such questioning. He is either adamantly confident that justice means devotion to the city or adamantly confident that justice means devotion to the family. The moment before he begins to yield to Haemon, Creon threatens to execute his fiancée before his eyes (758–61, 770–80). The moment before he completely yields to Teiresias, he bitterly denounces him as one who "loves to do injustice" (1059; see 1033–63, 1091–1114). Creon lacks the strength to face uncertainty. Just as he believes that "there is no greater evil than anarchy" (672) in the city or in the family, so he believes that there is no greater evil than anarchy within one's soul. But it is only if one is willing to experience such anarchy in one's soul, to wonder which beliefs are true and hence truly deserve to rule one's soul and one's life, that one has any hope of discovering the truth and of living a life based on the truth. Antigone demonstrates her superiority to Creon by daring to expose herself to the anarchic experience of wonder. Rather than simply clinging to, or simply jettisoning, her most cherished convictions about justice and about the possibility of happiness, as Creon does, she genuinely questions them. In her willingness to wonder about justice and piety, Antigone proves to be stronger, more courageous, more "manly," than Creon.[50]

[50] Knox maintains that Antigone "goes to her death unrepentant," that "she never retreats," and even that her suicide "too is defiant," since it triggers the suicides of Haemon and Eurydice which strike Creon down (1964, 62, 64, 67, 26). Knox's claim that Antigone killed herself with the intention of punishing Creon through the deaths of his wholly innocent son and wife is bewildering, given his assertion that Antigone's deepest motive is not hatred but love (116). But, in any case, Knox never presents any textual evidence for this claim about why she killed herself. Even though Knox concedes that Antigone experiences at least some self-doubt before her death, he tends to overstate her intransigence and tends simply to identify her heroic grandeur – indeed, all heroic grandeur – with intransigence (103–7; but see also 113). Antigone is the true hero because, unlike Creon, she "stands her ground and goes, still defiant, to her death" (62; see also 67–68). "The hero refuses to yield" (17). This "intransigence" is the defining characteristic of all Sophocles' heroes, who are modeled on Achilles, who "refuses harshly and bitterly" "to relent" (9, 51; see 8–27, 50–52). Knox consequently overlooks Antigone's impressive willingness genuinely to question herself, as well as Achilles' own willingness to question himself and even to yield in response to Priam's plea for compassion and understanding.

Through the character of Antigone in particular, the play invites the audience to think through the ultimate consequences of their beliefs about justice and piety. It invites the audience to go further along the path of doubt and questioning followed most clearly by Antigone. In this way, the play invites us to ascend from the pious heroism of Antigone to the humane wisdom of Sophocles.

Conclusion

Nietzsche, Plato, and Aristotle on Philosophy and Tragedy

Tragedy and philosophy appear to be natural enemies. By showing that the greatest human beings may suffer terrible misfortune, unjustly, and for reasons beyond our comprehension, tragedy seems to teach us that the world is out of joint, that it is fundamentally indifferent or hostile to our efforts to achieve happiness, justice, and understanding, and hence that it is fundamentally at odds with our deepest desires. Philosophy, on the other hand, seems to teach that the pursuit of wisdom through reason alone is the greatest good for a human being, that reason is therefore capable of both understanding the world and of guiding us to happiness, and hence that the world is, at the very least, not opposed to our deepest desires. It is not surprising, then, that Socrates, the hero and in a sense the founder of the philosophic tradition, as a tradition of moral and political philosophy, would denounce "the tragic life" as one that is surrounded by a multitude of lies (*Cratylus* 408c7–8) and would insist that Homer, "the most poetic and first of the tragic poets," be expelled from the most just political society, the one ruled by philosopher–kings (*Republic* 607a2–3).[1]

[1] As Lear puts it, "Plato treats acquaintance with Homer and the great Greek tragedians as a psychological catastrophe" (1997, 62). In Naddaff's words, Socrates desires "to rewrite Homer's epics as atragic" (2002, 42). See also Annas 1981, 96–101, 338–44; Halliwell 1996, 347. Nussbaum argues that, in the *Republic*, Plato criticizes "tragic values" but also claims that he recanted "aspects of his former criticism" later in his life (1986, 83; see as well 1992, 269). Euben goes so far as to argue that, in important ways, "the *Republic* is the last Greek tragedy" (1990, 269).

And it is not surprising that, when Nietzsche launched his attack on the tradition of philosophy, he did so in the name of tragedy.[2]

Yet, are philosophy and tragedy necessarily enemies? After all, even though Nietzsche attacks Socratic philosophy in the name of tragedy, he also calls himself a philosopher, indeed "the first *tragic philosopher*" (1969, 273 – emphasis in text). In the *Gay Science*, he suggests that *Thus Spoke Zarathustra*, which he regarded as his greatest work, is a tragedy (1974, 274; see also 347; 1969, 219–20).

Furthermore, even though Socrates issues a devastating attack on tragic poetry in the *Republic*, there are reasons for wondering whether that attack is as unconditional as it first seems. For example, in Book X, Socrates argues that Homer, "the first teacher and leader of all these fine tragic things" (595c1–2), evidently lacks wisdom because he had no followers. "But Glaucon, if Homer were really able to educate human beings, and make them better because he is in these things capable not of imitating but of knowing, do you think that he wouldn't have made many companions and been honored and cherished by them?" (600c2–6).[3] Yet the very fact that, as Socrates says, Homer was the "teacher and leader of all these fine tragic things" (595c1–2) and of tragedy itself (598d7-e2), and that he was "the most poetic and first of the tragic poets" (607a2–3), invites one to wonder whether the tragic poets – poets of such quality as Aeschylus, Sophocles, and Euripides – were not followers of Homer and hence whether Homer may not have been, in accordance with Socrates' own criterion, wise. This thought is also supported by what Socrates says in the *Apology*. There he declares that the tragic poets "know nothing of what they speak" (22a8-c6). But he also goes on to affirm that "to associate with," among others, "Orpheus and Musaeus and Hesiod and Homer" forever in Hades would be an "inconceivable happiness" (41a6-c4). Is it not reasonable to wonder, then, whether Socrates truly held the wisdom of Homer and the other tragic poets in such low esteem?

While Socrates issues a devastating attack on tragic poetry in the *Republic*, he also admits there that he has always loved such poetry,

---

[2] As Heidegger observes, "Experience of the tragic and meditation on its origin and essence pertain to the very basis of Nietzschean thought" (1991, 28–9).

[3] The translations from the *Republic* in this chapter follow Bloom 1991.

"since childhood," and declares that he would be "delighted" and "glad" to hear a persuasive defense of it (595b9-c3, 606e1–608a5; see also 388e2–3; compare as well *Apology of Socrates* 22a8-c8 with 40e4–41c8). The philosopher Aristotle seems to supply just such a defense. For he argues that tragedy is itself philosophic, that it plays an important and even a crucial role in leading the soul to philosophy. The question arises, then, whether philosophy and tragedy are truly at odds. Is the teaching of tragedy as bleak as it first seems to be? Is the teaching of philosophy as hopeful?

NIETZSCHE: THE COURAGEOUS TRUTHFULNESS OF THE TRAGIC HUMAN BEING

Nietzsche praises tragedy above all for its courage in the face of the truth. Philosophers since Socrates believe, as the very term "philosophy" – "love of wisdom" – implies, that the truth is loveable, and hence that the truth about the world is beautiful and comforting. They believe that the world is a cosmos rather than a chaos, that nature is friendly to man and welcoming of his longing for wisdom and justice and happiness, if he will only free his mind from the delusions of mere convention and live according to nature. But this belief, Nietzsche insists, is itself a delusion: "'According to nature' you want to *live*? . . . what deceptive words these are! Imagine a being like nature, wasteful beyond measure, indifferent beyond measure, without purposes and consideration, without mercy and justice, fertile and desolate and uncertain at the same time; imagine indifference itself as a power – how *could* you live according to this indifference? Living – is this not precisely wanting to be other than this nature?" (1989, 15 – emphases in the text). Now philosophers, at least Socratic philosophers, cannot bear to face the cruel indifference of nature to our moral and philosophic longings. Although such philosophers may dimly recognize the harshness of the truth they ostensibly love – and hence though it may be true that "every philosophy was in its genesis a long tragedy" (1989, 37) – philosophers nonetheless recoil from that insight. Plato, for example, "is a coward before reality" (1954a, 558–9). Accordingly, philosophy unself-consciously and self-deceptively imposes its

comforting moralities and ideals on chaotic nature and thereby "creates
the world in its own image" (1989, 16). But the tragic human
being faces the true chaos of the world unblinkingly, or at least as
unblinkingly as is possible for a human being. For "it might be a
basic characteristic of existence that those who would know it completely would perish, in which case the strength of a spirit should be
measured according to how much of the 'truth' one could still barely
endure" (49).

One might think that the tragic human being's willingness to face
such deadly truth is madness. Doesn't such truthfulness destroy all
possibility of human well-being and flourishing? As Nietzsche himself
asks, "*What* in us really wants 'truth' . . . Suppose we want truth: *why
not rather* untruth? and uncertainty? even ignorance?*" If nature truly is
so thoroughly indifferent to us, must we not conclude that ignorance of
this truth is "a condition of life and growth" (1989, 9, 101–2 –
emphases in text)?

Nietzsche suggests, however, that, while facing the truth, a truth
that may be "harmful and dangerous to the highest degree," may cause
one boundless suffering and misery, facing the truth, as the tragic man
does, may therefore ennoble human beings (1989, 49). For "Profound
suffering makes noble." . . . "[I]t almost determines the order of rank
how profoundly human beings can suffer" (220 – emphasis in text). The
alternative to noble suffering, according to Nietzsche, is not noble
contentment but rather "the universal green-pasture happiness of the
herd, with security, lack of danger, comfort, and an easier life for
everyone" (54). Nietzsche attacks those who follow "hedonism" and
"eudamonism" as follows: "You want, if possible – and there is no more
insane 'if possible' – *to abolish suffering*. And we? It really seems that *we*
would rather have it higher and worse than ever. Well-being as you
understand it – that is no goal, that seems to us an *end*, a state that soon
makes man ridiculous and contemptible – that makes his destruction
desirable. The discipline of suffering, of *great* suffering – do you not
know that only *this* discipline has created all enhancements of man so
far? That tension of the soul in unhappiness which cultivates its
strength, its shudders, face to face with great ruin, its inventiveness and
courage in enduring, persevering, interpreting, and exploiting mask,
spirit, cunning, greatness – was it not granted to it through suffering,

through the discipline of great suffering?" (153–4 – emphases in text). Nietzsche suggests here that, through the anguish of facing the ugly and painful truth about the world and its indifference to man, and above all through the heroic sacrifice of happiness and well-being that such courageous truthfulness entails, the tragic human being affirms his humanity and makes himself noble.

Yet Nietzsche also suggests that the tragic human being is not shattered by the spectacle of cosmic indifference, but even ultimately takes pleasure from it. Indeed, "The tragic man affirms even the harshest suffering: he is sufficiently strong, rich, and capable of deifying to do so" (1968, 543).[4] The true experience of tragedy, then, is not pity for the tragic hero or terror that one might suffer the hero's fate or horror at the harsh indifference of the world to man; it is rather an austerely satisfying feeling of power and pleasure in one's courage to face and to affirm "the terror and horror of existence" (1967, 42). "*Pleasure* in tragedy characterizes *strong* ages and natures: their *non plus ultra* is perhaps the *divina commedia*. It is the heroic spirits who say Yes to themselves in tragic cruelty: they are hard enough to experience suffering as a *pleasure*" (1968, 450 – emphases in text).[5] "The psychology of the orgiastic as an overflowing feeling of life and strength, where even pain still has the effect of a stimulus, gave me the key to the concept of *tragic* feeling, which has been misunderstood by Aristotle . . . Not in order to be liberated from terror and pity, not in order to purge oneself of a dangerous affect by its vehement discharge – Aristotle understood it that way – but in order to be oneself the eternal joy of becoming, beyond all terror and pity – that joy which included even the joy in destroying" (1954a, 562–3 – emphasis in text). This tragic joy or satisfaction in not only observing but also in willing the suffering of others and of oneself amounts, Nietzsche acknowledges, to a pleasure in

---

[4] Consider also 1974, 219: "*What makes one heroic?* – Going out to meet at the same time one's highest suffering and one's highest hope" (emphasis in text).

[5] In Heidegger's words, "Tragedy prevails where the terrifying is affirmed as the opposite that is intrinsically proper to the beautiful. Greatness and great heights subsist together with the depths and with what is terrifying; the more originally the one is willed, the more surely the other will be attained" (1991, 29).

cruelty. "What constitutes the painful voluptuousness of tragedy is cruelty; what seems agreeable in so-called tragic pity, and at bottom in everything sublime, up to the highest and most delicate shudders of metaphysics, receives its sweetness solely from the admixture of cruelty." Inasmuch as the world is indifferent to the deepest longings of our hearts and minds – for happiness and justice and wisdom – and inasmuch as the tragic human being not only has the courage to face the truth about the world, but also takes pleasure in facing that truth, the pleasure he takes must entail a pleasure in inflicting pain upon himself. "Finally, consider that even the seeker after knowledge forces his mind to recognize things against the inclination of the mind, and often enough also against the wishes of his heart – by way of saying No where he would like to say Yes, love, and adore – and thus acts as a transfigurer of cruelty. Indeed, any insistence on profundity and thoroughness is a violation, a desire to hurt the basic will of the mind which unceasingly strives for the apparent and superficial – in all desire to know there is a drop of cruelty" (1989, 158–9). While Nietzsche, then, attacks the *Socratic* tradition of philosophy in the name of tragedy, he makes it clear that the core of the *genuinely* philosophic, truth-seeking experience is identical to the core of the experience of tragedy: the noble courage and strength to face the painful truth and the austere and even cruel pleasure in forcing oneself to face the truth.[6]

SOCRATES: THE SOFTNESS OF THE TRAGIC HEROES

In his famous attack on the tragic poets in the *Republic*, Plato's Socrates apparently agrees with Nietzsche that, by portraying the greatest human beings as suffering beings, tragedy teaches that the world is fundamentally hostile to our aspirations for happiness. Yet, while Nietzsche claims that tragedy inspires hardness and courage among human beings by encouraging us to face "the terror and horror of

---

[6] As Heidegger explains in his account of Nietzsche's thought, "The tragic holds sway only where the 'spirit' rules, so much that it is only in the realm of knowledge and of *knowers* that the supremely tragic can occur" (1991, 30 – my emphasis).

existence," Socrates contends that tragedy inspires softness and even cowardice. At the beginning of Book III, after citing seven passages from the *Iliad* (4) and the *Odyssey* (3) in which Achilles, the goddess Circe, and Homer himself describe the nature of death and the afterlife, Socrates remarks: "We'll beg Homer and the other poets not to be harsh if we strike out these and all similar things. It's not that they are not poetic and sweet for the many to hear, but the more poetic they are, the less should they be heard by boys and men who must be free and accustomed to fearing slavery more than death . . . . Perhaps they're good for something else, but we fear that our guardians, as a result of such shivers, will get hotter and softer than they ought" (387b1-c5). Socrates then declares: "So we'd be right in taking out the wailings of renowned men and we'd give them to women – and not to the serious ones, at that – and to all the bad men" (387e9–388a1; see also 381e1–6). And he proceeds to cite passages from the *Iliad* that represent Achilles bewailing the death of his friend Patroclus, Priam the death of his son Hector, the goddess Thetis the imminent death of her son Achilles, and Zeus the imminent deaths of Hector and of Zeus's own son Sarpedon (388a5-d1). Socrates suggests that the tragic poets' description of the human condition is so terrifying, and their accounts of their heroes' and gods' sorrow over the death of their loved ones are so moving and so infectious, that they inspire us, their audience, with an overpowering fear and grief, and teach us that such fear and grief are proper responses to our mortal condition.[7] In contrast to Nietzsche, then, Socrates suggests that the manly and courageous spirit of tragic human beings is simply shattered by the tragic vision of life.

Yet Socrates' claim about the effects of tragedy is perplexing since his discussion centers on Achilles, to whom Nietzsche, for example, refers as "the greatest hero" (1967, 43). What can he possibly mean by suggesting that Achilles is soft and unmanly? Is this not a preposterous charge against the hero most famous for his courage?

---

[7] As Halliwell remarks, the tragic heroes embody "a sense of life which makes grief an imperative" (1996, 344). Naddaff goes so far as to claim that Socrates censors Homer "To create a truly masculine *aner*, a manly man without feminine traces" (2002, 46).

Socrates' account of tragedy focuses on Homer, the "leader" of
tragedy (*Republic* 598d8) and "the most poetic and first of the tragic
poets" (607a2–3; see also 595b9-c2, 605c10-d5). The context of
Socrates' discussion of Homer and the other tragic poets is the education of the guardians or rulers of a just city, guardians whose "nature" is
at least initially described here as "philosophic, spirited, swift, and
strong" (376b11-c5) and who will ultimately dwell in a city ruled by
philosopher–kings. His fundamental criticism of Homer and the other
tragic poets is that they would make such human beings unreasonably
soft and cowardly by filling them with fear.

In the first place, Homer and the tragedians inspire their audience to
fear the gods. For Homer depicts the gods as powerful and angry
beings, who inflict harm on one another as well as on human beings,
and he depicts his greatest hero, Achilles, as expressing a fear of the
gods. Socrates insists:

"We mustn't accept Homer's – or any other poet's . . . saying that
    Two jars stand on Zeus's threshold
    Full of dooms – the one of good,
        the other of wretched;
and the man to whom Zeus gives a mixture of both,
    At one time he happens on evil,
        at another good;
but the man to whom he doesn't give a mixture, but the second pure,
    Evil misery, drives him over the divine
        earth;
nor that Zeus is a dispenser to us
    Of good and evil alike" (379c9–e2)
And:
    "as Aeschylus says, that
    God plants the cause in mortals
    When he wants to destroy a house utterly" (380a1–4).

Moreover, the poets terrify us from childhood on by teaching that
the gods deceive us, that they are ubiquitous, but hide this fact, for
"The gods, like wandering strangers, Take on every sort of shape and
visit the cities" (381d3–4). The tragic poets present us with a world in
which we are always at the mercy of the gods, in which, at any moment,

they may suddenly ruin our happiness by destroying all that we hold
dear. And by presenting their heroes as being afraid of such ruin, the
tragedians suggest that fear of the gods is the proper response to the
world on the part of even the greatest of humans.

Socrates argues that the poets should instead teach that, since the gods
are perfect, they must be unchanging, self-sufficient, and uninvolved in
human affairs and hence must not punish or even reward us. The guardians, then, must accept specifically that the evils humans suffer are not
caused by the gods (see 379a7-c7, 380c6–381c2, 382e8–383a5).
Socrates concludes his discussion of what the guardians should be taught
about the gods by stating that the poets' depiction of the gods must be
expunged, "if our guardians are going to be god-revering and divine
insofar as a human being can possibly be" (383c3–5). Socrates reveals
here that the goal of the education of the philosophic guardians is to
make them as divine as possible and hence, it seems, as fearless and as
self-sufficient as the immortal gods themselves. And by suggesting that
the guardians are philosophic, Socrates seems to suggest that it is reasonable for human beings as a whole to strive to achieve a god-like self-
sufficiency and to believe that such happiness is within their grasp.[8]

But, a defender of the poets might ask, how reasonable is it for
mortal beings to model themselves on divine beings? As Homer's
Achilles points out, the gods are immortal and therefore "are free from
care" (*Iliad* 24.526). But precisely inasmuch as we human beings are
not immortal, is it not reasonable for us to be fearful, and to fear above
all the death that we and our loved ones must suffer? If happiness is
possible for such beings as ourselves, must it not incorporate an
awareness of the evil of death and hence a fear of death?

The fear of the gods inspired, according to Socrates, by the tragic
poets is rooted in our fear of death. We fear the gods specifically because
we fear the death they may inflict on our loved ones and ourselves.
Socrates accordingly proceeds to criticize Homer for teaching that
"Hades' domain exists and is terrible" (386b4) and for presenting his
greatest heroes as men who are terrified of death, their own and that of
their loved ones. For do you suppose anyone who believes this, Socrates
asks, "will be fearless in the face of death and choose death in battles

---

[8] As Nussbaum puts it in her account of the *Republic*, "We should imitate beings
who are completely without merely human needs and interests (1986, 158).

above defeat and slavery?" (386b4–6). The belief that death is an evil, for oneself and for those one loves, Socrates affirms, renders even the greatest human beings so soft and so cowardly that they will prefer slavery to death (see 387c3–5).

Yet the Homeric heroes that Socrates refers to here – Sarpedon, Odysseus, Priam, Hector, and above all Achilles – were clearly not cowards in battle, even though they all apparently believed that death was an evil. They were all clearly willing to fight and die rather than run away. In what sense does Socrates mean to suggest that they were soft?[9]

Socrates may mean to suggest that the Homeric heroes are soft, not because they are led by their fear of death to run away in battle, but because, rather than resigning themselves to their mortality and accept the hard truth that death is an inevitable evil, they are led by their fear of death to hope that the gods may protect them and their loved ones from that evil. For, as the passages Socrates cites and refers to here indicate, the gods depicted by Homer and the other tragic poets are not only angry and terrifying; they can also be loving and beneficent beings. Zeus loves Hector and his son Sarpedon. The goddess Thetis loves her son Achilles. Apollo protects his priest Chryses. And Zeus dispenses good to human beings as well as evil (388b8-d1, 392e2–394a7, 379c9-e2; consider as well 363a6-e3, 364c5–365a3). Furthermore, Socrates suggests through the passages he cites that, according to Homer and the tragic poets, the gods do protect some human beings from the evil of death. It is true that, in the seven passages Socrates cites at the beginning of Book III, the second one presents the judgment of Hades himself, the god of the underworld, that his domain is hateful to gods and men, and the fifth one presents the soul of Patroclus bewailing his death as he descends into Hades (386d1–2, 9–10). But it is also true that, in the third passage cited, Achilles concludes, after dreaming of Patroclus, that there is life after death, that the dead resemble the living, and that, specifically, his beloved Patroclus lives on in the House of Hades, in an afterlife, as a soul and a phantom, albeit without intelligence (386d4–5). To be sure, the dead Achilles is presented in the first passage declaring that he would rather live as a serf than be ruler over the dead (386c5–7). But the very section of the *Odyssey*

---

[9] The ensuing discussion of Socrates and Homer owes much to Bolotin 1995.

alluded to there presents Achilles in company with his beloved Patroclus and capable of taking pleasure in the news of the heroism of his still living son (11.465–540). Furthermore, the section of the *Odyssey* alluded to in the seventh passage cited by Socrates presents Achilles in seemingly pleasant conversation with Patroclus, Ajax, and Agamemnon (387a5–8; *Odyssey* 24.15–204). Finally, and perhaps most importantly, in the fourth and central citation of Socrates, the goddess Circe reveals to Odysseus that Teiresias lives on after death with intelligence (*Odyssey* 10.490–95). The poets, then, do not simply present death as an evil, but also offer hope for an afterlife of eternal well-being.[10] So Socrates may mean to suggest that the tragic, Homeric heroes are soft because they do not accept death as a natural necessity but regard it as an avoidable evil, and hope that the gods may rescue them from it. He may mean to suggest that the poets encourage us to be soft by encouraging us, not to run away in battle, but to hope that the gods may save us, and those we love, from the evil of death. Socrates' criticism of tragedy, then, may be this: by teaching that death is a terrible evil, tragedy teaches that human happiness is unattainable through our own efforts and that therefore our only hope for human happiness lies with the gods. For only they can possibly protect us and our loved ones from the evil of death. The seemingly bleak vision set forth by the tragic poets and their heroes is not simply bleak. It contains hope, a pious hope that Socrates suggests is unreasonable, self-indulgent, and soft.[11]

The suggestion that tragedy is fundamentally pious may seem surprising. At first glance, tragedy would seem to be at odds with piety, since heroic men do not deserve to suffer, and it would seem that, if

---

[10] See also Adeimantus's account of poets' claims that the gods grant eternal well-being to some humans – 363a6–e3, 364d3–365a3 – as well as Cephalus's haunting account of the poets' portrayal of the afterlife at 330d4–331b7; consider also *Odyssey* 11, 601–26.

[11] While I agree with Halliwell's suggestion that, in the *Republic*, Plato warns against "tragedy's tendency to deposit a corrosive pessimism about *human* possibilities," I do not agree with his claim that, in Plato's view, the mind of the tragic hero is "condemned by its own beliefs to abandoning any hope that its highest endeavours could be meaningfully satisfied by the world" (1996, 346 – my emphasis).

there are gods who care for us, if there are providential gods, they would not permit such suffering. Yet, Socrates suggests that, while tragedies may seem to call into question the existence of divine providence, they more emphatically teach us our need for divine providence. For, precisely if even great human beings suffer terrible things, is not the lot of human beings, when left on our own, a miserable one? Is man not miserable without God? And does this thought not inspire in us the longing to believe in gods who care for us, in gods who constitute our only hope for a relief from evils? Does it not inspire in us the hope that, beneath or beyond the surface of a world without providence, there is a providential order whose mysterious workings are not yet revealed to us, but whose existence our heartfelt longing for happiness points to?

Yet if Socrates means to suggest that the proper response to our mortality and that of our loved ones is not fear of death and hope that the gods may protect us from it, but resignation before the inevitability of death, one must wonder, why is such resignation reasonable? How can such resignation in the face of terrible evil be compatible with a happy or even a tolerable life? Socrates argues that the poets should teach that men who are decent will never lament or wail in the face of death because "for the decent man . . . being dead is not a terrible thing" (387d5–6). He suggests here that it is only possible to accept death without fear if one believes that death is not an evil. Yet Socrates offers no argument here for his contention that death is not an evil. He does, however, offer a second reason that the decent man will not lament or wail in the fact of death. The decent man "is most of all sufficient unto himself for living well and, in contrast to others, has least need of another" (387d11–e1). Since the decent man needs others less than other human beings, he is more self-sufficient than other humans. The happiness of the decent man is as self-sufficient as it is possible for human happiness to be. The decent man, then, evidently strives to be as self-sufficient as the gods.

Yet even the decent man is not truly self-sufficient. "Then for him it is least terrible to be deprived of a son, or a brother, or money, or of anything else of the sort . . . . Then he laments the least and bears it most gently when some such misfortune overtakes him" (387e3–7). Even the decent man, then, laments the loss of a loved one. But must he not consequently fear the death of a loved one, albeit less than other humans do? Furthermore, must he not fear his own death as an evil?

Finally, insofar as the self-sufficiency strived for by the decent man is not wholly achievable for human beings, is it a reasonable goal? Is the price of striving not to need others, and hence not to love others, a price worth paying for such beings as ourselves? Is there not something shallow and sterile about a life without loved ones?

After referring to Homer's moving representations of Achilles' grief over the death of Patroclus, Priam's grief over the death of his son Hector, Thetis's grief over the death of her son Achilles, Zeus's grief over the death of Hector, and Zeus's grief over the death of his son Sarpedon, Socrates remarks to his companion: "For, my dear Adeimantus, if our young should seriously hear such things and not laugh scornfully at them as unworthy speeches, it's not very likely that any one of them would believe these things to be unworthy of himself, a human being, and would reproach himself for them, if it should enter into his head to say or do such thing. Rather, with neither shame nor endurance, he would chant many dirges and laments at the slightest sufferings" (388d2–7). Socrates suggests that a decent human being should not only feel little grief over the death of a loved one but should laugh scornfully at the grief of Achilles over Patroclus and Priam over Hector. The decent man should find such grief so unreasonable that it seems ridiculous, a subject of comedy rather than tragedy. Socrates speaks here as though the model for a decent and reasonable human being is the young Cephalus, who laughs at the tales of Hades when he is young (330d7–e2; see 328c7–d4, 329b2–d5). But how reasonable is such a frivolous, heartless, and uncomprehending view of the grief of others? Furthermore, how sustainable is such laughter at death? After all, the very Cephalus who laughs at the tales of Hades when he is young is terrified by those tales when he himself is on the threshold of death (330d7–331a1; see also 328c1–3, 331d6–9). Is the light-hearted resignation of the young philosophic guardian described by Socrates not bought at the price of an inhuman and foolish blindness to the evil of death? Is the grief of an Achilles or Priam not closer to reason than the laughter of such a Cephalus-like guardian, at least insofar as Achilles and Priam recognize the genuine evil of death?

Socrates returns to his criticism of the tragic poets' depiction of the sorrows of their heroes in Book X. There, however, he himself stresses that the decent man will indeed grieve at the death of a loved one, just as the tragic poets teach, but that the decent man will do so only in private (603d5–604a8). Socrates acknowledges, then, that the tragic poets reveal the truth about the sorrows of the decent in the face of the evil of death. The poets, it seems, reveal the truth about the evil of death and the sorrows of the human condition.[12] But Socrates criticizes the poets for weakening our courage and reason by encouraging us to lament openly rather than suppress our grief. The tragic poet "awakens this [grieving] part of the soul and nourishes it, and, by making it strong, destroys the calculating part . . . When even the best of us hears Homer or any other of the tragic poets imitating one of the heroes in mourning and making quite an extended speech in lamentation, or, if you like, singing and beating his breast, you know that we enjoy it and that we give ourselves over to following the imitation; suffering along with the hero in all seriousness, we praise as a good poet the man who puts us in this state . . . . But when personal sorrow comes to one of us, you are aware that, on the contrary, we pride ourselves if we are able to keep quiet and bear up, taking this to be the part of a man and what we then praised to be that of a woman . . . . [W]hat is then held down by force in our own misfortunes and has hungered for tears and sufficient lament and satisfaction . . . is that which now gets satisfaction and enjoyment from the poets. What is by nature best in us, because it hasn't been adequately educated by argument or habit, relaxes its guard over this mournful part because it sees another's sufferings" (605b3–606b1).

Socrates' criticism here is that, by portraying openly and truthfully the private sorrows of decent human beings, of the human condition, tragic poets weaken our capacity to suppress our own sorrows by force and thereby weaken or even destroy our capacity to reason. Yet, while it is certainly true that one cannot think clearly about the world and about oneself when one is overwhelmed with sorrow, it would also seem to be true that one cannot think clearly about the world and about oneself

[12] I therefore think that Nussbaum goes too far when she claims, without qualification, of the *Republic*: "Plato's argument, repeatedly, is that correct beliefs about what is and what is not important in human life remove our reasons for fear" (1986, 386). See also her claim that "for Socrates a good person cannot be harmed" (1992, 268).

without facing the truth about the evil of death and the sorrows of our mortal condition. Would not a genuinely reasonable, philosophic life have to face this hard truth as the tragic poets encourage us to do?

Socrates goes on to suggest that it is the political community, speaking through the law, that demands that human beings hide their grief in the face of death on the grounds that "the human things" are not "worthy of great seriousness" (604b9-c1). The law demands that humans sacrifice their well-being, their friends and children, for example, for the sake of the community, and that they not regard such sacrifice seriously, as a serious loss. But, as Socrates himself acknowledges, the loss of loved ones is a real loss, as the poets point out, however much men may try to hide that loss. The demand that one not regard such sacrifice as a serious sacrifice is therefore not reasonable. But furthermore, how reasonable is it for a human being not to take "the human things," and hence, for example, our mortal nature and condition, seriously? In Plato's *Phaedo*, Socrates himself, on the day of his own death, declares that philosophers "themselves practice nothing but dying and being dead" (64a4–6). In this way, he suggests that reflection on death is at the center of the philosopher's activity. Are the tragedians, then, not right to encourage us to take death seriously, according to Socrates?

In Book X of the *Republic*, Socrates goes on to assert that death is not an evil for humans, that the soul is immortal, and that the good enjoy an everlasting happiness (608c1–621d3). In this way, he seems to end the dialogue by rejecting entirely the somber view of life set forth by the tragic poets. But, even leaving aside the question of whether any afterlife could be simply happy for such beings as ourselves (consider Aristotle, *Nicomachean Ethics* 1099b32–1100a30, 1101a22–1101b9), the claim that there is an afterlife in which the good are rewarded is an unproven assertion or myth, as Socrates himself acknowledges here, as well as in the *Phaedo* (*Republic* 611a10–612a5; *Phaedo* 63b5-c4, 84c5–7, 86d5-e4, 91a1-b7, 106c9-e7, 107a8-b9). The tragic portrayal of the evil of death, and of the sorrows of human beings in the face of death, then, would seem to be truthful. Are the tragic poets not right to draw our attention to the truth of our mortality and to the sadness such mortality bequeaths to any human life? Must the lover of wisdom not face that unlovely truth?

The *Republic* indicates that Socrates is indeed aware that the wisdom the philosopher seeks encompasses painful and ugly truths and hence that the austere capacity to endure pain is necessary for the philosophic life. To be sure, Socrates stresses in the dialogue the erotic character of the love of wisdom, and thereby suggests that the wisdom the philosopher pursues is simply and wholly beautiful, "an overwhelming beauty" (474b4–476d7, 485d3-e1, 508d4–509a7). But in the image of the cave, Socrates suggests that the philosopher must, at least initially, be *compelled* to seek wisdom. "Take a man who is released and suddenly compelled to stand up, to turn his neck around, to walk and look up toward the light; and who, moreover, in doing all this is in pain and, because he is dazzled, is unable to make out those things whose shadows he saw before. What do you suppose he'd say if someone were to tell him that before he saw silly nothings, while now, because he is somewhat nearer to what is, and more turned toward beings, he sees more correctly; and, in particular, showing him each of the things that pass by, were to compel the man to answer his questions about what they are? Don't you suppose he'd be at a loss and believe that what was seen before is truer than what is now shown? . . . And, if he compelled him to look at the light itself, would his eyes hurt and would he flee, turning away to those things that he is able to make out and hold them to be really clearer than what is being shown? . . . And if . . . someone dragged him away from there by force along the rough, steep, upward way and didn't let him go before he had dragged him out into the light of the sun, wouldn't he be distressed and annoyed at being so dragged?" (515c6–516a3). Through this strikingly unerotic account of the philosophic liberation from the illusions of the cave, Socrates indicates that the quest for wisdom is, in an important sense, a painful quest, and suggests that that quest entails facing such painful truths as the truth of our mortality (compare 515e1–4 with 330d1–331d9).

Socrates does insist, as he says in the *Apology*, that the philosophic life is the greatest good for a human being (38a1–7). The world is so built and man is so built that he can find his satisfaction and his joy in reflecting on the truth about the world.[13] In this respect, at least, nature is not indifferent but rather friendly to the human longing for

---

[13] For this formulation, see Strauss 1953, 75.

wisdom and happiness. But the happiness of the philosopher is not pure, but mixed with sadness. For, precisely insofar as the philosophic life is a happy one, the philosopher must be saddened by the truth that such happiness must end. As Diotima observes, and Socrates agrees, in the *Symposium*, "all human beings . . . want the good things to be theirs always" (205a5–8; see also 206a3–13).

The Socratic thesis is that the acquisition of wisdom is the greatest good, and hence that it is good for us human beings to know even the harsh truth about our mortality. Indeed, as already mentioned, Socrates declares in the *Phaedo* that philosophers practice nothing but dying and being dead (64a4–6). Yet, according to Plato's *Phaedo*, Socrates spends the time before his own death engaged, at least in part, in the unphilosophic activity of composing music and telling mythical tales in order to gratify his wish to believe that the soul is immortal (60c8–61b7, 61d10–e4, 70b5–7, 91a1-b7, 108c3–114d7). The dying Socrates does not simply or primarily reflect on death. Though it may be good to know one's mortality, it may not be good to reflect on that evil continuously. Perhaps the philosophic practice of dying and being dead consists not only of learning how to face and accept the necessity of death, but also of learning how and when to spare oneself the unnecessary pain of thinking relentlessly about one's own death.[14] As the Socratic Prospero says at the end of Shakespeare's *Tempest*, "Every *third* thought shall be my grave" (V.i.312 – emphasis added). But then the philosopher's happiness is a somber one, shadowed by the awareness of death. And so the tragic poets who draw attention to the sorrows of mortal life are not so very different from the Socratic philosopher who practices dying and being dead.[15]

Socrates' clearest criticism of the tragic poets is that they encourage us to wallow in grief at our mortality, as their heroes do. By presenting the sufferings of those whom they present as exemplary human beings, the

---

[14] On this point, see Ahrensdorf 1995, 147.

[15] I would therefore at least qualify Halliwell's account of "the Platonic contrast between two ultimate hypotheses about the world – the first that human lives are governed by external forces which are indifferent to, and capable of crushing, the quest for happiness; the second that the source of true happiness is located nowhere other than in the individual soul's choice between good and evil" (1996, 347).

tragic poets teach the terrifying lesson that human happiness is impossible in this life. More specifically, by teaching that there are mysterious and powerful gods who have the power to destroy us or to spare us from destruction, the poets inspire in their audience a religious terror. But by teaching us that the gods may spare us as well as destroy us, the poets teach the audience to place their hopes for human happiness in the gods and to devote themselves to appeasing the gods in some fashion. Socrates' fundamental criticism of the tragic poets is that, through their heroes, they point their audience away from reason and toward a fearful but also hopeful piety.

Yet this criticism assumes that the tragic poets view their heroes as exemplary human beings, that Homer, for example, simply admires his Achilles or that Sophocles simply admires his Oedipus. But is this true, even according to Socrates? At the end of Book II of the *Republic*, Socrates remarks to Adeimantus: "But Hera's bindings by her son, and Hephaestus' being cast out by his father when he was about to help out his mother who was being beaten, and all the battles of the gods Homer made, must not be accepted in the city, whether they are made with a hidden sense or without a hidden sense. A young thing can't judge what is hidden sense and what is not; but what he takes into his opinions at that age has a tendency to become hard and ineradicable" (378d3-e1; see also Xenophon *Symposium* 3.6). Socrates suggests here that Homer may not share the religious or the tragic perspective of his heroes. Socrates' criticism of the heroes of Homer and the tragic poets, then, may be a criticism that the tragic poets themselves share. Perhaps Socrates' blistering attack on the tragic poets in the *Republic* is directed at the surface and not at the inner, "hidden sense" of their poems. To examine the thesis, pointed to by Socrates, that the tragic poets themselves may be critics of the tragic view of life, we must turn to the full elaboration of that thesis in Aristotle's *Poetics*.

ARISTOTLE: THE PHILOSOPHIC EDUCATION
THROUGH TRAGEDY

Aristotle, like Nietzsche, defends tragedy, but he does so in the name of the life of reason. His key thesis is that tragedy – that is, the best tragedy – does not present its tragic heroes as exemplary human beings.[16] They are impressive, but flawed. Therefore, their suffering is brought down on themselves. Tragedy points above all, then, to the importance of wisdom as a means of avoiding the misery that is avoidable. Tragedy initially inspires pity for the hero and fear for ourselves. But ultimately tragedy purges or weakens our pity and fear by showing us that the heroes suffer as a result of a great error of understanding. In this way, tragedy ultimately teaches us that the greatest human being is the one who has the wisdom to avoid such error – namely, the wise or philosophic poet.

Aristotle claims that the pleasure of all poetry, including tragic poetry, originates in the philosophic pleasure of learning. For we human beings learn, and enjoy learning, by contemplating the imitation or representation of things. "For we rejoice in contemplating the especially accurate likenesses of things that, in themselves, we see with pain, such as the shapes of the most ignoble wild beasts and corpses. The cause of this, again, is that to learn is most pleasant, not only to the philosophers, but also to the others alike, though they share in this a little. For it is because of this that they rejoice in seeing a likeness, that, by contemplating, it is possible to learn and to calculate, what each one is, for example, that this one is that one" (1448b10–17). Aristotle suggests here not only that the pleasure of poetry is a theoretical or philosophic pleasure, a pleasure in knowing, but also that poetry offers indispensable assistance to philosophy. For through poetry – especially, presumably, tragic poetry – one can contemplate with pleasure what one would otherwise view with pain and revulsion, and therefore one can think clearly and deeply about matters that one otherwise would shrink from contemplating.[17] For example, it is very difficult, if not

---

[16] Aristotle's account of tragedy in the *Poetics* is, in large measure, of what tragedy should be and of what the "finest" tragedy is (see especially 1452b28–1453a30; consider as well 1455a16–1456b8.

[17] I must consequently disagree with Lear's argument that, according to Aristotle, "the pleasure we derive from tragedy is not primarily that which comes from satisfying the desire to understand" (1992, 321). I am inclined to disagree as well with Salkever's contention that "it is clear from the *Poetics* that nothing in the reading or viewing of tragedy can match 'the extraordinary pleasures' those who are 'philosophers by nature' can obtain from the careful

impossible, to view a corpse in person without being overwhelmed by grief or fear or disgust. But the viewing of a corpse on stage, within a tragedy – the corpse, say, of an Ajax or a Haemon – is an occasion to reflect on the significance of the deaths of those heroes and, more broadly, the significance of our mortal nature. By abstracting both from our direct relation to the dead and from the sights and smells of death, tragedy helps us to think about death without being overpowered by its immediate presence. While all poetry appeals to the philosophic love of learning, Aristotle indicates here that tragedy in particular helps us to face such "frightening and pitiful" truths as we would ordinarily find too painful to contemplate (1452a1–3).[18]

Aristotle then goes on to explain that tragedy also helps us to contemplate the world free of the passions that cloud our vision. For tragedy is a form of poetry that, "through pity and fear," carries out "the purgation of such passions" (1449b27–8). Tragedy, then, is the form of poetry that helps us to learn by helping to remove or weaken such passions, which are obstacles to learning, which prevent us from thinking and seeing the world clearly. Tragedy helps us to learn, not only by helping us to contemplate such painful truths as the truth of our mortality, but also by helping us to free ourselves from such passions as pity and fear, which may lead us to flee or deny such painful truths. Moreover, insofar as pity for the sufferings of tragic heroes and fear that we may suffer as they do inspire in us pious fears of the gods and pious hopes for their assistance, the liberation of our hearts from such passions would seem to constitute the liberation of our minds from religious passion. Aristotle suggests here, then, in contrast to Socrates, that tragedy provides an invaluable education for the philosophic soul by liberating that soul from those passions that most suggest to us that human happiness is unattainable in this life, that we cannot live well by

observation of plants and animals . . . to say nothing of the remote ecstasies of first philosophy" (1986, 303). See also Halliwell 2002, 199–200. I think Nussbaum is closer to the truth when she stresses that Aristotle "continues and refines the insights of tragedy" and highlights his belief in "the philosophical contribution of poetry" (1986, 421; 1992, 283).

[18] For the connection between deaths on stage and tragedy, see 1452b11–13, 1453b14–1454a34. Almost all of Aristotle's examples here of those actions that inspire pity and fear involve death. See Davis 1992, 28.

our own lights, and therefore that our only hope for happiness lies with the mysterious and fearsome gods.[19]

But how does tragedy arouse our pity and fear? How does it purge them? And, perhaps most importantly, does tragedy, according to Aristotle, purge pity and fear from our souls entirely or only in part? Does tragedy aim at leading us to become purely dispassionate, contemplative beings? Or does tragedy free us from pity and fear only to the extent that pity and fear are unreasonable?[20]

Aristotle suggests here that the experience of tragedy takes place in two stages. First we see great human beings – human beings who are "better" than we are now (1448a10–12, 16–18) – suffer "misfortune" (1451a14), within the course of a single day (1449b11–14). We pity them because of the sudden collapse of their good fortune and we fear that we too may suffer a comparably cruel fate. For if such grand, larger-than-life human beings could not avoid swift, unforeseen disaster, how can we hope to do so (see *Rhetoric* 1383a10–15)? Then – perhaps upon reflection, after studying the play or thinking back on it – we come to see that our pity for the heroes and fear for ourselves are unreasonable. In this way, it would seem, tragedy first arouses our pity and fear and then purges it from our hearts.

Yet, while it seems reasonably clear how tragedy arouses pity and fear, it is much less clear how tragedy frees us from those passions. How does this reversal of feeling, from pity and fear to their absence, occur? In the first place, and most simply, it would seem that tragedy weakens our pity and fear by exhausting our passions, for example, through

---

[19] Aristotle says twice that tragedy seeks to lead or conduct our souls ($\psi\nu\chi\alpha\gamma\omega\gamma\epsilon\iota$ – 1450a32–33, 1450b17–18). Regarding the question of piety in the *Poetics*, Aristotle remarks about "the things concerning gods": "For perhaps it is neither better to speak of them nor are they true, but they happen to be just as they are according to Xenophanes" (1460b36–1461a1). Xenophanes is reported to have said that he did not believe in the gods of Homer and Hesiod. See Diogenes Laertius 9.18 and Xenophanes fragments 11, 12 Diels, fifth edition, as well as fragments 15, 16, 19, 23–26, 32, 34D.

[20] For especially thought-provoking discussions of catharsis, see Lord 1982, 119–37, 159–64; Nussbaum 1986, 388–91; Halliwell 1986, 184–201, 350–6; Lacan 1992, 244–7; Lear 1992.

provoking our tears.[21] For example, in the *Iliad*, after hearing the heartrending speech of Priam and melting into tears, Achilles was able to reflect more dispassionately on the human condition because he "had satisfied himself through lamentation ... and the longing for it had gone from his heart and limbs" (24. 512–7). Similarly, when we see a tragedy, we may be moved to tears but, then, after having our fill of sorrow, we may be able to reflect with greater clarity and calm.

A true purgation of pity and fear, however, would presumably require us to grasp with our minds that our pity and fear are unwarranted. But how, or to what extent, does tragedy show that our powerful passions of pity and fear are not warranted? Aristotle's first answer to this question seems to be that it is by recognizing the necessity of the hero's suffering that we rid ourselves of pity for him and fear for ourselves. Aristotle stresses that "the work of the poet is not to speak of the things that have come to be but of such things as might come to be, as are possible, in accordance with the probable or the necessary . . . . For this reason poetry is more philosophic and more serious than history" (1451a37–1451b6). Furthermore, Aristotle emphasizes repeatedly that, whereas in bad tragedies events follow one another without probability or necessity, in the best tragedies events seem at first to occur in a wholly surprising and mysterious way, but then we recognize that they occur by necessity (1451b34–1452a24, 1454a33–36; see also 1450b28–35, 1451a11–15, 1451b8–10). Indeed, according to Aristotle, there should be nothing irrational in a tragedy, nothing mysterious or miraculous (1454a37-b8, 1460a26-b2, 1461b19–24). In contrast to Nietzsche, Aristotle contends that the best tragic poets present a rational account of the world, a world governed not by mysterious forces or gods but by intelligible, natural necessity. The "myth" that the tragic poets invent, the "myth" that is the "soul" of tragedy, is not divinely revealed or inspired, is not fantastic or mysterious or miraculous, but is rather the product of human art and human nature and comprehensible and clear to human reason (1450a37–38; see also 1451a22–24, 1455a29–34; but consider 1459a30–31).[22]

---

[21] Consider, on this point, Segal 1996.
[22] Halliwell goes so far as to suggest that "The price of Aristotle's philosophical rapprochement with the tragic poets turns out ... to be secularization" (1986,

Aristotle might seem to suggest, then, that it is by understanding the necessity of the downfall of the tragic hero that we are purged of pity for him and fear for ourselves. Yet, if, as Aristotle has suggested, tragedy presents great human beings, and if it presents their ruin as necessary, would it not teach that the natural human condition is so fragile that human happiness is simply impossible? Would it not plunge us into despair? Or would tragedy not inspire in us the desperate hope against hope that, by some miracle, by some divine assistance that overrules the sway of natural necessity, happiness may be attained by such beings as ourselves?[23] In this way, would tragedy not inflame our pity for the tragic hero, our fear for ourselves, and our hope in the gods?

Aristotle now explains, however, that the hero of the finest tragedy is not a simply great or admirable human being. Even though the heroes are "better [βελτιους]" than the common man, they must not, Aristotle insists, be "decent [επιεικεις]" (compare 1448a17–8 with 1452b30–36). Aristotle goes so far as to claim that the spectacle of a decent man's going from good fortune to bad fortune is not even frightening or pitiable but simply abominable or even sacrilegious (μιαρον – 1452b36). On the other hand, the spectacle of wicked men going from bad fortune to good fortune is "most untragic" of all, is not "philanthropic," and inspires neither pity nor fear (1452b37–38). Aristotle suggests here that tragedy should not shock our sense of justice, that it should not push decent human beings to despair of justice on earth or to hope against hope that justice must somehow be done, if not in this life, then in the next. To do so would be misanthropic rather than philanthropic, since philanthropy – loving that which is human – means assuring human beings that we can achieve justice on earth, on our own, without the assistance of superhuman beings (consider as well 1456a19–23).[24] Tragedy should arouse and

---

233; see 84–5, 89–92, 98–108, 165–7, 229–233). Consider as well Lord 1982, 172–4, 178–9.

[23] For a connection among fear, pity, and religious passion, consider *Politics* 1342a4–15.

[24] I therefore am inclined to disagree with Konstan's argument that φιλανθρωπον means "commiseration" regardless of "the merits of the

purge our sentiments of pity and fear, but it should also evidently avoid offending our sense of justice and inflaming our moral indignation by showing evil triumphant. Tragedy cannot free us from anger, and perhaps should not, since a measure of anger is necessary for decency (see *Nicomachean Ethics* 1125b26–1126b10). But tragedy can and should free us from the fear and pity that encourage us to fear the gods and to look to the gods for help.

Yet Aristotle insists that tragedy should not simply flatter our sense of justice by presenting the spectacle of the wicked being punished (1453a1–5). Tragedy should not offend the just hope that the good will be rewarded and the wicked punished, but it should beware of lulling us into a thoughtlessly complacent belief that justice is always done in this world and that the human condition is free from suffering. Tragedy must draw our attention to the apparent evils of our condition and must thereby arouse our pity and our fear. But it must also, somehow, free us from those passions.

Aristotle says (1453a5–7) that pity is aroused by undeserved misfortune, and fear is aroused by the misfortune of a human being like ourselves. He then goes on to describe who the tragic hero should be: "Such is one who is not surpassing in virtue and justice, who does not come into misfortune on account of vice or wickedness but on account of a certain error [ἁμαρτίαν], and who is one of great repute and good fortune, such as Oedipus and Thyestes and illustrious men of such families. It is necessary that the noble myth be simple rather than double, as some say, and that he come not into good fortune out of misfortune but the opposite, out of good fortune into misfortune, and not on account of wickedness but on account of a great error [ἁμαρτίαν], and that he be such as has been said or rather better than worse" (1453a7–17). Tragedy, then, first creates the appearance that the hero who comes into misfortune does not deserve to suffer so, and resembles us. The hero at first must seem virtuous or at least decent. But then, on reflection, we see that the hero brings his misfortune upon himself. He is responsible for his misfortune. His misfortune is

sufferer," though I would have to qualify the opposing claim that it simply means "morally satisfying" (Konstan 2001, 47; see also 2005, 46–7, 88).

avoidable. But how? Not through moral virtue, it seems, but through wisdom, the wisdom to avoid the error. For, as Aristotle makes clear in the *Poetics* as a whole, by the term ἁμαρτία, he means a mistake in one's understanding.

The term ἁμαρτία and its variants occur fifteen times in the *Poetics*.[25] The first time error is mentioned in the *Poetics* is when Aristotle speaks of comic heroes, whose "error" is not woeful or destructive (1449a33–36). More importantly, the second time the word appears, Aristotle criticizes all the poets who "err" (ἁμαρτάνειν – 1451a19–20) because, he says twice, they "think" (οἴονται – 1451a16, 21) that the unity of a plot consists of the unity of the hero (1451a15–22).[26] Then Aristotle uses the term twice in the course of explaining that the tragic hero comes into misfortune "not on account of wickedness but on account of a great error [ἁμαρτίαν]." In the remaining eleven times the word appears, it is used to describe the mistakes poets and their critics make in their understanding of poetry. Aristotle's account here indicates clearly that, according to him, the fundamental failing of the tragic hero is not moral but intellectual. The cause of the downfall of the hero is not a failure of justice or virtue, but a failure of understanding.

But why then does Aristotle insist that the tragic hero "is not surpassing in virtue and justice"? Why could the tragic hero not be superlatively just or virtuous but unwise? Aristotle suggests here that one who is not wise cannot be surpassing in justice and virtue. The downfall of the tragic hero is not an indication of the injustice of the world or of the fragility of all human happiness but rather a sign of the fragility of the good fortune of a man who may be somewhat virtuous but who is fundamentally unwise.

---

[25] See 1449a33–34, 1451a19–20, 1453a10, 1453a16, 1453a24, 1454b17, 1454b35, 1456b15, 1460b16, 1460b18, 1460b20, 1460b24, 1460b30, 1460b31, 1461b8. For valuable discussions, consider Lord 1982, 165–74; Nussbaum 1986, 382–3; Halliwell 1986, 220–2.

[26] See also 1456b15–17: "For who would suppose that what Protagoras censures was done in error [ἡμαρτῆσθαι] because [Homer], thinking [οἰόμενος] to pray, gives a command, saying, 'of anger, sing, goddess?'"

The recognition of the tragic hero's error is evidently the moment of true catharsis. First, the hero must seem undeserving of misfortune, a man without vice or wickedness, a man of considerable virtue and justice. The swift and terrible misfortune of so seemingly great a man arouses our pity for him and our fear for ourselves. But then we see that the hero brought on his own misfortune by committing a great error. Our pity is purged because we see that, in some sense, he did deserve his suffering. And our fear is purged because we see that he is not like us, at least insofar as we can attain the wisdom he lacks. Tragedy, then, points to wisdom as the cardinal virtue. The tragic hero suffers, it seems, because of his lack of wisdom. Tragedy at first seems to be an abominable story of a perfect man suffering undeserved misfortune, but then it is revealed to be the cautionary tale of a flawed man who, through his failure to be as wise as he could have been, brings about his misfortune.[27]

But does tragedy, then, purge us entirely of our pity for the tragic hero and fear for ourselves? Is it reasonable to conclude that the lack of wisdom of the hero is responsible for all of his suffering? Is it reasonable to conclude that we can be immune to all of the sufferings of the hero, if only we are wise?

Aristotle suggests that such a conclusion would not be reasonable. For he proceeds to argue that a tragedy should not simply be a morality tale in which the good triumph and the wicked suffer. A tragedy that

---

[27] Lear argues that, according to Aristotle, tragedy does not educate its audience because the primary audience is "a virtuous person . . . [who] is in no need of education" and "we should not be trained to find *any* pleasure in real life tragic events, as we do find in the tragic portrayals of the poets." Therefore, Lear concludes that, according to Aristotle, "If poetry has positive value, it must lie outside the realm of ethical education" (1992, 319–21 – my emphasis). I suggest that Lear overlooks here a crucial Aristotelian distinction between ethical virtue and wisdom and hence between "ethical education" and theoretical education. The morally virtuous person is not simply wise, and may, in crucial respects, require wisdom in order to be virtuous. As Nussbaum puts it, "however good each person is, there remains room for improvement, advice, further experience" (1992, 282). Furthermore, if, according to Aristotle, there is a theoretical pleasure in learning (*Poetics* 1448b10–17), and if it is possible to learn important and beneficial truths even from "real life tragic events," then it seems unreasonable to insist, as Lear does, that, according to Aristotle, one must not take "any" pleasure from contemplating such events.

resembles the *Odyssey*, "one which ends in opposite ways for the better and worse," seems best, he explains, not because of the excellence of the poem, but because of "the weakness of the spectators" (1453a30–35). The pleasure of such happy endings, where those who are most hateful to one another become friends and no one kills or is killed, is proper to comedy, not tragedy (1453a35–39). It is weak, then, especially weak-minded, to believe that the good and the bad suffer opposite fates. For all human beings must face the evils of their common mortal condition. All human beings must face the deaths of their loved ones, for example. A key feature of comedy, Aristotle indicates, is that it abstracts from death. But tragedy seems to be closer to philosophy than comedy because it faces and helps us to face the harsh truth about our human condition. Tragedy does not, it seems, give in to human weakness. Comedy invites us to believe that the good and the bad suffer opposite fates, but tragedy reminds us that all humans suffer the same mortal fate. Comedy tempts us to forget our mortality, but tragedy does not. The tragic hero's error leads him to suffer avoidable misfortune, but even a wise hero cannot avoid the ills attendant on mortal beings. Wisdom would enable him to avoid avoidable, but only avoidable, misfortune.

Aristotle suggests, then, that tragedy does not purge us entirely of pity and fear. Insofar as we come to recognize that the tragic hero erred, that he compounded the suffering of his life, we will not fear or pity his fate. But insofar as his suffering was truly due to the natural necessity of such mortal beings as ourselves, we will reasonably fear and pity his fate. Tragedy helps us to clarify which misfortunes are due to our avoidable errors and which are due to natural necessity. In this way, tragedy points to our need for wisdom. But it also brings into sharp relief the indelibly somber character of even the wisest human life.[28]

---

[28] I therefore think that Lear goes too far in his conclusion that, "In Aristotle's conception of tragedy, the individual actor takes on the burden of badness, the world as a whole is absolved . . . Even in tragedy, perhaps especially in tragedy, the fundamental goodness of man and world are reaffirmed" (1992, 335). Halliwell also goes too far, I believe, in suggesting that Aristotle's "conception of tragedy entails that the genre" will not ever even "confront us with the stark idea that the world is radically blind to or heedless of human aspirations to happiness" (2002, 226; consider also 1986, 235–7).

If Aristotle is right, the greatest tragic poets were themselves philosophic. But is Aristotle right? For Aristotle, the most illuminating example of tragedy is Sophocles' Oedipus plays. Aristotle praises *Oedipus the Tyrant* nine times in the *Poetics*, and suggests three times that it is either the "finest" and "best" tragedy or among the very finest and best. (1452a24–26, 1452a32–33, 1453a7–12, 1453a17–22, 1453b6, 1453b29–31, 1454b6–8, 1455a16–18, 1460a27–32; 1452a32–33, 1453a17–22, 1455a16–18).

I have argued in this book that Sophocles' Theban plays do indeed confirm the thesis that this tragic poet, at least, was philosophic. Through our analysis of the magnificent heroes of these plays – from the anti-religious political rationalism of Oedipus the Tyrant and the religious anti-rationalism of Oedipus at Colonus to the pious heroism of Antigone and the cautious political rationalism of Theseus – we finally encounter the true model of rationalism in Sophocles himself, who exhibits a genuinely philosophic clarity, intransigence, and humanity. The outlook of Sophocles, then, is closer to the rationalism of Socrates than it first seems. But, as I have shown in this chapter, the outlook of the classical philosophers is less optimistic, more somber, and therefore closer to the outlook of the tragic poet Sophocles than it first seems. It is my hope that this study will substantially broaden and deepen our understanding of both classical rationalism and tragedy and that it will stimulate further political and philosophic studies of the great classical tragic poets.

Bibliography

Adams, S. M. 1957. *Sophocles the Playwright*. Toronto: University of Toronto Press.

Ahrensdorf, Peter J. 1995. *The Death of Socrates and the Life of Philosophy*. Albany: State University of New York Press.

Annas, Julia. 1981. *An Introduction to Plato's Republic*. Oxford: Clarendon Press.

Anzieu, Didier. 1966. "Oedipe avant le complexe ou de l'interpretation psychanalytique des mythes." *Les Temps Modernes,* 245 (October): 675–715.

Beer, Josh. 2004. *Sophocles and the Tragedy of Athenian Democracy*. Westport, CT: Praeger.

Benardete, Seth. 1999. *Sacred Transgressions: A Reading of Sophocles' Antigone*. South Bend, IN: St. Augustine's Press.

——— 2000. *The Argument of the Action: Essays on Greek Poetry and Philosophy*. Chicago: University of Chicago Press.

Bloom, Allan. 1991. *The Republic of Plato*. 2nd edition. New York: Basic Books.

Bloom, Harold. 1988. "Introduction." In *Modern Critical Interpretations: Sophocles' Oedipus Rex*. Ed. Harold Bloom. New York: Chelsea House, pp. 1–4.

Bolotin, David. 1980. "On Sophocles' *Ajax*." *St. John's Review*, 32:1 (July).

——— 1995. "The Critique of Homer and the Homeric Heroes in Plato's *Republic*." In *Political Philosophy and the Human Soul*. Eds. Michael Palmer and Thomas Pangle. Lanham, MD: Rowman and Littlefield, pp. 83–94.

Bowra, C. M. 1944. *Sophoclean Tragedy*. Oxford: Clarendon Press.

Calme, Claude. 1996. "Vision, Blindness, and Mask: The Radicalization of the Emotions in Sophocles' *Oedipus Rex*." In *Tragedy and the Tragic*. Ed. M. S. Silk. Oxford: Clarendon Press, pp. 17–37.

Carter, D. M. 2007. *The Politics of Greek Tragedy*. Exeter, UK: Bristol Phoenix Press.

Dannhauser, Werner J. 1974. *Nietzsche's View of Socrates*. Ithaca: Cornell University Press.

Davis, Michael. 1992. *Aristotle's Poetics: The Poetry of Philosophy*. Lanham, MD: Rowman and Littlefield.

Dodds, E. R. 1968. "On Misunderstanding the *Oedipus Rex*." In *Twentieth Century Interpretations of Oedipus Rex*. Ed. Michael J. O'Brien. Englewood Cliffs, NJ: Prentice-Hall, pp. 17–29.

Edmunds, Lowell. 1996. *Theatrical Space and Historical Place in Sophocles' Oedipus at Colonus*. Lanham, MD: Rowman and Littlefield.

Ehrenberg, Victor. 1954. *Sophocles and Pericles*. Oxford: Basil Blackwell.

Euben, J. Peter. 1986. "Introduction." In *Greek Tragedy and Political Theory*. Ed. J. Peter Euben. Berkeley: University of California Press, pp. 1–42.

——— 1990. *The Tragedy of Political Theory*. Princeton: Princeton University Press.

——— 1997. "Oedipean Complexities and Political Science." In *Corrupting Youth: Political Education, Democratic Culture, and Political Theory*. Ed. J. Peter Euben. Princeton: Princeton University Press, pp. 179–201.

Foley, Helene P. 1996. "Antigone as Moral Agent." In *Tragedy and the Tragic*. Ed. M. S. Silk. Oxford: Clarendon Press. pp. 49–73.

Freud, Sigmund. 1927. *The Interpretation of Dreams*. Trans. A. A. Brill. New York: Macmillan.

Fukuyama, Francis. 1989. "The End of History?" *The National Interest* 16 (Summer), pp. 3–18.

Fustel De Coulanges, Numa Denis. 1900. *La Cité Antique*. Paris: Libraire Hachette.

Goethe, Johann Wolfgang von. 1984. *Conversations with Eckermann*. Trans. John Oxenford. San Francisco: North Point Press.

Gould, Thomas. 1988. "The Innocence of Oedipus: The Philosophers on the *Oedipus Rex*." In *Modern Critical Interpretations: Sophocles' Oedipus Rex*. Ed. Harold Bloom. New York: Chelsea House, pp. 49–63.

Grene, David. 1967. *Reality and the Heroic Pattern: Last Plays of Ibsen, Shakespeare, and Sophocles*. Chicago: University of Chicago Press.

Griffith, Mark. 2005. "The Subject of Desire in Sophocles' *Antigone*." In *The Soul of Tragedy: Essays in Athenian Drama*. Eds. Victoria Pedrick and Steven M. Oberhelman. Chicago: University of Chicago Press, pp. 91–135.

Halliwell, Stephen. 1986. *Aristotle's Poetics*. Chapel Hill: University of North Carolina Press.

———— 1996. "Plato's Repudiation of the Tragic." In *Tragedy and the Tragic*. Ed. M. S. Silk. Oxford: Clarendon Press. pp. 332–49.

———— 2002. *The Aesthetics of Mimesis: Ancient Texts and Modern Problems*. Princeton: Princeton University Press.

Hegel, Georg. 1962. *Hegel on Tragedy*. Eds. Anne and Henry Paolucci. Garden City, NY: Anchor Books.

Heidegger, Martin. 1980. *An Introduction to Metaphysics*. Trans. Ralph Manheim. New Haven: Yale University Press.

———— 1991. *Nietzsche*, Vol. II. Trans. David Farrell Krell. Harper: San Francisco.

———— 1998. *Einführung in die Metaphysik*. Tübingen: Max Niemeyer Verlag.

Jebb, Richard C. 1955. *Sophocles: Oedipus Coloneus*. Cambridge: Cambridge University Press.

————1966. *The Oedipus Tyrannus of Sophocles*. Cambridge: Cambridge University Press.

———— 1979. *Antigone*. Cambridge: Cambridge University Press.

Johnson, P. J. 1997. "Woman's Third Face: A Psycho-Social Reconsideration of Sophocles' *Antigone*." *Arethusa,* 30: 369–98.

Kaufmann, Walter. 1968. *Tragedy and Philosophy*. Princeton: Princeton University Press.

Kitto, H. D. F. 1958. *Sophocles: Dramatist and Philosopher*. Oxford: Oxford University Press.

Knox, Bernard. 1964. *The Heroic Temper: Studies in Sophoclean Tragedy*. Berkeley: University of California Press.

———— 1998. *Oedipus at Thebes*. New Haven: Yale University Press.

Konstan, David. 2001. *Pity Transformed*. London: Duckworth.

———— 2005. "Aristotle on the Tragic Emotions." In *The Soul of Tragedy: Essays in Athenian Drama*. Eds. Victoria Pedrick and Steven M. Oberhelman. Chicago: University of Chicago Press, pp. 13–25.

Lacan, Jacques. 1997. *The Seminar of Jacques Lacan: Book VII, The Ethics of Psychoanalysis 1959–1960*. Trans. Dennis Porter. New York: W. W. Norton.

Lane, Warren J., and Lane, Ann M. 1986. "The Politics of *Antigone*." In *Greek Tragedy and Political Theory*. Ed. J. Peter Euben. Berkeley: University of California Press, pp. 162–82.

Lattimore, Richmond. 1958. *The Poetry of Greek Tragedy*. Baltimore: Johns Hopkins University Press.

Lear, Jonathan. 1992. "Katharsis." In *Essays on Aristotle's Poetics*. Ed. Amélie Oksenberg Rorty. Princeton: Princeton University Press, pp. 315–40.

———— 1997. "Inside and Outside the *Republic*." In *Plato's Republic: Critical Essays*. Ed. Richard Kraut. Lanham, MD: Rowman and Littlefield, pp. 61–94.

Locke, John. 1988. *Two Treatises of Government*. Ed. Peter Laslett. Cambridge: Cambridge University Press.

Lord, Carnes. 1982. *Education and Culture in the Political Thought of Aristotle*. Ithaca: Cornell University Press.

Meier, Christian. 1993. *The Political Art of Greek Tragedy*. Trans. Andrew Webber. Baltimore: Johns Hopkins University Press.

Mills, Sophie. 1997. *Theseus, Tragedy and the Athenian Empire*. Oxford: Clarendon Press.

Mogyoródi, Emese. 1996. "'Tragic Freedom and Fate in Sophocles' *Antigone*: Notes on the Role of the 'Ancient Evils' in 'the Tragic.'" In *Tragedy and the Tragic*. Ed. M. S. Silk. Oxford: Clarendon Press. pp. 358–76.

Montaigne, Michel de. 1958. *The Complete Essays of Montaigne*. Trans. Donald Frame. Stanford: Stanford University Press.

Naddaff, Ramona A. 2002. *Exiling the Poets: The Production of Censorship in Plato's Republic*. Chicago: University of Chicago Press.

Nietzsche, Friedrich. 1954a. *Twilight of the Idols*. In *The Portable Nietzsche*. Trans. Walter Kaufmann. New York: Viking Press. pp. 463–563.

———— 1954b, *Thus Spoke Zarathustra*. In *The Portable Nietzsche*. Trans. Walter Kaufmann. New York: Viking Press. pp. 103–439.

———— 1967. *The Birth of Tragedy*. Trans. Walter Kaufmann. New York: Vintage Books.

———— 1968. *The Will to Power*. Trans. Walter Kaufmann and R. J. Hollingdale. New York: Vintage Books.

———— 1969. *Ecce Homo*. Trans. Walter Kaufmann. New York: Vintage Books.

———— 1974. *The Gay Science*. Trans. Walter Kaufmann. New York: Vintage Books.

———— 1989, *Beyond Good and Evil*. Trans. Walter Kaufmann. New York: Vintage Books.

———— 1997. *Daybreak*. Trans. R. J. Hollingdale. Cambridge: Cambridge University Press.

Nussbaum, Martha. 1986. *The Fragility of Goodness: Luck and Ethics in Greek Tragedy and Philosophy*. Cambridge: Cambridge University Press.

———— 1992. "Tragedy and Self-Sufficiency: Plato and Aristotle on Fear and Pity." In *Essays on Aristotle's Poetics*. Ed. Amélie Oksenberg Rorty. Princeton: Princeton University Press. pp. 261–90.

O'Brien, Michael J. 1968. "Introduction." In *Twentieth Century Interpretations of Oedipus Rex*. Ed. Michael J. O'Brien. Englewood Cliffs, NJ: Prentice-Hall, pp. 1–16.

Opstelten, J. C. 1952. *Sophocles and Greek Pessimism*. Trans. J. A. Ross. Amsterdam: North-Holland.

Ormand, Kirk. 1999. *Exchange and the Maiden: Marriage in Sophoclean Tragedy*. Austin: University of Texas Press.

Racine, Jean. 1965. *Phèdre*. Paris: Libraire Larousse.

Rehm, Rush. 1992. *Greek Tragic Theatre*. London: Routledge.

Reinhardt, Karl. 1979. *Sophocles*. Trans. Hazel Harvey, and David Harvey. New York: Barnes and Noble Books.

Rocco, Christopher. 1997. *Tragedy and Enlightenment: Athenian Political Thought and the Dilemmas of Modernity*. Berkeley: University of California Press.

Rorty, Richard. 1989. *Contingency, Irony, and Solidarity*. Cambridge: Cambridge University Press.

——— 1991. *Objectivity, Relativism, and Truth*. Cambridge: Cambridge University Press.

Ruderman, Richard S. 1999. "Odysseus and the Possibility of Enlightenment." *American Journal of Political Science*, 43: 138–61.

Salkever, Stephen. 1986. "Tragedy and the Education of the *Demos*: Aristotle's Response to Plato." In *Greek Tragedy and Political Theory*. Ed. J. Peter Euben. Berkeley: University of California Press, pp. 274–304.

Saxonhouse, Arlene. 1986. "From Tragedy to Hierarchy and Back Again: Women in Greek Political Thought." *American Political Science Review*, 80: 403–18.

——— 1988. "The Tyranny of Reason in the World of the Polis." *American Political Science Review*, 82: 1261–75.

——— 1992. *Fear of Diversity: the Birth of Political Science in Ancient Greek Thought*. Chicago: University of Chicago Press.

Schwartz, Joel D. 1986. "Human Action and Political Action in *Oedipus Tyrannos*." In *Greek Tragedy and Political Theory*. Ed. J. Peter Euben. Berkeley: University of California Press, pp. 183–209.

Scodel, Ruth. 1984. *Sophocles*. Boston: Twayne Publishers.

Segal, Charles. 1966. "Sophocles' Praise of Man and the Conflicts of the *Antigone*." In *Sophocles: A Collection of Critical Essays*. Ed. Thomas Woodward. Englewood Cliffs, NJ: Prentice-Hall, pp. 62–85.

——— 1981. *Tragedy and Civilization: An Interpretation of Sophocles*. Cambridge, MA: Harvard University Press.

———— 1986. "Greek Tragedy and Society: A Structuralist Perspective."
In *Greek Tragedy and Political Theory*. Ed. J. Peter Euben. Berkeley:
University of California Press. pp. 43–75.

———— 1993. *Oedipus Tyrannus: Tragic Heroism and the Limits of Knowledge*.
New York: Twayne Publishers.

———— 1995. *Sophocles' Tragic World*. Cambridge, MA: Harvard
University Press.

———— 1996. "Catharsis, Audience, and Closure in Greek Tragedy." In
Tragedy and the Tragic. Ed. M.S. Silk. Oxford: Clarendon Press.
pp. 149–72.

———— 2001. *Sophocles' Oedipus Tyrannus*. New York: Oxford University
Press.

Silk, M.S. 1996. "General Introduction." In *Tragedy and the Tragic*. Ed.
M.S. Silk. Oxford: Clarendon Press. pp. 1–11.

Silk, M.S., and Stern, J.P. 1981. *Nietzsche on Tragedy*. New York:
Cambridge University Press.

Slatkin, Laura. 1986. "Oedipus at Colonus: Exile and Integration."
In *Greek Tragedy and Political Theory*. Ed. J. Peter Euben. Berkeley:
University of California Press, pp. 210–21.

Sophocles. 1966. *The Oedipus Tyrannus*. Ed. Richard C. Jebb. Cambridge:
Cambridge University Press.

———— 1975. *Fabulae*. Ed. A.C. Pearson. Oxford: Oxford University
Press.

Strauss, Leo. 1953. *Natural Right and History*. Chicago: University of
Chicago Press.

Tessitore, Aristide. 2003. "Justice, Politics, and Piety in Sophocles'
Philoctetes," *Review of Politics*, vol. 65: 61–88.

Tocqueville, Alexis de. 2000. *Democracy in America*. Trans. Harvey C.
Mansfield and Delba Winthrop. Chicago: University of Chicago Press.

Tyrrell, Wm. Blake, and Bennett, Larry J. 1998. *Recapturing Sophocles'
Antigone*. Lanham, MD: Rowman and Littlefield.

Van Nortwick, Thomas. 1998. *Oedipus: The Meaning of a Masculine Life*.
Norman: University of Oklahoma Press.

Vellacott, Philip. 1971. *Sophocles and Oedipus: A Study of the Oedipus
Tyrannos*. New York: Macmillan.

Vernant, Jean-Pierre, and Vidal-Naquet, Pierre. 1988. *Myth and Tragedy
in Ancient Greece*. Trans. Janet Lloyd. Brooklyn, NY: Zone Books.

Waldock, Arthur. 1966. *Sophocles the Dramatist*. Cambridge: Cambridge
University Press.

Walker, Henry J. 1995. *Theseus and Athens*. Oxford: Oxford University Press.

Whitman, Cedric H. 1971. *Sophocles: A Study of Heroic Humanism*. Cambridge, MA: Harvard University Press.

Wilson, Joseph P. 1997. *The Hero and the City: An Interpretation of Sophocles' Oedipus at Colonus*. Ann Arbor: University of Michigan Press.

Winnington-Ingram, R. P. 1980. *Sophocles: An Interpretation*. Cambridge: Cambridge University Press.

Wohl, Victoria. 2002. *Love Among the Ruins: The Erotics of Democracy in Classical Athens*. Princeton: Princeton University Press.

Zeitlin, Froma. 1986. "Thebes: Theater of Self and Society in Athenian Drama." In *Greek Tragedy and Political Theory*. Ed. J. Peter Euben. Berkeley: University of California Press, pp. 101–41.

Index

CPSIA information can be obtained at www.ICGtesting.com
Printed in the USA
LVOW08s2042301115

464710LV00002B/576/P